AMERICAN
VISIONS

ALSO BY EDWARD L. AYERS

Southern Journey: The Migrations of the American South, 1790–2020

The Thin Light of Freedom: The Civil War and Emancipation in the Heart of America

What Caused the Civil War?
Reflections on the South and Southern History

In the Presence of Mine Enemies:
Civil War in the Heart of America, 1859–1863

The Promise of the New South: Life after Reconstruction

Vengeance and Justice: Crime and Punishment in the Nineteenth-Century American South

AMERICAN VISIONS

The United States, 1800–1860

Edward L. Ayers

W. W. NORTON & COMPANY
Celebrating a Century of Independent Publishing

About the cover artwork:
Robert S. Duncanson, *View of Cincinnati, Ohio, from Covington, Kentucky* **(1851)**
Robert S. Duncanson (1821–1872), the first prominent Black American landscape
artist, painted the scene adapted for the cover of this book—a view of the sprawling
city of Cincinnati across the Ohio River from the rural landscape of Kentucky.
The painting depicts the border between slavery and freedom, with a Black laborer,
presumably enslaved, at the center of the scene. Himself the grandson of an enslaved
man from Virginia, Duncanson was born free in New York and raised in Michigan. In
1840 he moved to Cincinnati, where, despite Ohio's notorious Black Laws and other
obstacles, Duncanson was able to launch a career as an artist that eventually won him
national and international renown.

Copyright © 2023 by Edward L. Ayers

For information about permission to reproduce selections from this book,
write to Permissions, W. W. Norton & Company, Inc.,
500 Fifth Avenue, New York, NY 10110

For information about special discounts for bulk purchases, please contact
W. W. Norton Special Sales at specialsales@wwnorton.com or 800-233-4830

Manufacturing by Lakeside Book Company
Book design by Lisa Buckley
Production manager: Anna Oler

ISBN 978-0-393-88126-4

W. W. Norton & Company, Inc., 500 Fifth Avenue, New York, N.Y. 10110
www.wwnorton.com

W. W. Norton & Company Ltd., 15 Carlisle Street, London W1D 3BS

1 2 3 4 5 6 7 8 9 0

For Abby, always

Contents

Preface

This book is about visions, imagined paths between things as they are and what they might become. To a remarkable extent, the visions that have defined the United States appeared in the first two-thirds of the nineteenth century. Fundamental elements of national life crystallized then, from the country's borders to the shape of its politics, from its religious identity to the themes of its literature. Americans of all kinds fashioned, word by word, a vocabulary to describe the new nation taking shape before their eyes.

People across North America and beyond felt the rising power of the new United States at the beginning of the nineteenth century. Indigenous peoples from the Atlantic to the Pacific confronted the armies, settlers, missionaries, and agents of the expansive nation. The imperial powers of Britain, France, and Spain reckoned with the new country's ambitions. Mexico and Canada struggled over the future of North America. Democratic hope and possibility grew for white American citizens, even as slavery and dispossession gripped millions of others. The Americans who claimed to speak for the nation declared the continent theirs through the will of God or the inevitable working of economic progress. Others denied such boasts, instead championing ideals of universal human equality and dignity.

A broad cast of characters, their lives woven together in the time they shared, shaped the volatile new nation. Frederick Douglass, Ralph Waldo Emerson, and Harriet Beecher Stowe became famous then and remained so. Writers who struggled in their own times—Edgar Allan Poe, Herman Melville, and Henry David Thoreau—won veneration after their deaths. Nat Turner and John Brown ruptured history; Charles Grandison Finney and Joseph Smith transformed faith. P. T. Barnum pioneered American showmanship, Stephen Foster sought a distinctly American music, Samuel F. B. Morse and Samuel Colt became synonymous with their innovations, and John James Audubon and Louis Agassiz celebrated nature while denigrating most of humankind. Indigenous leaders William Apess and Black Hawk, female activists Angelina Grimké and Margaret Fuller, Black speakers Maria Stewart and Frances E. Watkins, and abolitionists Sojourner Truth and William Wells Brown spoke words powerful then and now.

Each person in this diverse cast articulated a vision, some in the language of religion, art, and literature, others in politics and power, and others in commerce and invention. People at the margins moved the center, the disenfranchised moved power, and the eccentric moved the expected. Individuals dismissed for their skin, sex, or peculiarity spoke for an America of freedom and connection, of possibility and responsibility. They did so from the traditions of the Declaration of Independence and the New Testament, from the individuality of art and literature, from traditions of African and Indigenous cultures, and from a recognition of the mutual dependence of the human and the natural world. They articulated such powerful visions by confronting the moral failings of the nation. They faced opposition and obstruction, and they confronted their own limitations of understanding and compassion, but they glimpsed aspects of what America might be.

The young United States veered in unexpected directions in this era. It seemed impossible in 1800 that American slavery would spread over an area the size of continental Europe and lead the United States into a war against another republic. Few white people imagined that Native peoples would sustain their cultures and contest the power of the new nation for generations to come. Only the Mormon devout believed that their church would grow into a global faith. Few would have expected that, centuries later, "OK" would become the world's most frequently used phrase, that millions of Americans would remember the tune to "Oh! Susanna," or that young schoolchildren would learn about Johnny Appleseed.

Americans have often turned to familiar stories to tame the confusion of this era, the complexities of remembering and forgetting. These decades are commonly described as the "age of Jackson" and "the rise of the common man," the era of "expansion" and "manifest destiny," the "Second Great Awakening" and the "antebellum era." Such terms domesticate the lurching history of the new United States, leaving out too much of the dissent and struggle that shaped America's history. We might better call this the era of the new nation, the story of government, economy, culture, and identity invented on the spot, of progress and wrong weaving together in ways that defined America's understanding of itself.[1]

The central concerns of this era still matter in the United States. Debates over the pursuit of Black freedom, the place of women in private and public life, the rights of Indigenous peoples, and the inclusion of new immigrants have not ceased. The early appearance of those struggles revealed, during the deepest darkness in American history, that a concern for rights of some can grow into respect for the rights and dignity of all. The language of empathy, inclusion, and mutual understanding forged in the first decades of American history, like the language of exclusion and possession forged at the same time, created a vocabulary of national self-reflection that is resonant still.

My own time studying American history has led me to revisit the visions of the nation's defining era. I am an optimistic person who has written and taught about the worst wrongs in American history—slavery, war, violence, injustice—for forty years. I have done so believing that by addressing those evils we can perceive and counter their insidious legacies. Grappling with past injustices seemed a way to secure our progress.

But it is sometimes hard to sustain that optimism when ugly scenes from the new United States reappear: nativists and racists march, apocalyptic prophecies and conspiracies proliferate, and religious faith is wielded as a political weapon. Those who would rule the United States with such purposes claim the sanction of history. They dress in the garb of the frontier and battlefront; they wave flags and guns in defiance of democratic change; they declare ownership of an America seized through the violence of white settlers. Self-proclaimed patriots deny the wrongs of the past and refuse reconciliation or recompense for its victims. They seek control over history, expunging evidence of injustice in the name of national pride.

But we can choose to remember a fuller American history, one that is more truly patriotic, one that evokes the nation's highest ideals of equality and mutual respect in the face of the nation's failings. Bold men and women in the new United States spoke without permission and often in defiance of those who held power. They evoked humane understanding in speeches, novels, paintings, and songs; they deflated pretension and hypocrisy; they wrote with care of the beauty and fragility of the natural world. Their visions remain powerful—and necessary—generations later.

AMERICAN
VISIONS

Chapter One

REVELATIONS

1800–1829

Prophets

The Native peoples of North America had shown themselves shrewd and adaptable in their centuries of interaction with Europeans. They welcomed some of what traders, priests, and diplomats offered even as they pursued goals that had nothing to do with European desires or understanding. To the west, north, and south of the new United States, eight hundred thousand Native people traded with the British, Spanish, and French for furs and hides. Powerful circuits of trade radiated from the Great Lakes, coordinated by European men and Native women. Other circuits of trade and power, shifting and growing, ranged through the Spanish territories to the south and west.[1]

The emergence of the United States in the East held little immediate consequence for these complicated webs of trade and diplomacy. The expedition of Meriwether Lewis and William Clark, begun in 1803 through the lands of the Louisiana Purchase and beyond, revealed that the Native population of North America was complex beyond comprehension. Whatever fate awaited the United States would be tied to those Native peoples and alliances they might strike among themselves and with European powers.

East of the Mississippi, Native peoples had long confronted the people they called Americans, Europeans who had declared themselves independent of other Europeans. Indigenous peoples, diverse in language, religion, history, and loyalty, had struggled for centuries over ways to deal with the white Americans pushing on them from the east, north, and south. The Americans brought welcome trade, but they also brought alcohol, violence, disease, disruption, and religions that challenged Indigenous beliefs and hierarchy. In the South, some among the Cherokee, Chickasaw, Muscogee, and Choctaw had begun to adopt American ways to their ends. They grew cotton and spun cloth, raised cattle and hogs, learned English and listened to Christian missionaries.

Unlike the French and British, the Americans demonstrated a relentless hunger for Native land. They would purchase it with cash and annuities, take it with threats and bloodshed. The American population grew beyond reckoning. Endless numbers of settlers rushed in after the speculators and agents who signed treaties. The settlers showed little respect for boundaries and precedent. They took what they could, often with violence. Their greed threatened trade and accommodation that had bound people for generations.

At the beginning of the nineteenth century, nearly half of the land claimed by the United States in fact lay under the control of Native peoples who had not ceded their territories. From the Great Lakes to the Gulf of Mexico, Indigenous nations had no intention of surrendering their lands to American settlers. They would leverage their connections with European nations far more powerful than the United States to resist and channel the flood of settlers who pushed from the East. The Americans had only a small army and weak officials who seemed unable to control the ravenous settlers who arrived in ever greater numbers.

A Native prophet arose to warn his people that they could no longer accommodate the Americans. In the Indiana Territory in 1805, Tenskwatawa, of the Shawnees, emerged from a trance to tell all who would listen that Native peoples were one, that they must set aside their tribal identities to find common purpose against the white people. The Great Spirit had given the land to them, not to the whites, who were a mere foulness that had washed up from the waters to the East. Tenskwatawa, whose name meant "the Open Door," told pilgrims to his village that they must give up the ways of the Americans: the woven clothing and hats, the domestic animals and dogs, the alcohol and religion. Even firearms should not be used for hunting, only defense.[2]

The Prophet and his followers built, in 1808, a new town, which the white people called Tippecanoe or Prophetstown, devoted to the Master of Life. Sixty cottages surrounded a longhouse and hewn logs for benches where people could listen to Tenskwatawa, who, white visitors reported, spoke powerfully, "with his eyes closed," in a "solemn voice." Young men traveled great distances to hear the Prophet. All Native visitors found welcome in the House of the Stranger, a space set aside for new arrivals to the town.

Prophetstown stood positioned between the Wabash and Tippecanoe Rivers, ideal for defense and for trade. Surrounding villages and cornfields stretched for a mile distant and word of the place spread for hundreds of miles in all directions. Six thousand people gathered in Prophetstown, making it the largest settlement on the western frontier, larger than Pittsburgh or Cincinnati. The town boasted its own warriors, religious figures, and diplomats. Many white leaders in Washington and governors in the territories feared and despised Tenskwatawa. Many Indian leaders did as well, for they benefited from dealings with the Americans that the Prophet challenged and threatened to upset.[3]

The Prophet's older brother, Tecumseh—an impressive warrior, religious figure, and diplomat—grew in public stature. Tecumseh called on William Henry Harrison, the territorial governor, at his fort in 1810, traveling with an honor guard of seventy-five men. The local white newspaper translated the speech Tecumseh delivered during the visit. The Great Spirit, he instructed Harrison, had given the lands "as common property to all the Indians" and they "could not, nor should not be sold without the consent of all." All the "tribes of Indians on the continent formed but one nation" and "they would have no more chiefs, but in future to have everything done under the direction of the warriors." Tecumseh ended his speech with a penetrating question to his white listeners: "How can we have confidence in the white people—when Jesus Christ came upon the earth you kill'd him and nail'd him to a cross, you thought he was dead but you were mistaken."

The white people, Tecumseh warned all Native people who would listen, "are like poisonous serpents: when chilled they are feeble and harmless; but invigorate them with warmth, and they sting their benefactors to death." The red men wished for peace, "but where the white people are, there is no peace for them." The white people "have destroyed many nations of red men because they were not united, because they were not friends to each other." The white men, he told those he hoped to recruit, are only men; they could be defeated.[4]

In 1811 and 1812, three major earthquakes, interspersed with many smaller shocks, radiated from a place called New Madrid, on the Mississippi River. Strange disruptions in the land and air shook the country all the way to the Atlantic. Bells clanged and clocks tolled in distant cities. Steeples swayed and compass needles swung.

The New Madrid earthquakes shattered Native lives along the Mississippi. The tremors and floods destroyed farmland, dislocated villages, and swamped hunting fields. Solid land became quicksand. Networks of exchange broke among the Cherokees, Delawares, and Shawnees. Some Native leaders saw in the earthquakes a sign that Tecumseh and Tenskwatawa were right. A chief of the Potawatomi told his people that the "Great Spirit is angry" because "many children have sold their lands" to white settlers and speculators.[5]

The Creeks, Choctaws, Cherokees, and Chickasaws in the Southeast fought among themselves over the best ways to deal with enemies who schemed to take their land. A Cherokee man named Sequoyah stood in the middle of these conflicts. Born the son of a white man and a Native mother in eastern Tennessee about 1770, Sequoyah became a skilled silversmith and trader. He joined with those who signed a treaty that traded eastern lands for allotments in the Arkansas Territory. Sequoyah experimented with a radical idea: producing a syllabary of the Cherokee language. Sequoyah, like most Cherokee, neither spoke nor read English, but he saw the advantages of written language. After years of trial and error, he devised a system in which eighty-six symbols represented syllables in Cherokee. He adopted English letters from a spelling book, turning some of them upside down.

Sequoyah traveled to the Cherokee territory in Arkansas and told leaders of his system. He confronted skeptics, who doubted that one man could devise an entire written language, so he proved the system by teaching his young daughter, Ayoka, the symbols. She sent her father a message, which he opened before the Cherokee council to demonstrate its power. Sequoyah returned east, carrying a speech from one of the Arkansas Cherokee leaders. Reading it aloud, he persuaded eastern leaders as well of his gift.

The new written language, easily learned, spread quickly. White missionaries were surprised and puzzled to see symbols carved into trees and fences, and then to learn that Cherokee people were sending letters to one another. Resistant to the idea of the Cherokee syllabary at first—since reading the symbols meant knowing Cherokee, which few white people did—the missionaries came to see its power. With Cherokee help, they translated the New Testament, Cherokee laws, and eventually, a newspaper into the language. Sequoyah's syllabary gave the Cherokee a valuable tool and pride, but also helped spread among them the ideals of literacy and of Christianity that eroded traditional authority.[6]

Capital, Banner, and Anthem

Dolley Madison faced a problem. Her husband, James, had been elected president of the United States in 1808. That much was not unexpected, for James Madison had drafted much of the Constitution and served as secretary of state and ally of Thomas Jefferson through his eight tumultuous years as president. People respected Madison's character even though they worried whether his slight frame and diffidence could bear the weight of the office. His wife, seventeen years younger, offered a welcome counterpart to her husband. She used her charm, intelligence, and taste to make his presidency, and the fragile country over which he presided, a success.[7]

Mrs. Madison did not have much to work with in Washington City. Visionary plans for a city-to-be left the current city with looming gaps between buildings connected by muddy roads. The executive mansion was poorly suited to public events and, in fact, had rarely been used for such. Americans remained unsure of how to adorn such a place, for they had rejected British pretension and viewed French style with suspicion. Americans remained uncertain about many things, in fact, including how to make their elaborately balanced government work. The early years of the republic had been filled with the rumor and reality of cabal and conspiracy, of dueling and scandal.[8]

Dolley Madison worked to change the tenor of Washington, beginning with the interior of the executive mansion. Carefully selecting American-made furniture and furnishings, she sought to create a space that embodied the spirit of the new republic, confident and modern yet welcoming and republican. The statues and paintings of the house celebrated American scenes and heroes, featuring a (copy of a) portrait of Washington by the American artist Gilbert Stuart. Mrs. Madison bedecked the parlor in sunflower yellow, framed with yellow draperies around the windows, yellow sofas and chairs, and a rising sun in yellow damask on the fireboard before the fireplace. Mirrors reflected the splendor of the room and those fortunate enough to visit it. She made the larger Oval Room even more impressive, featuring red velvet curtains. She presented herself in simple but elegant dress. Observers agreed that Dolley Madison had found a style worthy of a great if still emerging nation.[9]

Mrs. Madison helped Mr. Madison knit together a government of far-flung places and character. Men and women who had never seen a piano or tasted champagne had to be made comfortable alongside those who had dined in the grand houses of London and Paris. Men who schemed at the head of factions had to chat with one another in the polite company of women. New Englanders and southerners, easterners and westerners, had to mingle with those whose manners did not always please them. Diplomats who arrived in fine golden carriages jostled among people who had not traveled beyond the borders of their home states before their Washington sojourn. Political work was accomplished in this congenial setting, the work of finding common purpose and direction for a divergent nation.[10]

During the season when the federal government was in session, Dolley Madison hosted events almost every evening in the executive mansion. People came by the hundreds—so many, in fact, that the gatherings became known as "squeezes," as guests happily jammed into parlors and hallways. The executive mansion became popularly known as the White House in 1810, a name more domestic and welcoming than the previous President's Palace.[11]

The building, like all of those in Washington City, had been constructed by enslaved labor. The cooks who prepared the food and carried the trays among the guests were Black and held in slavery. The Madisons claimed some of those "servants" as their property and hired others from neighboring slaveowners. White guests generally did not comment on the Black people on whose skill and care they depended. Dolley's favorite cousin, Edward Coles, a young man from Virginia who anguished over his inheritance of enslaved people as he served as personal secretary to Dolley's husband, sarcastically congratulated Madison for presiding over a "great Republic" where the "revolting sight" of slavery filled the capital's streets. Dolley Madison, raised as a Quaker in Philadelphia but now accustomed to service by enslaved people, smoothed over the contradictions in the nation's raw capital as best she could.[12]

Not far away, in a city James and Dolley Madison knew well, the Virginia General Assembly gathered in Richmond in the fall of 1811, bringing in leading men and their families from across the state and beyond. The capital of Virginia boasted Thomas Jefferson's austerely beautiful state capitol building, modeled on a Roman temple, the nation's first neoclassical public building. Richmond also possessed flour mills that drew power from the canal that bypassed the rocky turbulence of the falls on the James. Almost half of Richmond's population of five thousand was African American, most of them enslaved, with hundreds of free Black people living among them. Memories of Gabriel Prosser's rebellion and its bloody repression in 1800 lingered a decade later. Rumors of complicit Frenchmen and Quakers, of revenge against enslavers and white women, of Biblical injunction and sanction had never been put to rest.[13]

The winter social season of that year, remarked one young woman, proved the "gayest winter Richmond had ever known and often we went from one entertainment to another and even a third on the same evening. There was dancing for the young people and cards for the old." On December 26, over 640 people bought tickets to Richmond's theater. Groups of girls filled boxes, their Grecian dresses accentuating their figures, young men hovering about. African American people, both enslaved and free, stood on the floor. Wealthy white men sported canes and cravats, their wives bearing elegant jewelry and the latest hairstyles from England and France. The program promised over four hours of entertainment, two full-length plays interspersed with comic songs, children's performances, dances, and a solo by the leading female of the cast.[14]

Early in the show, a candelabra, its ropes caught in pulleys, tipped toward a backdrop. Flames leapt to the paint-covered hemp sheet and then to the pine ceiling, the raw wood spotted with beads of rosin. Within minutes, the roof hissed with flames that spread to other backdrops. The crowd, trapped by narrow hallways and doors, panicked and were trampled by those behind them. Many tried to help others escape. A muscular doctor lowered a dozen women and girls to an enslaved blacksmith, Gilbert Hunt, who rushed to the theater to offer aid. In ten minutes, the building's roof and stairs collapsed, killing those above and below. The Richmond theater fire marked the worst public disaster of the new nation. Members of the United States Congress wore black for the next month; all balls and parties were canceled in Washington. Disturbing rumors circulated that the fire had been set by enslaved people as a signal for an insurrection.[15]

Ministers in cities and towns far from Richmond judged the conflagration a divine sign against the "prevailing, but most unchristian, and most baneful Amusement" of the theater, a token of "Divine displeasure." One sermon declared that "all those who encourage this sinful practice of plays, &c. are not worthy in this respect to be called Christians." Baptists and Methodists, already opposed to theater-going and devoted to spreading the word of salvation, grew even stronger. A camp meeting near Richmond attracted four thousand people, their singing echoing a half mile away.

Evangelical leaders later remembered that Richmond changed profoundly and immediately after the fire. "Never perhaps has the sudden destruction of men, women, and children, in one overwhelming ruin, produced a greater moral effect," recalled one minister. "All classes of community bowed down before the Lord." New charitable organizations served the poor. Aristocratic fashions gave way to more restrained hues. Card-playing virtually stopped. Local newspapers began to carry religious news.

The religious revolution, however, was more complete in memory than in actuality. The conversion of the nation to evangelical religion had far to go. The veiled deism and skepticism of Thomas Jefferson and other national leaders still held adherents. A future bishop in the Episcopal Church in Virginia admitted that he expected any educated man he met in those days to be "a skeptic, if not an avowed unbeliever." Across the country, in raucous cities and on the ragged frontier, the number of unchurched far outnumbered those who claimed formal membership.[16]

As Richmond struggled to recover, the new nation gambled for high stakes as it challenged the world's most powerful empire. The British undermined Americans' determination to dominate the continent and seized American sailors on the seas. In what enemies called, jeeringly, "Mr. Madison's War," in 1812 the United States declared that it would no longer tolerate Britain's intrusive power on the seas and on America's borders. New England Federalists, seeing in the war a Republican grab for power and an unjustified animus against the British, voted against the war and withheld support, threatening to secede. A war launched to protect the new nation might destroy it in its infancy.

The war against Britain went badly until, on one front after another, it began to go well for the United States. On the Great Lakes, outnumbered British and Native fighters were overrun by Americans fortified by militia on horseback from Kentucky. Tenskwatawa, the Prophet, watched the Battle of the Thames from behind British lines and retreated with them, an exile from the lands he believed a gift from the Great Spirit. His brother

Tecumseh was killed in the battle. Kentucky militiamen flayed the corpse of the man they believed to be Tecumseh, using strips of his skin to sharpen their razors.[17]

On the Chesapeake Bay the Royal Navy longed to punish the hypocritical Virginians who preached liberty while growing rich from bondage. About 3,400 Black Virginians managed to escape to freedom aboard British ships from plantations and towns along the rivers and bays. Most were young men, though women and children increasingly found British allies as well. The runaways directed the British to the most strategic targets as well as to places where enslaved relatives or friends might seize freedom.[18]

The British, ranging at will through the Chesapeake, aimed their contempt toward Washington City. Retaliating for the burning of the Canadian capital of York by the Americans in the preceding year, the British commanders relished the humiliation of the American capital. Dolley Madison rushed to the roof of the White House with a spyglass. With President Madison away surveying the troops, his wife determined to stay as long as possible and defiantly oversaw preparations for a dinner that evening. She gathered state papers and folded away the red velvet curtains of the Oval Room into trunks. Finally, with news of the impending enemy, Dolley Madison ordered her Black servants to unscrew the portrait of George Washington from the wall. When they could not, they dismantled the frame and entrusted the painting to two passing white men to protect it from certain capture, display, and gloating in the streets of London. The British troops, arriving at the presidential home, enjoyed the elegant dinner that had been set out for guests. They then methodically burned the house and all its furnishings.[19]

The British ridiculed the Americans who "would tamely allow a handful of B Soldiers to advance thro' the heart of their Country, and burn, & destroy the Capitol of the United States." Americans agreed. As the treasurer of the United States wrote, "I feel myself humbled & degraded. I have no longer a country or a Government that I can speak of with pride." He had expected the war to elevate America, to win "the lasting respect of all Nations. What an Illusion!"[20]

The Royal Navy, having destroyed the symbolic heart of the new nation, turned toward Baltimore, a city that had sent fast, armed privateers to prey on British ships. The British commanders, determined to devastate Baltimore, deployed a fleet of over fifty warships in the attack. Fort McHenry guarded the harbor with thick walls and more than fifty pieces of artillery. Baltimore residents dug a mile of trenches and earthworks, clogged the harbor to keep the invading force as far away as possible, and recruited ten thousand volunteers for battle on land.

The British launched bombs from the bay, firing 1,500 Congreve rockets from vessels named *Devastation, Terror, Volcano, Aetna,* and *Meteor.* The bombs, each weighing two hundred pounds, screamed through the air before exploding and raining shrapnel on those below. The shattering attack lasted all night, finally falling silent at seven o'clock the following morning. From inside the fort, where only five soldiers had died from the rockets, the Americans raised an enormous American flag crafted by a local woman and her female assistants.

Seeing the flag in the morning mist through a spyglass, a young American lawyer and slaveholder who had initially opposed the war, Francis Scott Key, composed a verse on the back of a letter. The "rocket's red glare" and the "bombs bursting in air," the words declared, had failed to destroy America's vision of itself. Key's song was a hymn of deliverance, grateful for the "heav'n rescued land" and "the power that hath made and preserved us a nation." Key invented the phrase "the star-spangled banner" to describe the flag. He sneered at the British for deploying mercenaries and enticing enslaved people.[21]

Key set the new words to a song whose tune people already

knew, "The Anacreontic Song," a song from a men's club in Britain. At least eighty-four other songs had adopted the tune in America, including one written by Key a decade earlier. At a local printing shop in Baltimore, a teenage apprentice printed a broadsheet of Key's verses. Over the next two weeks the stanzas appeared in newspapers in Baltimore and Washington; two weeks later, readers in three dozen newspapers from Vermont to Georgia, from New Hampshire to Mississippi, could sing the patriotic words to a tune they had learned from the enemies they taunted.

In New Orleans, the Tennessee militia leader Andrew Jackson won an astonishing victory against the British and then turned his forces against Native peoples in the Southeast. As word arrived of Jackson's triumph and of the Treaty of Ghent that ended the war, white Americans celebrated. Congress rebuilt the President's House in Washington and Dolley Madison purchased new furniture. The government of the United States emerged from the War of 1812 with unlikely victories and a consecrated flag yet profoundly divided in ways that would soon become alarmingly evident.[22]

Bondage

In the wake of the war with the British, Andrew Jackson's defeat of the Creeks and negotiation with the Cherokees helped the United States acquire the rich lands that stretched from Georgia through Alabama and Mississippi. Land speculators and their lawyers rushed to monopolize the best tracts; outlaws and swindlers hovered around Mississippi River towns; squatters staked out land to which they did not have title; banks of dubious standing distributed bills of uncertain value; and people paid prices for land they could not recover if prices declined.

Slavery gained new economic life as manufacturers in Britain and the American Northeast turned to American planters for cotton to feed burgeoning textile mills. Slaveholders pushed into new plantation lands where upland cotton flourished, its tenacious fibers pulled from seeds by cotton gins spreading among plantations. The long-planned end of America's involvement in the international slave trade in 1808, rather than slowing slavery's growth, converted the enslaved population of the young United States into a perpetual source of profit. "Georgia traders" prowled among the plantations and towns of Virginia and Maryland, offering high prices for "likely" boys and girls, strong men and fertile women. By 1820, some 350,000 enslaved people lived west of the Appalachians, nearly the number who had lived in Virginia in 1810.[23]

In the face of the disheartening spread and strengthening of slavery, Black Americans pursued the promises of the Revolution and the Declaration of Independence with determination and hope. They founded societies devoted to abolition, confident that, as one Black activist declared in 1806, the new nation was "rising above the mean prejudices imbibed against" people of color and assuring that "equal justice is distributed to the black and the white." Free Black people, encouraged by steps toward abolition taken by northern states, believed that the tides of history ran toward freedom.

By mobilizing themselves through education, respectability, and prosperity, Black men and women in Philadelphia, New York, and other cities demonstrated the capacities of all Black people to thrive in freedom. They believed that the language of inalienable rights and universal freedom would gradually but certainly erase the archaic vestiges of prejudice based on skin color. Black leaders found white allies eager to move the United States toward its founding ideals.[24]

Black Americans also sought to unite with Black people in other nations. Paul Cuffe, the son of an emancipated Ashanti father and a Wampanoag mother from Cape Cod, built a lucrative shipping business that sent vessels throughout the Atlantic in the decades during and following the Revolution. Cuffe, a devout Quaker, warned white Americans that, in their accelerating and expanding domestic slave trade, they were "preparing instruments for their own execution." The only way to avoid disaster was to abandon slavery, but few would do so, Cuffe argued, until advocates of Black people had secured "safe ground" for any slaves they freed. The "peace and tranquility of the world" depended on finding that ground. Cuffe longed for "the liberation of the African race" and believed that in Africa they could "rise to be a people." Cuffe took ten Black American families of about forty people to the British colony Sierra Leone, on Africa's western shore. They sailed on Cuffe's own ship, carrying a year's provisions.[25]

The American Colonization Society, founded in 1816, damaged Cuffe's vision of a global Black community. The ACS recruited Henry Clay, a slaveholding senator from Kentucky, to assume the presidency of the society. The goal of the new organization, Clay assured his listeners, was to protect white Americans from the growing numbers of free Black people in their midst, who constituted "a useless and pernicious, if not dangerous portion of its population." Because of "the unconquerable prejudices resulting from their color, they never could amalgamate with the free whites of this country." Faced with this threat, Clay warned, the United States must find a way to "drain them off." White Americans, innocent agents of a system of slavery imposed by the British, could create a peaceful future for slavery in their new nation. The ACS chartered a colony they called Liberia; the capital, originally named Christopolis, became Monrovia, in hopes that President Monroe might support their efforts.[26]

Free Black people denounced colonization from the outset. Having fought with "undaunted courage" for the new nation in the Revolution, they claimed the United States as their "native soil." A meeting in Philadelphia, attracting three thousand people, unanimously denounced the purposes of the American Colonization Society: "WHEREAS our ancestors (not of choice) were the first cultivators of the wilds of America," they proclaimed, "we their descendants feel ourselves entitled to participate in the blessings of her luxuriant soil, which their blood and sweat manured." They would not forget their kindred held in bondage and would never "separate ourselves voluntarily from the slave population in this country."[27]

Black people in Virginia, confronting daily threats from the domestic trade in enslaved people, tried to make use of the opening created by the American Colonization Society. Lott Cary, an enslaved Black man in Richmond who taught himself to read, write, and maintain business ledgers while he worked in a tobacco warehouse, purchased the freedom of himself and two of his children. In 1821, Cary led a group of Black men and their families to Liberia, supported by themselves and the white members of First Baptist Church. Cary did not hide his hatred of slavery: "I am an African, and in this country, however meritorious my conduct, and respectable my character, I cannot receive the credit due to either," he announced in his farewell sermon to Virginia. "I wish to go to a country where I shall be estimated by my merits, not my complexion, and I feel bound to labor for my suffering race." White Virginians joined with Black Virginians to send more than three thousand people to Liberia by the end of the 1820s.[28]

Some white Virginians struggled with themselves over slavery in the new nation. Edward Coles, a relative of Dolley Madison and neighbor of Thomas Jefferson, knew he would inherit a plantation and its enslaved people even though he intended to free any human property that came to him. Coles wrote an anguished letter to Jefferson to "entreat and beseech" the great man "to exert your knowledge and influence in devising and getting into operation some plan for the general emancipation of slavery." Jefferson held a particular duty to do so, Coles urged, because of the great statesman's "known philosophical and enlarged view of subjects, and from the principles you have professed and practiced through a long and useful life." Jefferson replied warmly, praising Coles for bringing the subject forward but would not lead a march toward freedom. "This enterprise is for the young, for those who can follow it up and bear it through to its consummation. It shall have all my prayers, and these are the only weapons of an old man." Jefferson urged Coles to remain in Virginia to preside as a benevolent master until some undefined process of general education of white people allowed slavery to end peacefully, until some future effort enabled the formerly enslaved to be colonized in some place other than the United States.[29]

Disappointed by Jefferson's response, Coles set out on his own path. In 1817, Coles sold his Virginia land and headed west to look for a place where he and seventeen of the enslaved people he had inherited would be free of slavery. He found fertile land in Illinois just across the Mississippi River from the promising town of St. Louis. On the riverboat journey to the new lands, Coles gathered the enslaved people around him to promise land so "that the descendants of Africa might demonstrate that they were well able to care for themselves and enjoy the blessings of liberty and thus promote universal emancipation." He hoped to establish a model for other Virginia slaveholders. Even though many white Virginians regretted slavery's hold on their state, few followed Coles's example. Instead, they sought to diminish slavery in Virginia by selling men, women, and children to the cotton regions farther south, where they would chop and dig plantations on land taken from Indigenous peoples.

Ambiguities of slavery, identity, and freedom in the new nation created some openings for free Black people scattered throughout the South. Black families with both free and enslaved members waged decades-long legal suits to secure freedom for themselves and their descendants. Some families established a place for themselves by gaining property and going to court to protect themselves. Others purchased security through their mastery of trades and businesses. Some free people of mixed white and Black ancestry, especially in cities, set themselves apart from Black people with darker skin while others allied themselves with those in slavery.[30]

Amid the uncertainty and contradictions of slavery and Black freedom in the 1810s, a political crisis revealed the stark divisions facing the nation. Slaveholders had moved into rich river lands in the territory of northern Missouri, using forced labor to gain advantage over settlers reliant on free and family labor. Under the slaveholders' power, and in the face of white hostility to Black people, in 1819 Missouri applied for statehood with slavery.[31]

The debate over Missouri's admission to the Union inflamed a nation already under intense pressure from a severe financial downturn. The opponents of slavery shuddered as they witnessed the acquisition of Florida from Spain in 1819, which threatened to add another slave state, and as they confronted slavery's spread across the Mississippi River and into regions where cotton would not grow. Advocates of slavery, for their part, bristled as abolitionists celebrated the Haitian revolution and campaigns against slavery in Britain's and Europe's colonies in the New World.[32]

Slaveholders recognized that if the free states were a majority in the United States Senate, the movement against slavery would threaten the institution's future. After bitter debate and unprecedented slurs against the North and the South, Congress admitted Missouri as a slave state, counterbalanced by the admission of Maine—formerly part of Massachusetts—as a free state. Slavery would be prohibited everywhere in new territories north of Missouri's southern border.

Americans, Black and white, saw the problem of slavery with a new clarity. They were forced to recognize that the United States, so recently unified by victory in war with Britain, might break into separate and competing nations. While politicians in Washington managed to patch together deals to avert disunion, no one was satisfied by the outcome. After 1820, slavery would cloud every hope and dream of the American people.

The crisis over slavery soon erupted in the wealthiest city in the slave South: Charleston, South Carolina. In the summer of 1822, officials in Charleston heard rumors of a planned slave revolt. White men swept through Black neighborhoods and households, rounding up suspects and forcing them to testify against one another. The evidence proved tangled and contradictory, but eventually a story emerged that white people believed and acted upon. The story settled on Denmark Vesey, a powerful free Black man who had purchased his own freedom, as the villain of the piece, the mastermind. Biblical quotations in the court proceedings testified that the language of the Bible, read or heard or whispered, fired the imaginations and hearts of enslaved people. America's enslaved people and the people of Israel shared a powerful vision of eventual deliverance.[33]

White officials arrested 131 people, hanged 35, and transported 37 from the United States. Vesey, called on in prison by the leading Baptist minister of the state, was offered prayers, but "would hear nothing they had to say," for it "was a Glorious cause he was to die in." He was hanged. White Charleston mobilized by building a "Citadel" for their arms, forbbidding Black sailors to leave their ships to come on shore, and policing the mails and newspapers to stop the contagion of antislavery in the words of politicians and abolitionists.[34]

White Americans recognized the growing international contempt for the slavery they embraced ever more tightly. In 1824, the

Marquis de Lafayette, the French hero of the American Revolution, came to the United States on a tour to help unify the scattered new nation. The sixty-seven-year-old traveler visited all twenty-four states, from Maine to Louisiana. Lafayette embodied virtuous and selfless service. Revered by Thomas Jefferson as well as John Adams, Lafayette knew no regional prejudice or party identity. Americans used their speeches, editorials, songs, and trinkets to celebrate themselves along with Lafayette, boasting of their unexampled combination of freedom and prosperity, claiming to lead a global march of progress and democracy. The hero's aristocratic ancestry, rank, and bearing made his respect and affection for the democracy of the new United States more flattering.[35]

Lafayette, for all his politesse, quietly reminded Americans that the United States had not indeed "perfected" free government. Lafayette's antislavery efforts in Europe were well-known, and he had corresponded with American friends about his hopes that the United States would end slavery. Astounded and dismayed by the cancerous growth of slavery he witnessed in the South and the callous racism he found everywhere, Lafayette demonstrated his respect for Black Americans. In New Orleans, Lafayette publicly thanked the Black soldiers who had helped Jackson defeat the British in 1815, shaking the hands of each veteran. "I have often during the War of Independence," he told the group, "seen African blood shed with honor in our ranks for the cause of the United States." The marquis made a point of talking with a delegation of Creeks who met with him in Alabama.[36]

For much of his journey, Lafayette invited the company of Frances Wright, a Scottish advocate for liberty in many forms. Like Lafayette, the twenty-nine-year-old "Fanny" Wright had used an inheritance to disdain convention and expectation. She had visited the United States several years before and in 1821 published *Views of Society and Manners in America*, praising the United States and applying for American citizenship. Lafayette responded warmly to Wright's book and invited her to join him in the America they both loved. Wright and her sister accepted the invitation, traveling on their own along Lafayette's route.[37]

Wright, like the marquis, held no racial prejudice and could not comprehend the taboos, fears, and suspicions white Americans attached to dark skin. Though kindly received by Jefferson as well as by James and Dolley Madison, Wright was appalled by what she saw of slavery in Virginia. The slave trade to South Carolina and Georgia had infected the old plantation districts of eastern Virginia, where enslaved people were treated much like cattle: "They are advertized in the same way, exposed and sold in the same way, driven in the same way and spoken of and treated in the same way." The celebration of Lafayette by slaveholders across the South, day after day, weighed on Wright. "They who so sin against the liberty of their country, against those great principles for which their honored guest poured on their soil his treasure and his blood, are not worthy to rejoice in his presence," she wrote with clenched teeth.[38]

Disheartened, Wright found inspiration in an unlikely source. Robert Owen, after a series of humane and profitable reforms at his textile mill in Scotland, came to America to invest in a bold experiment in 1824. He believed that a small community, focused on diversified work and mutual welfare, offered the best chance for a healthy social order. Owen thought America held the keys to the world's future. He and his sons traveled to the Wabash River in Indiana, not far from Prophetstown, where Owen purchased 180 buildings and several thousand acres previously occupied by a religious group of poor immigrants from Germany who had established a thriving town they called Harmony on the site.

Hoping for broad support, Owen spoke in early 1825 to the House of Representatives in Washington, attended by the outgoing president, James Monroe, and the president-elect, John Quincy Adams. Owen celebrated the principle of "mutual co-operation" as more productive and profitable than self-interest. Some of those who heard Owen dismissed him out of hand, but others found in his message a thrilling prospect. Fanny Wright, listening to Owen in Washington, counted herself among the converts.

Wright visited Harmony—soon to be christened "New Harmony" by Owen—where she saw a vision of a world as it could be, filled with purpose and cooperation. As she continued her journey down the Mississippi River to New Orleans, Wright confronted a terrifying contrast. "Slavery I expected to find here in its horrors, and truly in all its horrors it is found." In New Orleans, "every man's hand is against the hapless slave and every law of man's creation." Returning north on the river, struck by the beauty along the way, she could "have wept as I thought that such a garden was wrought by the hands of slaves!"[39]

Wright determined to extend Owen's principles to enslaved people. Combining practicality with idealism, Wright would buy enslaved people who would gain education and skills to establish new lives in freedom while they repaid the price of their purchase. Children would learn "order and co-operation from the schoolroom into the field," with enough play to keep "their minds cheerful, and their bodies vigorous."

Wright thought that, for once, her sex might prove an advantage, protecting her from violence that might meet a man proposing to challenge slavery. She set out to raise money for a farm in western Tennessee, bought on public land, to be worked by fifty to one hundred enslaved people. Wright expected her model to spread rapidly and widely as planters saw the benefits of such a system. Wright purchased 320 acres as well as six men and four women. She named the enterprise after the Chickasaw word for the river that watered the land: Nashoba. Lafayette reluctantly agreed with Wright's plan, though warning of its dangers. James Monroe approved of the project and Thomas Jefferson sent a long letter praising her effort.

Wright worked her way from New York back to the South in

late 1829, lecturing to packed houses—and vicious opposition—along the way. She spoke of freedom in all its forms: for working people, for religious dissent, for the rights of women. Americans flocked to see Fanny Wright even though they often came to mock or denounce her, throwing vegetables, burning garbage, and extinguishing lights to disrupt a woman who dared speak to a "mixed" audience of men and women. She "has with ruthless violence broken loose from the restraints of decorum," railed a paper from Louisville, to leap "over the boundary of feminine modesty, and laid hold on the avocations of man, claiming a participation in them for herself and her sex." A defiant Wright reprinted the denunciation in the *Free Enquirer*, a paper in New York that promoted her radical cause.[40]

Unable to raise the money to sustain Nashoba, Wright chartered a ship to take her, a male ally, and thirty-one enslaved people from Nashoba to Haiti. The Haitians celebrated Wright and provided excellent farms for the Black people she brought with her. Leaving Haiti for Philadelphia, Wright discovered that she had become pregnant while in a relationship with the man who had accompanied her to Haiti. Though she had pledged never to marry, Wright had also lectured that both parents held responsibility for any child they created together.

Before her pregnancy became evident, Wright returned to the Northeast. In her final speech in New York, three thousand people—many of them women—crowded into the theater to hear Wright declare all people "occupants of the same earth, citizens of the same country, creatures of the same form and nature." Free public secular education held the key for American progress, and Wright pleaded for her listeners to pursue that noble purpose. She sailed to England soon thereafter, where she married the father of her child and removed herself from public view for several years.[41]

Wright's American crusade would long be remembered for its bravery and its iconoclasm. Her principles of female independence, economic equality, and outspoken defense of justice would inspire many. The charge of "Wrightism" would be leveled against those who dared challenge convention in any way.

Heaven

Americans in the early nineteenth century enjoyed a religious freedom unknown in Europe. With established churches discredited by their connection with Britain, people sought new forms of faith. They found many ways, mostly in evangelical churches, but others in visions of American prophecy.

Christian ministers worried that religious faith would dissipate in newly settled areas, where authority had grown weak and moral chaos threatened. Denominations fought against one another over matters of doctrine and within themselves over issues of governance. In this time of spiritual disarray and decline, people prayed for a revival of faith, for the creation of a Christian nation before the centrifugal forces of settlement pulled the new country apart. Many found themselves believing that the fate of the world depended on the moral regeneration of America.

Charles Grandison Finney grew up in Henderson, one of Upstate New York's many raw communities. In 1818, twenty-six years old, tall, handsome, athletic, and ambitious, Finney had never heard sermons that moved him. Studying law with a local magistrate, his mind "not made up as to the truth or falsehood of the Gospel and of the Christian religion," Finney purchased his first Bible to trace the origins of Scripture quoted in legal cases. Intrigued but not persuaded, he listened at prayer meetings at a nearby Presbyterian church, noting that even eloquent and impassioned prayers seldom received answers. Confronted with the failure, Finney felt driven near "sceptism," for "it seemed to me that the teachings of the Bible did not at all accord with the facts which were before my eyes." He struggled, night after night, with unresolved doubt and suspicion. People in the congregation prayed for his awakening, but many doubted it would come. Finney shared their doubts, though he studied the Bible as he worked in the law office, hastily covering his spiritual reading with law books when people visited on business.[42]

Suddenly, in the autumn of 1821, Finney's mind was opened "by an inward voice." Stopping in the street of the village of Adams, New York, near Henderson, the young man saw, "as clearly as I ever have in my life, the reality and fullness of the atonement of Christ." Finney heard that God required him only "to give up my sins, and accept Christ." Finney knew "that God wanted me to preach the Gospel, and that I must begin immediately." Finney discovered that he no longer had a "disposition to make money. I had no hungering and thirsting after worldly pleasures and amusements in any direction. My whole mind was taken up with Jesus and His salvation; and the world seemed to me of very little consequence."[43]

Finney immediately began to minister to neighbors who gathered to hear him. Young people "were converted one after another, with great rapidity." The word "spread among all classes; and extended itself, not only through the village, but out of the village in every direction." Finney, for all his success, struggled to persuade some who believed in Universalism, in the salvation of all souls without the intervention of miracles or the divinity of Christ. He also confronted a learned Calvinist, who argued that salvation "was made for the elect and available to none else." Finney, untutored in theology, could not believe that Christ would withhold salvation from any who accepted Him. Prominent allies offered to pay Finney's tuition if he would study theology at Princeton, but he declined because he "did not expect or desire to labour in large towns or cities, or minister to cultivated congregations. I intended to go into the new settlements and preach in school-houses, and barns, and groves."

Finney had no new theology or vision. His was a struggle with sin and doubt experienced by generations of Christians before and after him, a conviction of salvation promised to all who accepted Christ. Anyone could receive the gift, Finney preached, and yet the promise of that gift divided the young from the old, the educated and uneducated. Finney, threatened with tarring and feathering in one community, strode to the pulpit in a crowded church to speak as "a fire and a hammer breaking the rock."

Evangelical Protestantism did not establish easy dominion anywhere in the new United States. What Finney called "nothingism" dominated, for most Americans did not belong to a church of any denomination. Deism, skepticism, and Universalism challenged the vision of the Trinity, of miracles, and of submission that men such as Finney preached so passionately. Later generations would talk of the early nineteenth century as the Second Great Awakening, embracing the story the advocates of Protestantism told about their triumphs, but Christians knew that people awakened could fall back to sleep. As their very revivals testified, faith demanded constant renewal in the face of sin, lassitude, and new preaching.

Faced with the challenge of ministering to the most mobile and literate population in world history, Christians turned to the printed word. Christians needed "powerful action" because they confronted "vicious literature" everywhere they looked, the output of what they called the "satanic press," the "loathsome swarms of 'literary vermin' to 'corrupt the land,' to deprave the hearts, and ruin the souls of our citizens." Cheap books of religious skepticism, seduction, and murder spread in competition with Bibles and tracts, often winning. To counter such a flood, the American Bible Society formed in 1816 in New York City, attracting officers such as Justice John Marshall of the Supreme Court and Francis Scott Key.

The American Bible Society adopted "stereotyping," plates that permitted pages to be printed in unlimited numbers without resetting type, along with new steam-powered presses and advanced papermaking. The Society distributed Bibles in the slums of the nation's cities and in remote cabins, selling to those who could afford the books so they could give others away for free. Through these means, Bibles proliferated in the 1820s; many households owned a Bible and no other book. The language of the King James Bible echoed throughout America, its cadences, names, and parables familiar to believer and unbeliever alike.[44]

The American Tract Society grew alongside the American Bible Society. The Tract Society established depositories across the country, distributing almanacs with "facts relative to the present state of the world," newspapers that boasted "lively talent in a style of its own," and brief books for young children. Tracts, the Society declared, "are needed in *the most simple style*, and especially *narratives* calculated to engage and fasten the attention." The American Sunday School Union launched in 1824 to educate the nation's burgeoning young population. The leaders of the Union acknowledged that "there is no such thing as a *natural taste* for religious reading," which had to compete with "books abounding with foolishness, vulgarity, and falsehood." Fired with purpose and facing devious competition, the Sunday school proponents produced fourteen million pages in 224 publications in their first year and ever more thereafter. If the Kingdom of God did not flourish in America, it would not be for want of printed inspiration.[45]

The expanding Christian denominations sought to translate their social power into political power. In 1826, the Presbyterian General Assembly urged members of their denomination to boycott every company that carried mail by stage, steamboat, or canal packet on Sunday. Americans had sought to protect the

Christian Sabbath before, but now an expanding post office system of the United States brought the dilemma of Sunday delivery into every community. That same postal system empowered citizens to work together with "the uniformity of a disciplined army" so that "whole states may be deluged with tracts and other publications."[46]

Sabbatarians, outraged that the federal government's post offices undermined the holiness of the Sabbath, organized vast petition campaigns to protest: "We will let Congress know that our rulers shall obey us; that *WE are their MASTERS!!*," they thundered. "Monster petitions" bearing thousands of names flooded into Congress, every major Protestant denomination lending its weight. Opponents of the Sabbatarian crusade warned that such efforts by Protestants would be the "entering wedge" of an "*ecclesiastical hierarchy*" that would trample the rights of Jews, Catholics, and others who did not subscribe to their selfish demands. The Sabbatarian campaign failed, but the Christian crusade to dominate government at every level continued.[47]

Gold Plates

Joseph Smith embodied the longing that traditional Protestantism failed to fill for many Americans. His family, like so many, had moved repeatedly to gain a foothold in an America that seemed full of elusive promise. In Upstate New York, the Smith family supported themselves by selling painted oilcloths, baskets, and brooms, hawking cakes on court days, and digging wells for neighbors. The children did not have much time for school, and so picked up what they could learn from one another and their parents. In 1820, the Smiths put money down to purchase a hundred acres on time, building a cabin to house six boys and two girls, ranging in age from two to nineteen. They struggled to meet the payments.[48]

The Smith family members were divided regarding matters of faith. Their village of Palmyra claimed a Methodist church, a Quaker assembly, a Presbyterian church, and a large Baptist meetinghouse. The mother and some of the children attended the Presbyterian church, but the father and other children stayed home. Joseph grew disgusted by the rivalries and jealousies among the churches, contests inflamed when revivals set believers of one denomination against other Christians. The revivals created "a stir and division amongst the people." Rather than bringing people closer to God, "All their good feelings for one another (if they ever had any) were entirely lost in a strife of words and a contest about opinion."[49]

Smith agonized over his sins, real and imagined. In 1820, when he was fourteen, he went to the woods, like Charles Finney, to ask God's direction. He experienced a "a pillar of light above the brightness of the sun at noon day come down from above and rested upon me and I was filled with the spirit of god and the Lord opened the heavens upon me and I saw the Lord and he spake unto me saying Joseph my Son thy sins are forgiven thee. Go thy way walk in my statutes and keep my commandments." Like Finney, Smith felt his soul "filled with love." But when Joseph told a Methodist minister of his conversion, he was met with disdain. Such visions were all too common, the pastor told Smith, fleeting and often imaginary. The days of miracles had ended with the apostles. Only patient prayer, sermons, and meetings could sustain salvation.[50]

Smith kept his struggles to himself. The handsome young man struck no one as unusually preoccupied with things of the spirit, but on an early fall evening in 1823, after the other members of the household had gone to bed, he prayed. The room grew as bright as daylight. Suddenly, "a person appeared in the light standing above the floor. He had on a loose robe of most exquisite whiteness. The visitor announced himself as the angel Moroni and instructed Smith that God had chosen him for an arduous task.

Moroni told Smith of a book, "written upon gold plates, giving an account of the former inhabitants of this continent and the source from whence they sprang." The book contained "the fulness of the everlasting Gospel . . . as delivered by the Saviour to the ancient inhabitants." Along with the book lay "two stones in silver bows" that God had prepared "for the purpose of translating the book." The plates and the tools were buried on a hill about three miles away, among scattered trees. Smith knew the place and went there to find the promised gift. Moroni had warned Joseph not to be tempted by the earthly luster of the gold, but when the young man saw the plates he succumbed to their beauty and reached out to touch them, only to be shocked and rebuked by the angel. Smith was not ready, the angel told him, and should leave the plates and the stones until he was twenty-one and ready to assume the burden and responsibility.

That evening, Joseph Smith told his family of the vision and of his journey. His mother recalled them "seated in a circle, father, mother, sons and daughters." They gave the "most profound attention to a boy, eighteen years of age; who had never read the Bible through in his life." Though the "sweetest union and happiness pervaded our house, and tranquility reigned in our midst," Joseph warned that the "world was so wicked that when they came to a knowledge of these things they would try to take our lives." The family would have to keep the secret even though they knew that God would soon share with them "a more perfect knowledge of the plan of salvation and the redemption of the human family." The Smith family proceeded as if nothing had happened, waiting for the plans to unfold as God intended.

Seeds

New settlements in the west attracted people who found little comfort in communities back east. One such person was a New Englander named John Chapman, who devoted his life to spreading the gift of apple trees to new and struggling farms where they might not grow otherwise. Traveling alone, often barefoot and dressed in secondhand clothes, sleeping without shelter, Chapman shared saplings and seeds with farming households bereft of sweetness and variety in their diets. He accepted payment in whatever a family might be able to offer, perhaps a worn shirt, a shared meal, or a place to sleep on the floor near a fire. Chapman paid special attention to young children and shy wives often neglected by male visitors.[51]

Apples did not naturally flourish in North America, where they tended to be small and hard, misshapen and bitter. Farmers could grow more attractive apples only by grafting, binding a favored variety of a tree to an existing root. John Chapman knew that most new homesteads could not afford the time, stock, or skill for such cultivation, so he helped by bringing saplings and seeds to isolated farms as he moved from Pennsylvania to Ohio.

In his travels, Chapman came across the writings of Emanuel Swedenborg, a wealthy Swedish polymath who had written volumes in the preceding century telling of his visits with angels and his detailed knowledge of hell and heaven. One young girl on the frontier was spellbound as she heard Chapman talk: "I stood back of my mother's chair, amazed, delighted, bewildered, and vaguely realizing the wonderful powers of true oratory." Chapman told of Swedenborg's principle of correspondences, in which everything earthly held a heavenly counterpart. Nature radiated meaning if people would only pause to respond to the messages of streams, mountains, and apple trees, if they realized how close heaven hovered to those who opened their eyes.[52]

John Chapman's eloquence and determination confronted challenges in the late 1820s, as agricultural reformers worked to persuade farmers with their own gospel. Only lazy and thoughtless farmers, correspondents declared, would grow trees from seeds when it had been proven that grafted trees produced superior fruit. Attacks on apples came from another direction as well: a burgeoning temperance movement driven by evangelical Protestants. In the view of those reformers, the kind of fruit produced from Chapman's stunted trees was good for only one thing: being pressed into cider, a cider easily and frequently fermented into alcohol. "It takes a long time to make a man a drunkard on cider," one temperance advocate declared, "but when made, he is thoroughly made, is lazy, bloated, stupid, cross and ugly, wastes his estate, his character, and the happiness of his family."[53]

To these reformers of farming and moral character, John Chapman appeared an agent of slovenly agriculture and intoxication. Later, histories of frontier days would tell of the harmless eccentric "Johnny Appleseed," who peddled strange gospels of heaven along with speckled and stunted fruit. Pushed aside in his own day, the mythical figure grew famous in articles and poems, the gentle and isolated wanderer embodying a story of the American frontier cleansed of dispossession and despoliation.

The young United States pushed in every direction at once in the first decades of the nineteenth century. Rather than maturing and settling, the new nation uprooted itself over and over. The United States congratulated itself on its military victories, territorial expansion, and prosperity for white people. Some people thought they saw in the disarray promises of a future of peace and order, even as others warned of a grievous future for a nation that refused to reckon with the wrongs that grew within.

Chapter Two

RECKONINGS

1820–1832

Who Reads an American Book?

In 1820, an editor of the *Edinburgh Review*, though "a friend and admirer" of America, chastised the young nation for its claims to be "the greatest, the most refined, the most enlightened, and the most moral people upon earth." After all, despite decades of independence, "In the four quarters of the globe, who reads an American book? or goes to an American play? or looks at an American picture or statue?" The British critic expressed a hard truth.[1]

Over the first two decades of the nineteenth century, several isolated people had attempted to write an American book people wanted to read. Some Americans sought to position themselves within the traditions and fashions of the British literature they knew and respected; others sought distinctively American voices and themes. Without an American publishing industry to print and distribute their books, these authors found themselves with few compatriots and few readers.

Despite these disadvantages, several American writers forged literary identities for themselves. Some managed to find audiences on both sides of the Atlantic, while others would be discovered decades later. They each crafted their visions alone, in places apparently uncongenial to visions.

Charles Brockden Brown sought to comprehend the nation taking shape around him. A native of Philadelphia born in 1771, the young man composed novels, stories, and essays at a rapid pace, the most haunting of them written in feverish visions in the years around 1800. Brown imagined a fantastical America that belied its placid surface of farmers and shopkeepers. He searched for the meaning of borders and boundaries, physical and psychological, between men and women, citizens and aliens, white people and people of color, America and the world, slavery and freedom.[2]

Brown, a precocious but sickly boy, had seen his Quaker father imprisoned for refusing to fight against the British in the war for independence. He watched as Philadelphia changed after the Revolution, the tides of trade washing away older standards of deference, classical learning giving way to practical arts, people of unknown origins presenting themselves as people worthy of trust. Brown experimented with one form after another to explain the transformations, from learned essays to imagined dialogues.

Influenced by Mary Wollstonecraft and other models from England, Brown decided that novels provided the clearest insight into the confusing scenes that surrounded him. In his late twenties, Brown launched out on several novels at once. For one, *Wieland*, he drew on the true story of a New York farmer who killed his wife and children in a religious vision. For two others, *Arthur Mervyn* and *Ormond*, he portrayed the terrifying scenes of the yellow fever epidemic in the 1790s that devastated Philadelphia and other American cities, and that killed his best friend. For another, *Edgar Huntly*, Brown translated stories of attacks by American Indians on isolated white settlers into a novel drenched in blood. In each novel, irrational and unnamed forces drove people insane, tricked them into killing those they loved. Ventriloquism and sleepwalking offered putatively rational and scientific explanations for acts of horrific violence. Brown chronicled the vertigo of a society that had dispensed with the customs and respect of the past.

Brown's books had no means of sale and distribution, for the literary trade of the United States relied on volumes imported from England or peddled from town to town by itinerants. Pressed with the need to make a living and start a family, Brown turned to forms of writing better suited to the means at hand: the periodicals and newspapers that filled the new nation. He wrote in favor of the Louisiana Purchase and against racism, attacking "that arrogance, which would confine to one race, the characteristics of the species." He died in early 1810, only thirty-nine years old, from tuberculosis, leaving a young wife and four small children in Philadelphia, his work and his promise unfulfilled. Brown's dark and convoluted novels would inspire writers who followed over the next several decades, in America and in Britain.[3]

Washington Irving determined to bridge American and British tastes, seeking polish and calm in all he wrote. Born in 1783 and growing up in polyglot Manhattan, in 1809 Irving published a parody history of New York, based on the nonexistent papers of one recently deceased fictional Diedrich Knickerbocker. The parody was a hit, widely read and profitable. Irving, only twenty-six, found himself famous, but he had no other writing to offer, no clear sense of direction or purpose. When presented an opportunity to travel to Britain in 1815 as part of the family business, he took it for lack of better occupation.[4]

In Scotland, Irving visited the famous novelist Walter Scott, who had expressed admiration for Irving's *A History of New York*. Scott encouraged Irving to write about the Hudson River Valley he had evoked in his history spoof. Scott also suggested that Irving read German folktales for inspiration. Irving followed both pieces of advice, writing two stories set in New York. A friend in Manhattan arranged for publication in the United States of a series of installments, to be gathered into *The Sketch Book* under the pseudonym of Geoffrey Crayon. Most of the sketches were of Britain, but the installments that included the American stories immediately sold out.

In "Rip Van Winkle," as generations of readers would know, a shiftless Dutch colonist, henpecked by his nameless wife, saunters off to the woods, falls asleep, has a strange dream, and returns to his village to find that he has been gone twenty years. In the meantime, the American Revolution has come and gone. The portrait of the king above the tavern has been replaced with a portrait of George Washington, and an unfamiliar flag of stars and stripes waves atop a pole in the town square. Rip's daughter takes him in and he spends the rest of his days smoking contentedly and telling of his strange adventure. Rip's long nap allowed Irving, as an American expatriate, to step around the two wars fought between two countries he sought to please. The other American story in the collection, "The Legend of Sleepy Hollow," portrayed an awkward schoolmaster, Ichabod Crane, tormented by a vision of a headless hessian soldier chasing him through the dark American forest.

The Sketch Book became a sensation on both sides of the Atlantic, selling more copies than the poems of Lord Byron. One British critic admitted that, to his surprise, "everywhere I find in it the marks of a mind of the utmost elegance and refinement, a thing as you know I was not exactly prepared to look for in an American." Washington Irving suddenly became famous and prosperous. Every major American author for the next forty years would try to follow Irving's example, tapping into the larger and more profitable British market at the first opportunity, trying to satisfy two audiences at once. The lack of copyright protection and the ease of unauthorized reprinting in both countries meant that authors needed to publish on both sides of the Atlantic.[5]

In Upstate New York, James Fenimore Cooper, born in 1789, had been promised a bountiful inheritance of $50,000 in his father's will. Cooper borrowed against the expected funds, mortgaging lands and juggling debts, but mismanagement by older brothers and declining land prices on the New York frontier forced Cooper to find other ways to pay his bills. One evening in 1820, reading aloud a new English novel to his young family, Cooper cast the book aside and declared with disgust that "I could write you a better book than that myself!" His wife jokingly challenged him to live up to his boast and Cooper, with little else to occupy his time, plunged into the task.[6]

Cooper wrote as fast as he could and paid for the printing of the book himself. The volume, thanks to his hasty and illegible writing, was filled with errors. The book failed to find readers, but Cooper began a second book even before the first one appeared. This one, *The Spy*, evoked New York during the American Revolution. Cooper admitted that "the task of making American manners and American scenes interesting to an American reader" would be "arduous," but he believed that a stirring novel of American resolve, resourcefulness, and loyalty to the revolutionary cause would appeal to a new generation of confident Americans. Cooper moved to a hotel in New York City, where he handed chapters to the printer as he finished drafting them. *The Spy* appeared at the end of 1821 and sold briskly in New York and Philadelphia.[7]

Encouraged, Cooper wrote *The Last of the Mohicans* in 1824. The combination of the resolute white hero and the noble but doomed Indian, a scene that had played out in the white imagination for generations, proved irresistible to white readers. The book proved immediately and enduringly popular in the United States and, more importantly in financial terms, Britain. Cooper, in books he published in rapid sequence, invented a character variously named Natty Bumppo, Hawk-eye, the Deerslayer, and Leather-Stocking, the prototype of the solitary hero who would stand at the center of American culture for two centuries. Cooper and his family, their finances finally settled after years of struggle and turmoil, left New York for England, intending to stay a year. They would be gone instead for eight.

An American author boldly set out to emulate and then challenge Cooper. Born in 1793 to a childhood of genteel poverty in Maine, John Neal had made himself into a specialist in penmanship, a reluctant student of the law, and a frequent failure in business. In Boston, he "began to cast about for something better to do—something, at least, that would pay better; and after considering the matter for ten minutes or so, determined to try my hand at a novel." Novels had grown popular in Britain and America with Sir Walter Scott's stirring historical dramas.

Neal had already published *Keep Cool: A Novel Written in Hot Weather*, in 1817 under the name of "Somebody." *Keep Cool* told of a white man who, after killing another man in a duel, retreated to the wilderness to live among Native people. Inspired by Cooper's *The Spy*, Neal wrote four more novels in 1822 and 1823. *Seventy-Six*, a story of the Revolution, did well, despite being, apparently, the first to use "son of a bitch" in print.[8]

Neal moved to London, where he wrote pseudonymous essays that analyzed one hundred American writers in alphabetical order. Neal told his British readers that they paid attention to the wrong American books, for the bestselling volumes by Irving and Cooper were merely British books transposed in their settings. The writers worth paying attention to were Charles Brockden Brown and John Neal. Brown's works, he enthused, are "full of perplexity—incoherence—and contradiction," words that Neal intended as praise. Even better than Brown was Neal, "the most original writer, that America has produced." Neal "overdoes everything—pumps the lightning into you, till he is out of breath, and you, in a blaze," his five novels burst forward "as course of experiments" that tested the "forbearance of the age." Neal's books did indeed test forbearance, for they told of interracial marriage, rape, incest, and open sexual desire.

Neal, despite his self-promotion, failed to eclipse Cooper's growing popularity in Britain and the United States. Neal returned home, where his neighbors expressed outrage for his harsh judgments of American writers. When Neal arrived in Portland, residents posted broadsides denouncing their native author, attacked him in the streets, and blocked his admission to the bar.

He would overcome their objections in coming years to edit an influential magazine, write short stories, perform as a flamboyant public speaker, advocate feminism, open the first gymnasium in America, oppose slavery, and eventually prosper as a businessman and civic leader in Portland.

Neal abandoned novels but encouraged those who might follow. Do not forget, he urged, that "there are abundant sources of fertility in their own beautiful brave earth" of America. Neal's tempestuous novels of the 1820s particularly impressed two aspiring young writers: Nathaniel Hawthorne and Edgar Allan Poe. Poe would, twenty years later, rank John Neal "first, or at all events, second among our men of indisputable genius."[9]

More immediately successful than the confrontational John Neal was Catharine Sedgwick, a young novelist who wrote of Christian women who used their faith to navigate a patriarchal world filled with the challenges of faith, property, and marriage. Raised in New England in a family of stern Calvinist belief, Sedgwick moved steadily toward Unitarianism and its message of human goodness and free will. She published, anonymously, *A New-England Tale* in 1822, telling of a heroine overcoming adversity through simple honesty and concern for others. Another novel, under her own name, did well, portraying the jumbled class relations and blurred religious distinctions of America in the 1820s.

Finding herself selling better than Washington Irving and James Fenimore Cooper, Sedgwick peered back into early New England for her next novel, *Hope Leslie*. Published in 1827, Sedgwick's novel was the first to portray Native people with the complexity of white characters. In words that echoed Tecumseh's in the previous decade, a Pequot woman asks of the Puritans who beheaded a sixteen-year-old boy, "You English tell us that the book of your law is better than that written in our hearts, for ye say it teaches mercy, compassion, forgiveness—if ye had such a law and believed it, would ye thus have treated a captive boy?" *Hope Leslie* endured as one of the most popular novels of the era, challenging the simple portrayal of Native people put forward by male authors.[10]

The first American stories, poems, and novels experimented to see what American writing might be. Together, they created characters, plots, and scenes that would recur throughout generations of American literature. Already, at the beginning of the new nation, American writers wrestled with the meaning of Native people for a white readership, finding guilt and anxiety, disdain and compassion. These first writers, too, made the American landscape an active agent in their works, locating scenes of danger and madness in limitless forests, humor in isolated hollows and villages. In a nation reputed to be without history, authors pushed into the past nevertheless, to the Puritans, the early days of settlement, and the tumult of the Revolution.

Much of what would emerge as American literature, in other words, began to appear in the first American books.

Capturing Nature

Americans killed wild animals in uncountable numbers. The centuries-old fur trade had already decimated populations of deer and beaver. Buffalo would soon follow. Battles against bears and wolves filled the stories of settlement. Guns made it possible to kill birds in enormous numbers, without skill or restraint, devastating passenger pigeons that passed in flocks so great they darkened the sky.

One young immigrant devoted himself to painting images of all the birds of North America before they disappeared, killing them to do so. Arriving in Pennsylvania from Haiti by way of France in 1803 at the age of eighteen, John James Audubon developed an early and enduring fascination with the birds he saw migrating each year near his new home. On his own, he developed a technique to pose freshly killed specimens as if they were living, painting them quickly before they began to decompose. He drew and painted the birds in apparent action, striving to capture their feathers, eyes, beaks, and feet in exact detail.[11]

After failing in various businesses, Audubon opened a store on the Ohio River in Kentucky. There, he met a visiting author peddling what Audubon considered less-expert paintings of American birds. Determined to create his own comprehensive collection of paintings, Audubon won a letter of introduction from his congressman—Henry Clay—for a journey from Kentucky down the Mississippi River to document the birds in the new states and territories. Leaving his wife and two young sons behind, Audubon drifted downriver on a flatboat, paying his fare by hunting game during the boat's frequent stops. In New Orleans, Audubon supported himself by painting portraits and giving lessons. In every moment, including some in which he should have been earning a living for his family, he continued to shoot and paint the birds that surrounded him.

Finally exhausting himself and his possibilities in Louisiana, Audubon traveled to Philadelphia, New York, Pittsburgh, Louisville, and back to Louisiana to find support for his ever-growing collection of bird paintings. Failing, he decided, like other American authors and painters, to turn to Britain. In 1826, Audubon displayed his paintings in several British cities, whose newspapers praised his work for its "semblance of life and motion," creating "an aviary of skies, where birds of all plumage and of all dispositions are sporting around."

Audubon staged himself as part of the show, posing as the "American Woodsman." A portrait of him painted in Britain showed hair flowing on his shoulders, a rough fur coat, a rifle in his hands, and a distant prey in view. At forty-one, Audubon had finally become what he had always dreamed of being, an American admired for his skill in science and art. Unfortunately, Audubon embodied other traits of the United States emerging in the 1820s. He enslaved people and decried emancipation, and he resorted to shady business dealings and plagiarism in his determination to beat others to market and to win acclaim.

Audubon determined to gather his work into the largest book ever published so that he could present his birds in the "size of life." He recognized the challenges—"I must acknowledge it renders it rather bulky, but my heart was always bent on it, and I cannot refrain from attempting it so." *The Birds of America* would be breathtakingly expensive, but if Audubon could sell several hundred copies to individuals and institutions, he could finally provide his long-suffering wife and children the living he had promised.

Audubon helped develop an engraving and printing process worthy of his art. His patrons would receive portraits of large birds and small, in sets of five, five times a year. Completing the work of collecting and painting all the birds Audubon promised would require another decade of migration back and forth across the Atlantic, journeys through the forests, swamps, and shores of America from Maine to Florida to Texas. The "Great Work" accrued one image at a time, the exotic bounty of the United

States captured for the world to see. He would eventually complete the work in 1838, when his interests shifted to quadrupeds.[12]

A young immigrant and self-taught painter, not unlike John James Audubon, sought to capture the American landscape even as it changed before his eyes. Arriving from England in 1818 at age seventeen, Thomas Cole and his family moved from one city to another as his father tried and failed to establish a wallpaper business. Along the way, Cole met an itinerant portrait painter who introduced him to an instruction book. "This book was my companion day and night," Cole recalled, "nothing could separate us—my usual avocations were neglected—painting was all in all to me." As he engraved patterns for calico and wallpaper, "in my imagination I pictured the glory of being a great painter."[13]

In 1823, Cole moved with his family to Philadelphia, where he decorated stage sets and transparencies displayed during Lafayette's triumphal tour. Visiting the galleries of the Pennsylvania Academy of the Fine Arts, Cole found himself drawn to paintings of landscapes. Though the genre fell in prestige below that of history, Bible, and mythological painting, landscape required no skill in portraying people, a craft Cole had not been able to acquire from his books. Fortunately, a taste for landscape painting had grown among Americans with money to spend on such works, their interest developed through travel, reading, and tourism in England and Europe. Influential landscape artists, funded by these patrons, sought out places untouched by the industry and cities growing rapidly in the eastern United States, looking for places that came to be known as "picturesque."

From New York, the Hudson River Valley beckoned tourists with the Catskill Mountain House on a palisade high above the Hudson. Guidebooks told visitors of picturesque scenes nearby, of falls, lakes, and vistas. Cole began painting those scenes, carefully omitting evidence of human intervention. Word quickly spread in

New York of the talented young artist. Only in his mid-twenties, Thomas Cole suddenly emerged as a leading American painter.

In 1827, Cole painted scenes from Cooper's bestselling *The Last of the Mohicans*, depicting a uniquely American history in a genre long devoted to biblical and classical themes from the European past. Cole chose four powerful scenes from Cooper's novel, each featuring Native people and the mixed-race heroine, Cora. Cole's paintings confronted white Americans with Native people more complex and imposing than they had known before. The American Indians in the paintings bore the grandeur of figures caught amid tragic choices, shown in acts of diplomacy, governance, and violence. Cole combined sketches of landscapes from the White Mountains of New Hampshire with those of the Hudson River Valley to create a fitting epic scale, one that collapsed several scenes in the novel into compelling tableaux. A giant circle of the Native council, judging whether the heroine should live or die, evoked a history larger than any scene in the brief national history of the United States. The paintings conveyed a rare respect for Native people.[14]

John Neal returned from London to discover Thomas Cole and others who painted landscapes near New York. These artists "are better than we deserve, and more than we know what to do with," Neal gushed. "Their progress too, is altogether astonishing, if we consider the disadvantages under which they have laboured, with no models, no casts, no academy figures, and little or no opportunity for them to see the old masters gathered together, where they could either be copied or studied with impunity."[15]

Thomas Cole traveled to Britain after his early success to expand his influence and to learn. Like John James Audubon, who published *The Birds of America* at the same time Cole painted *The Last of the Mohicans*, Cole found in the Old World a fascination with the New World and a curiosity about the artists who imagined they could bridge the two. Painters, like novelists, would market American difference even as they sought the approval of Europe, navigating the Atlantic as well as the North American continent. The approbation of Britain and the Continent would sustain those who sought to represent the United States.

Hero and Despot

Andrew Jackson had navigated the chaos of the southern frontier as the eighteenth century became the nineteenth. Moving west from the Carolinas into eastern Tennessee, with little education but raw ambition, Jackson made himself into a lawyer and then, in middle Tennessee, a planter. He led a coffle of enslaved people from the Mississippi River to begin his plantation, married well, and rose into leadership of local and state militia. That position empowered him to lead volunteers against the British and Indians in the South in the War of 1812. After his victories, newspapers across the nation filled columns with praise for the man his troops had named "Old Hickory," the hardest wood in the southern forest. Congress commanded a gold medal struck in his honor. Building on his fame, Jackson represented Tennessee in the House of Representatives and Senate in Washington. There, politicians saw in the American hero the foundations of national political alliances that would benefit them all.[16]

Despite his popularity, Jackson lost the presidency in 1824 to what he and his supporters claimed to be a corrupt bargain between John Quincy Adams and Henry Clay. Four years later, the Tennessean and his men determined to overwhelm what they saw as a self-satisfied elite in Washington. Jackson surrounded himself with twenty longtime friends and allies who wrote a campaign biography, answered the many slurs on his reputation, and prevented Jackson from entangling himself—as he was inclined to do—in ugly exchanges that filled the papers and the mail. In Tennessee, Jackson's team subscribed to eighteen newspapers and worked with counterparts across the country to build a national coalition. In places large and small, newspapers reprinted each other's praise and attacks. Local committees staged marches and parades, and handed out trinkets and badges provided by central organizers.[17]

Jackson's message was simple and direct. The new United States belonged to households overseen by white men. Those men must be unobstructed by Indians or any foreign power. Slavery and the slave trade should be unimpeded. Government at every level should remain inexpensive and unobtrusive, serving only to enable settlement quickly and at low cost. Concentrations of power were inherently corrupt and dangerous, whether in banks, corporations, or publicly funded canals and turnpikes. Money should be tangible and material, not based on paper and promises. Those who would challenge such visions were devious and unprincipled, enemies to the republic.[18]

Jackson projected an image of virility even though his health had been decimated by the long-ago battles in which he won his reputation. The former general was nearly toothless, coughed up phlegm, and suffered constant pain from bullets lodged in his body. Jackson managed to sustain his reputation with the aid of a full-time painter who portrayed him in guises of a general or a gentleman farmer as the occasion demanded.[19]

The strategies of mobilization worked: a million white men voted in 1828, more than four times as many as in the previous presidential contest. The election forged a complex political machinery that created alliances across twenty-four states, uniting workingmen in eastern cities with farmers on barely cleared land in the West and South.[20]

News of Jackson's political triumph arrived just as his wife,

Rachel, died in December 1828. Jackson blamed his enemies for her death, for they had charged her with bigamy decades before. In office, Jackson sought, but failed, to resolve a crisis that grew up around the marriage of a cabinet member to a young woman of contested reputation. Jackson found himself impotent against enemies who delighted in chaos and scandal, who dragged the private into the public. The politics of personality and publicity, essential to Jackson's rise, could punish as well as reward.[21]

The Indians' Advocate

By the late 1820s, the position of the Native peoples of the South had grown ever more desperate. The Creek, Cherokee, Choctaw, and Chickasaw lived directly in the path of the cotton frontier, occupying the richest lands along the largest rivers. Some Native men sought personal advantage rather than the collective good of their people, selling lands from their nations to the United States without the agreement of others. Many members of these so-called Civilized Tribes had adopted Christianity and learned to read and write English. Some of the Native people trafficked in Black slaves and worked them on their farms to produce cotton. Those slaveowners had mastered the details of markets and property as practiced by white people.

Other Natives rejected the religion, slavery, or ideas of property put forward by white people, whom they avoided by retreating to remote homesteads. No matter what strategy Indian people followed, white settlers and officials took Native land in whatever way suited them.

The Cherokees built a capital at New Echota in north Georgia in 1824. The village contained a court building, a church, and plans for other public buildings. They published a newspaper, *The Cherokee Phoenix and Indians' Advocate*, printed in Sequoyah's

Cherokee syllabary as well as English. The paper was edited by Elias Boudinot and Samuel Worcester, a missionary. Boudinot, born in Georgia of Native and white ancestry, educated in Christian schools in New England and married to a white woman, documented the unceasing assault on Cherokee lands. White men covetous of Creek and Cherokee land increased their incursions, thefts, and threats, their violations inflamed by the discovery of gold on Cherokee land in Georgia in 1829. Georgia expelled any white man who would aid the Cherokees. Samuel Worcester challenged the law and was sent to prison. He appealed the case to the United States Supreme Court.[22]

Finally coming to believe that the removal of his people to lands west of the Mississippi was inevitable, Boudinot counseled the Cherokee to sign a treaty with the United States. Most Cherokees rejected this plan, led by Principal Chief John Ross, also of mixed ancestry and educated in Christian schools. After growing wealthy as a planter and businessman, Ross worked in Washington to win rights for the Cherokee. In 1829 and 1830, Congress divided over a bill to remove the Native peoples of the South. The bill's outcome in doubt, the White House warned legislators that the Indian Removal Act was the president's "favorite measure." Those who did not support the measure would be known as "traitors and recreants."[23]

Opposition to Jackson's demands for dispossession gathered force and numbers. "Now is the time when every Christian, every philanthropist and every patriot in the United States ought to be exerting themselves to save a persecuted and defenceless people from ruin," urged Jeremiah Evarts of the American Board of Commissioners for Foreign Missions. His articles were reprinted in more than a hundred newspapers across the United States, and a pamphlet assembled from those articles reached more than half a million people in 1829.

As Evarts traveled to build support for the cause, he called on Lyman Beecher in Boston, one of the most influential advocates for Protestant reform. The family's oldest daughter, Catharine, felt the injustice. At the Hartford Female Seminary, where she was director, Catharine Beecher met with several friends to consider opposition to Jackson's impending bill. Among those friends was Lydia Sigourney, a popular writer. They decided to circulate a letter "addressed to the benevolent ladies of the United States."

Though Beecher, Sigourney, and their allies worked anonymously, the letter's authors proudly announced that it came from the hands of women. This "Ladies' Circular" urged its readers to use both "prayers and exertions to avert the calamity of removal." Quoting treaties that clearly established the promises the United States had made to the Cherokee, the circular told women they were above "the blinding influence of party spirit." Disenfranchised, women "have nothing to do with any struggle for power" and so could act from purely benevolent purposes. Those who read the circular should not pause, for a delay of "*a few weeks*" would decide the question, after which "sympathy and regret will be in vain."

The Ladies' Circular spurred women to action across the North. One petition from Pittsburgh bore the names of 670 women. The major religious publications printed the circular on their front pages, only a few with mild admonishments to women not to venture too far into the public realm. The circular, the first petition put forward by American women on their own, caused Catharine Beecher such anxiety that she refused to acknowledge authorship and experienced "many narrow escapes from falsehood in efforts to preserve our secret." Thomas Hart Benton, chairman of the Senate Committee on Indian Affairs, launched an elaborate parody of the petitions, pretending that, with the help of a "famous corset-maker" to "draw me up a little," he would "march in bonnet, cloak, and petticoats, than in hat, coat, and pantaloons."[24]

Both the harsh debates over removal and the petitions pitched the South against the North. While a defender of the Native people disparaged the "force and terror" inflicted by state governments that imposed "grinding, heart-breaking" law over them, a Georgia senator contemptuously replied that no worthy treaty could be made with "a petty dependent tribe of half-starved Indians." Northern philanthropists, he sneered, should send food and clothing to aid the "half-starved and naked wretches" instead of supporting a newspaper that spread lies on their behalf. The struggle went on for months, neither side relenting. Six-hour speeches led to eight-hour rebuttals.[25]

The opposition to Jackson's Indian Removal Act changed the North. The Ladies' Circular demonstrated that women could mobilize for political purposes, using the power of the petition to gather their voices. The effort revealed, too, that Christian faith could exert influence beyond personal salvation and stir people to action. Jackson's many opponents saw that he could be challenged politically, even if he might triumph through brute force and threat.

Appeals to the World

Free Black people in the North, their numbers enlarged by manumissions and emancipation by states in the years after the Revolution, launched crusades to end slavery in the United States. Outraged by the presumptions of the colonization movement, they built networks of self-determination and self-protection to promote the immediate abolition of bondage in the new nation. Some white people devoted themselves to the vision of Black freedom.

David Walker, a free Black man from North Carolina, had been in Charleston near the time of the tumult over Denmark Vesey in 1822. Walker then moved to Massachusetts, where he opened a used clothing shop in Boston, married, joined a Methodist church, and opposed the colonization movement that would send free Black Americans to Africa. Walker allied himself with *Freedom's Journal*, the first African American newspaper, founded in New York in 1827 by John Wilk, Peter Williams Jr., and other free Black leaders. They intended the paper to serve as "a medium of intercourse between our brethren in the different states of this great confederacy." *Freedom's Journal* attacked the American Colonization Society and celebrated the accomplishments of people of African descent in Haiti, in Africa, and in the United States. Walker, ever more prominent as a leader, addressed the Massachusetts General Colored Association in 1828, an organization created two years earlier "to unite the colored population" throughout the nation.[26]

In his speeches, organizing, and writing, David Walker developed ideas he published in 1829 in his *Appeal to the Coloured Citizens of the World*. His thesis was direct: the Black people of the United States were "the most wretched, degraded and abject set of beings that ever lived since the world began, down to the present day." Why? Because "the white Christians of America, who hold us in slavery, (or, more properly speaking, pretenders to Christianity,) treat us more cruel and barbarous than any Heathen nation did any people whom it had subjected."

With these words, Walker confronted white Americans' understanding of themselves as the embodiment of enlightened Christian democracy. Walker attacked Thomas Jefferson, whose death a few years earlier had elicited praise and mourning across the United States. Jefferson lied and misled on every front, Walker raged, poisoning the minds of the white people who so admired him. Jefferson opined that Black people were inherently inferior and so would have to be removed "beyond the reach of mixture" so they would not pollute white democracy. Jefferson had characterized Black people as unattractive, lazy, sexually licentious, and "dull, tasteless" in their imagination and reasoning. "Mr. Jefferson's remarks respecting us," Walker concluded, "have sunk deep into the hearts of millions of the whites, and never will be removed this side of eternity."

The *Appeal* shifted from one kind of rhetoric to another, sometimes reassuring white people that all Americans could live together if white people repented, other times acknowledging that white Americans showed no signs of changing their minds, hearts, or acts. Sometimes Walker chastised his fellow Black people for submitting to injustice, but other times told them to trust in God for deliverance. Walker wrote an anguished text for an anguished time, when it seemed that nothing people of goodwill said or did made any difference.[27]

Walker hoped that "all coloured men, women and children, of every nation, language and tongue under heaven, will try to procure a copy of this Appeal and read it, or get some one to read it to them." His rows of exclamation points and lines of bold type indicated where a reader might speak with special force and emphasis. The pamphlet was carried by Black sailors into Georgia, North Carolina, South Carolina, and Louisiana. State legislatures rushed to pass harsher laws against literacy among enslaved people. In the third edition of the *Appeal* Walker ridiculed white people for "the fearful terror they labor under for fear that my brethren will get my Book and read it." He sarcastically paraphrased the Declaration of Independence: "'we hold these truths to be self-evident, that all men are created equal,' &c. &c. &c."[28]

Native Americans, like Black Americans, spoke with disdain and outrage of the injustices they suffered at the hands of white people. William Apess, descended from the Pequot as well as a white ancestor, gave voice to the Natives of New England. A devout Methodist, in 1829 Apess published his autobiography, *A Son of the Forest*. Apess told how he had suffered abuse and neglect as a child, leaving at fifteen to fight for the United States in the War of 1812. Seeking respite and self-reformation afterward, Apess turned to the Pequot community he had not known since his childhood. There, he found his identity and his cause. Apess traveled throughout New England, preaching to audiences of white, Native, and Black people, fusing the language of Christianity with respect for the humanity of Indigenous people. He became friends with many in the free Black community of Boston.

In 1833, Apess published "An Indian's Looking Glass for the White Man," imploring white people to reflect on the value they placed on "skin," on color. In the world of nations, Apess reminded them, white people constituted "but a handful," yet if all the peoples of the world came together in one place, "and each skin had its national crimes written upon it—which skin do you think would have the greatest?" Apess gave white people a hint: "Can you charge the Indians with robbing a nation almost of their whole continent, and murdering their women and children, and then depriving the remainder of their lawful rights, that nature and God require them to have?" And who had robbed Africa of people "to till their grounds and welter out their days under the lash with hunger and fatigue under the scorching rays of a burning sun?"

Apess confronted his readers with the words of the religion they shared: "Did you ever hear or read of Christ teaching his disciples that they ought to despise one because his skin was different from theirs?" Jesus Christ and "his Apostles certainly were not whites—and did not he who completed the plan of salvation complete it for the whites as well as for the Jews, and others? And were not the whites the most degraded people on the earth at that time?" Apess, himself of mixed ancestry, scoffed at the phobia against amalgamation. "I can assure you that I know a great many that have intermarried, both of the whites and the Indians—and many are their sons and daughters and people, too, of the first respectability." And yet it was illegal in Massachusetts for a clergyman or justice of the peace "to encourage the laws of God and nature by a legitimate union in holy wedlock between the Indians and whites."[29]

The movements to end slavery and to stop Native expulsion spoke to each other in a new American language, a language that combined the moral certainty of Christian faith with the secular certainty of the Declaration of Independence. Both languages defended the value of the individual person as an object of rights and as an advocate for the rights of others. Women—white, Black, and Indigenous—rose to become eloquent and passionate advocates of American equality.

Water, Steam, and Rail

Robert Fulton and Robert Livingston, having shown steam power river-worthy on the Hudson in New York in 1807, in 1811 determined to prove that steamboats could navigate even the long and turbulent Ohio, Missouri, and Mississippi Rivers. They shipped, piece by piece, a hundred-ton steam engine overland from New York to Pittsburgh, where workmen assembled a boat of spruce and oak, painted it sky blue, and named it *New Orleans* in hopeful honor of its destination. Twice the size of most other craft on the river, the *New Orleans* placed its heavy engine between paddle wheels on each side, driving the boat at up to ten miles per hour. The loud, fiery, and smoky craft passed through the devastation and turbulence of the New Madrid earthquakes without pause.[30]

Another steamboat company sent its *Enterprise* south with cannonballs and guns to Andrew Jackson in New Orleans. After the victory there in 1815 against the British, the *Enterprise* left New Orleans for an upriver trip to Ohio, a journey of more than two thousand miles, the first steamboat to overcome the currents of the mighty rivers. Soon, thousands of others would follow, uniting the Northwest and Southwest in a way impossible only years before, pushing into smaller rivers to carry cotton from new plantations to New Orleans.[31]

In the 1810s a former mayor of New York City, DeWitt Clinton, promoted a canal that would traverse a natural passage between the Hudson River and Lake Erie. After the federal government declined to support the canal, New York's state legislature stepped up. Clinton traveled the proposed route, gathering over a hundred thousand signatures on a petition, spinning visions of boats laden with "flour, pork, beef, pot and pearl ashes, flaxseed, wheat, barley, corn, hemp, wool, flax, iron, lead, copper, salt, gypsum, coal, tar, fur, peltry, ginseng, beeswax, cheese, butter, lard, staves, lumber," and other goods from "all parts of the world." Such a canal would "create a new era in history," he rhapsodized, a work "more stupendous, more magnificent, and more beneficial, than has hitherto been achieved by the human race."

Skeptics and opponents could not slow the tide of enthusiasm built through Clinton's crusade. Engineers and workmen progressed from one successful stage to the next, gathering expertise, confidence, and investment in the enterprise. The canal was itself simple: a ditch four feet deep and forty feet wide, dug by men and aided by horses and oxen. Nothing could proceed until the way had been cleared of roots and stumps, so workmen devised a machine with wheels sixteen feet in diameter that held another wheel two feet smaller wrapped with a chain and attached to a team of four horses that pulled enormous stumps out of the ground.[32]

By 1821, nine thousand men worked on the canal. New towns arose along the canal even before its completion in 1825. Freight and people moved on canal boats seventy feet long and only inches narrower than the eighty-three locks on the canal. The boats were pulled by two horses on the towpath beside the canal, horses often tended by boys—"the most profain beings that now exist on the face of this whole earth without exception," complained one local man. Traffic on the canal surged immediately, bonds returned high returns, and New York paid the debt on the project ahead of schedule. Throughout the Northeast and Midwest other states rushed to build their own canals, also financed by bonds and state borrowing.[33]

Cities and states looked to the new technology of railroads to complement and compete with canals. Martin Van Buren, a leading politician of New York, in 1829 warned against railroads, an innovation that would endanger the employment of "captains, cooks, drivers, hostlers, repairmen and dock tenders . . . not to mention farmers supplying hay for horses." Worst of all "'railroad' carriages are pulled at the enormous speed of fifteen miles per hour by 'engines' which [endanger] life and limb of passengers, roar and snort their way through the countryside, setting fire to crops, scaring livestock, and frightening our women and children. The Almighty certainly never intended that people should travel at such breakneck speed."[34]

States without New York's favorable geography for a central canal turned to the railroad as an alternative and a complement to shorter canals. The railroad had been used on a small scale in Britain, but Baltimore decided on a more ambitious gamble on the new machinery. The Fourth of July 1828 saw Baltimore, the nation's third-largest city, celebrating with a joyous parade to mark the launching of a "rail-road." The last living signer of the Declaration of Independence, ninety-year-old Charles Carroll, turned the first soil for the Baltimore and Ohio. Twenty-two thousand Baltimore citizens—a quarter of the population—invested in the line, buying stock in their city as well as the technology.

The plans for the B&O were audacious, cutting across a challenging landscape to reach four hundred miles to the Ohio River in present-day West Virginia. The Alleghenies through which the B&O would pass offered an "inexhaustible profusion of coal" to fuel the engines. Railroads would be many times faster than canal boats, rocketing ahead at a previously unimaginable twenty-five miles an hour. Despite their remarkable speed, one enthusiast predicted, railroads would soon offer "little travelling palaces" to allow passengers to "eat, drink, sit, stand or walk, and sleep, just as they do in steam boats."[35]

A newspaper proclaimed that the B&O promised, in a phrase that would soon become a cliché, the very "annihilation of time and space." Though space and gravity could not be "wholly conquered by the ingenuity of man," they are to be "subjected to his dominion." Vast mountain ranges would submit to the "pressure of unconquered steam." Reaching deep into the American interior, the B&O would bring "an empire to our doors." The first steam engine on rails, the American-built *Tom Thumb*, a vertical black boiler perched on a heavy wooden frame, evoked images of a teakettle, but within two years the B&O delivered, in just one six-day period, nearly 1,500 barrels of flour, 86 tons of granite, and over 2,000 passengers to and from the city.[36]

The South proved just as eager to adopt the latest technology as the North. The South, in fact, had already benefited disproportionately from leading innovations: the introduction of the textile industry in Britain and New England, the spread of the cotton gin, and the profusion of steamboats on southern rivers in the 1820s. Enterprising planters in South Carolina looked to adopt railroads as quickly as their northern counterparts. Charleston worried that it was falling behind Savannah in the cotton trade and that its earlier glory as the most prosperous city in North America for white people was fading. Leading men advocated for a 136-mile railroad to Hamburg, South Carolina, across the Savannah River from Augusta, Georgia, to speed cotton transport from the booming upcountry of the state.

Six months after the ceremony in Baltimore, the South Carolina legislature chartered three railroads. Soon, the *Best Friend of Charleston* locomotive ran seventy-three miles and enjoyed the first post office contract in the country for a railroad. Enslaved labor built much of the line, "doing the work in the very best manner." The company claimed that its locomotives covered more miles daily than any other railroad in the world and cost much less per mile to build than any northern counterpart. Georgia, Mississippi, Alabama, and Tennessee began to dream of railroads of their own. The South and slavery joined the first stages of the technological transformation of the nation from its outset.[37]

Whether in literature, politics, reform, or economy, an expectation of change defined America's vision of itself, a place where nothing long remained what it had been. The United States became a land of perpetual becoming.

Chapter Three

REBELLIONS

1827–1836

Freedom's Advocates

The Reverend Richard Allen's African Methodist Episcopal Church in Philadelphia created a base for Black self-determination and inspired people throughout the North and into the South. It was in Allen's church that Jarena Lee, a young widow with two children, felt called during a service. As a male minister struggled in his preaching, Lee stood in a pew and compared herself to Jonah; she was also prevented from her divine mission of spreading the gospel. The Reverend Allen rose before the shocked congregation to defend the woman's right to preach.

In 1827 alone, Jarena Lee would travel 2,325 miles to deliver 178 sermons, journeying north to Maine and west to Ohio to speak in churches, barns, storehouses, and meeting halls, converting thousands. "Why should it be thought impossible, heterodox, or improper, for a woman to preach?" she asked. "Did not Mary, a woman, preach the Gospel?" Lee would preach for the next thirty years, joining a growing chorus of Black voices.[1]

Another young Black woman followed a journey of freedom and self-assertion. Maria Miller had been born in Hartford, Connecticut, in 1803. Orphaned and without siblings, at the age of five she found herself indentured to a white minister's family. In her teens, Miller joined a Black church in Hartford, where she studied the Bible and improved her writing ability in a Sunday school. Eager to escape the site of her indenture and hungry for greater experience, Miller moved to Boston. There, the young woman met James W. Stewart, a veteran of the War of 1812 and a successful shipping agent. Like other Black sailors, Stewart worked to secure greater freedom and equality for Black Americans. Miller and Stewart were married in 1826.

For three years, Mrs. Maria W. Stewart enjoyed what she recalled as "the sunshine of prosperity." She established friendships with other prominent Black women in Boston and came to know David Walker and his wife. Walker's business in secondhand clothing for sailors put him in the same business circles as James Stewart, who outfitted ships and supplied sailors, many of them Black. Walker worked as an agent for *Freedom's Journal*, a paper read aloud in the meeting rooms where Black Bostonians gathered. He was also at work on his *Appeal to the Coloured Citizens of the World*, which circulated through the hands of those sailors landing in southern ports. His words of defiance, driven by the Bible and the Declaration of Independence, inspired the young Mrs. Stewart.

Two months after the publication of Walker's *Appeal*, in December 1829, James W. Stewart suddenly died. Though he was considerably older than his wife, his death nevertheless shocked the Black community. Maria Stewart's expectations of a comfortable life disappeared as creditors exerted claims on her late husband's estate. Years of lawsuits followed, each one diminishing Stewart's inheritance and standing. In August 1830, David Walker also died, followed by the death of the minister most important in the young widow's life. Stewart made a public profession of her belief in Christ in 1831 and drew the conviction that she must speak out.

The twenty-eight-year-old Maria Stewart composed an essay she titled "Religion and the Pure Principles of Morality, the Sure Foundation on Which We Must Build." She delivered it to the office of the *Liberator* headed by the young white editor William Lloyd Garrison. A wealthy Black supporter from Philadelphia, James Forten, a proud veteran of the American Revolution, provided funding, inspiration, and credibility for Garrison's paper. Black men worked as agents of the *Liberator*, seeking subscribers and contributors among free Black communities along the east coast from Maryland to Massachusetts and into Canada and Haiti.

Garrison, like Stewart, found inspiration in the words of David Walker. Largely self-taught after growing up in Newburyport, Massachusetts, Garrison had worked as a printer on reform newspapers. Only twenty-six years old, Garrison launched the *Liberator*, on January 1, 1831, the anniversary of the abolition of the African slave trade and the founding of the Haitian republic. In October, he published Stewart's remarkable declaration.

As a widow, Stewart spoke with a freedom denied married women or women who had never married. Stewart urged her fellow Black Americans to prepare for God's deliverance. Her personal anguish and sense of abandonment charged her writing, delivered in the cadence of the Bible. When she saw how few Black men and women "care to distinguish themselves either in religious or moral improvement, and when I see the greater part of our community following vain bubbles of life with so much eagerness," she admitted, "I really think we are in as wretched and miserable a state as was the house of Israel in the days of Jeremiah."[2]

But it was the United States that bore the sin. "Oh, America, America, foul and indelible is thy stain! Dark and dismal is the cloud that hangs over thee, for thy cruel wrongs and injuries to the fallen sons of Africa," Stewart thundered. "The blood of her murdered ones cries to heaven for vengeance against thee. Thou art almost become drunken with the blood of her slain; thou hast enriched thyself through her toils and labors; and now thou refuseth to make even a small return." Stewart warned white Americans that "too much of your blood flows in our veins, and too much of your color in our skins, for us not to possess your spirits." The day of justice would come, for "it is the blood of our fathers, and the tears of our brethren that have enriched your soils. AND WE CLAIM OUR RIGHTS."

"All the nations of the earth are crying out for Liberty and Equality. Away, away with tyranny and oppression!" Stewart proclaimed. "Shall Afric's sons be silent any longer?" She struggled with a troubling question: if, as she argued, Black people enjoyed a special relationship with God, why did God allow them to suffer so? In Virginia, a young enslaved man had long wrestled with the same questions. A different vision drove him to act.

Rebellions against Slavery

Virginia enslavers sold people to the cotton lands of the South in ever-growing numbers in the 1820s and 1830s, and yet slavery still dominated the demography, economy, and politics of the state. Counties in the eastern half of Virginia, to the Blue Ridge Mountains and up to Washington, DC, possessed Black majorities. Free Black people lived throughout eastern Virginia, concentrated in cities and scattered in rural communities, accounting for about one Black person in ten. Free and enslaved Black people worked, had children, and worshipped together.[3]

Black Virginians had long adapted evangelical Christianity to their own visions. Since the late eighteenth century, when the gospel of salvation had spread rapidly through Methodist and Baptist churches, some Black people listened attentively. They had no formal churches of their own, but they met in isolated places beyond the scrutiny of white people. They found inspiration in the deliverance of the Israelites, in the glory of the Exodus, in God's judgments against enslavers who held others in bondage. The Black congregations found inspiration, too, in the story of Jesus and his followers, of men and women favored by God despite, or even because, of their poverty. The persecution of the Jews and the physical suffering of Jesus evoked their own experience. The boundary between the world of the Bible and the world of Virginia seemed permeable, the days of miracles and prophecy still at hand.

In many Virginia communities, Black Christians outnumbered white Christians. Though many of the people in slavery held to faiths brought from Africa or to no faith at all, by 1830 over a hundred thousand Black people in Virginia worshipped Christ. Most attended churches overseen by white people, but they also prayed and gathered beyond the hearing or sight of those who would supervise their spiritual as well as their earthly lives. Free and enslaved Black preachers traveled throughout the countryside, ministering to individuals and to impromptu congregations. They did not wait to be ordained, nor did they desire that sanction. Some had learned to read; others interpreted the Bible from what they heard.

Nat Turner, a thirty-year-old enslaved man in Southampton County, Virginia, had seen signs that he stood in divine favor. Though his secular life had inflicted humiliations, whippings, and powerlessness common to those in slavery, Nat saw indications, over many years, that some great purpose lay in store for him. He held himself aloof from his fellows, and yet they listened to him. He baptized a young white man despite the prohibition against such actions. He traveled from one farm to another, gaining a following. He saw signs in the sky, like those in the Bible, that foretold struggle and deliverance. He gathered allies who would help him overthrow their oppressors when the time arrived. In August 1831, that time came. Nat and his band traveled through Southampton County to the county seat of Jerusalem, killing white families who held slaves.[4]

Word spread quickly, first to the state capital in Richmond and then across the nation. The governor received news that "devastation" had descended on Southampton County, an old tobacco district about seventy miles to the southeast of the city: "an insurrection of the slaves in that county had taken place." The governor was told that "several families had been massacred and that it would take a considerable military force to put them down." Horrifying reports came in from Southampton: "Whole families, father, mother, daughters, sons, sucking babes, and school children, butchered, thrown into heaps, and left to be devoured by dogs and hogs, or to putrify on the spot." Reports soon arrived, too, of the Black people who had been killed in retaliation or panic. Virginia newspapers told of the "slaughter of many blacks, without trial, and under circumstances of great barbarity."

After the spasm of killing, white leaders downplayed the scale if not the ferocity of the insurrection and the reaction it unleashed, insisting that only forty or fifty enslaved men participated, many of them coerced. Just a few men led the violence, they reassured white people, enslaved men by the name of Nelson, Artist, and Turner, all but one of whom had been killed. But Virginia governor John Floyd, informed by reports from across the state, came to believe that hundreds of enslaved conspirators had been ready to strike alongside Turner and might remain so. Indeed, every Black preacher "east of the Blue Ridge, was in on the secret," Floyd believed, inflamed and influenced by "northern prints."

The man known as Turner escaped and so his role grew. One Richmond paper explained the insurrection in just two sentences: "A fanatic preacher by the name of Nat Turner (Gen. Nat Turner) who had been taught to read and write, and permitted to go about preaching in the country, was at the bottom of this infernal brigandage. He was artful, impudent, and vindictive, without any cause or provocation that could be assigned." The origin of the violence lay in too much education, too much freedom, and too little supervision among enslaved people. "This Nat seems to be a bold fellow, of the deepest cunning, who for years has been endeavoring to acquire an influence over the minds of these deluded wretches," another correspondent wrote. Turner's legend rose over the next two months as he eluded capture and rumors mounted.

Turner's escape through September and October, followed by his capture, imprisonment, trial, and execution in early November, gave time for the story to be fashioned by many hands. Thomas Ruffin Gray, a young, well-connected but bankrupt local lawyer, persuaded the jailor in Southampton to allow him to interview Turner while he awaited trial and execution. Gray conducted the conversation four days before Turner's trial in November 1831 and secured copyright for the work the day before the execution. Gray had fifty thousand copies of the twenty-three-page pamphlet printed, and put it on sale for twenty-five cents two weeks later under the title *The Confessions of Nat Turner*. To prove its authenticity, the publication bore an affidavit attesting that six witnesses had heard Turner acknowledge the faithfulness of the transcription. The pamphlet also included a trial transcript, the names of the white victims, and a list of the Black people tried in the court. The first printing sold out, soon followed by a second.[5]

The words imputed to Turner in the *Confessions* testified to an interpretation of the Bible that Thomas Gray would not have possessed or imposed. Turner drew inspiration primarily from the Gospel of Luke and from Revelation. Like Luke, Turner felt himself transformed from a life of self-denial, setbacks, and doubt into a state of grace. Turner resisted the knowledge that he had been chosen with a divine mission and grew sick with its implications. Like many in the Bible, he feared deeds he had been commanded to perform. Like a prophet, Turner had to persuade men who had not received his revelations to join him in the divine purpose.[6]

Gray claimed that Turner, "for natural intelligence and quickness of apprehension, is surpassed by few men I have seen." He judged that the enslaved man was not a coward, a drunkard, or a fraud, as some claimed, but rather "a complete lunatic," his mind "warped and perverted" by religious delusion. Gray warned white Christians with good intentions to be more careful, for Turner showed how the word of God could be distorted in the "dark, bewildered, and overwrought mind" of a "gloomy fanatic."

The true breadth or depth of the Southampton rebellion would never be known. The killing of all the leaders other than Turner meant that their planning and intentions would remain mysteries. Officials in Southampton and in Virginia ignored testimony that would have implicated other enslaved people or suggested that the insurrection had been more carefully planned and purposeful than it appeared. Despite the supposed irrationality of the attacks, Turner and his allies had carefully singled out the families of slaveholders and especially those with ties to his former owner, Samuel Turner.[7]

Virginia executed Nat Turner in November 1831. As in Charleston, officials seemed determined to give a single name and a face to rebellion, to identify a leader who had been caught, tried, and executed, to remove an isolated source of infection so that a mythical world of enslaved peace and order could be restored. Whatever his words, to white people Turner's confessions testified to the dangers of literacy among Black people, of unsupervised preaching, of free Black people living among enslaved people, of unimpeded movement around the community. After Southampton, Virginia's Black people would live under greater scrutiny and constraint than ever before.

When the Virginia legislature convened a few weeks after Turner's execution, the members of the General Assembly of the nation's largest and most powerful slave state publicly debated how they might free themselves of slavery. They expressed few concerns about further revolts or the welfare of Black people—whom they considered comfortably situated in slavery—but confessed many concerns about the effect of slavery on white society, economy, and character. The delegates were pressed into debate by petitions sent to Richmond from twenty-seven counties, signed by more than two thousand white citizens. All the petitions agreed that free Black people should be taken from the Commonwealth. Almost half urged that the state purchase and remove a prescribed number of enslaved people each year, and a sixth called for a gradual end to slavery. Only one of the petitions, from a Quaker meeting, referred to slavery as wrong in and of itself. The other petitioners complained instead of the "fatal, paralyzing, destroying mischief" of free Black people, people "degraded, profligate, vicious, turbulent, and discontented."[8]

The Virginia legislature ended weeks of passionate and public debate by simply declaring any action against slavery to be "inexpedient" at the time. The harsh words against slavery hung in the air, the anger against the North seething, the defense of slavery piecemeal and unsatisfying. Eastern Virginia fell into persistent conflict with western Virginia, where nonslaveholding white farmers resented the domination of the state by enslavers and their interests.

Into this situation strode a young man, Thomas Roderick Dew, to provide intellectual weight and gloss to the ugly debate.

Dew, a professor of history, metaphysics, and political law at the College of William & Mary, educated in Europe, deployed his erudition to frame slavery in a global and historical context in a *Review of the Debate in the Virginia Legislature of 1831 and 1832.* The young professor disparaged the lawmakers as inexperienced and hasty, foolishly debating "before the world" matters of profound and complex importance. Their plans for gradual emancipation were "puerile conceits" that should never have been aired. Dew demonstrated to his own satisfaction that every plan put forward for Virginia was "subversive of the rights of property and the order and tranquillity of society." He marshaled statistics to prove that colonization, the panacea long promoted by so many educated white men in the South and beyond, was impractical demographically, economically, and politically.[9]

Dew invoked Lord Blackstone and Adam Smith to declare slavery "perhaps the principal means for impelling forward the civilization of mankind." All white people in Virginia benefited from Black slavery, Dew declared, for "color alone is here the badge of distinction, the true mark of aristocracy, and all who are white are equal in spite of the variety of occupation." The enslaved people were loyal to their owners, for "a merrier being does not exist on the face of the globe, than the negro slave of the United States." Slavery was not inferior to free labor, for the North's current prosperity was the result merely of unjust tariffs, a wrong that could be righted once people understood the true nature of things. The growing domestic slave trade would take care of Virginia slavery, shipping people farther south in ever-increasing numbers, leaving only profit and opportunity for white people.[10]

The *Liberator* published news of the "Insurrection in Virginia" days after Nat Turner's rebellion. "What we have long predicted—at the peril of being stigmatized as an alarmist and declaimer—has commenced its fulfillment," Garrison grimly noted. Garrison had earlier declared that "if any people were ever justified in throwing off the yoke of their tyrants, the slaves are that people," but counseled enslaved people to "suffer, as did our Lord and his apostles, unresistingly, knowing that the Almighty will deliver the oppressed in a way which they know not." Now, the violence Garrison had predicted had come to pass; what had been imagination "is now a blood reality." Some in Virginia blamed the *Liberator*, only a few months old, with inflaming Nat Turner. The charges helped spread the influence of the struggling paper far beyond its subscriber rolls.[11]

Maria Stewart published her first article in the *Liberator* soon after the Southampton revolt. A few months later, in April 1832, she arranged to speak in the African Meeting House's first-floor room, since the beautiful sanctuary was closed to female speakers. She addressed the Afric-American Female Intelligence Society. She told the women gathered before her that the future of Black America depended on them. "O woman, woman! Upon you I call; for upon your exertions almost entirely depends whether the rising generation shall be any thing more than we have been or not."[12]

Stewart was not finished. Early in 1833 she delivered in Boston's African Masonic Hall one of the first speeches by an American woman before men as well as women, white people as well as Black, and charged them all with a share of responsibility. "O, ye fairer sisters, whose hands are never soiled, whose nerves and muscles are never strained, go learn by experience!" she admonished white women. Stewart wistfully and angrily observed that "had we had the opportunity that you have had, to improve our moral and mental faculties, what would have hindered our intellects from being as bright, and our manners from being as dignified as yours?" Had Black women "been nursed in the lap of affluence and ease, and to have basked beneath the smiles and sunshine of fortune, should we not have naturally supposed that we were never made to toil?"

Maria Stewart gave a farewell address at the African Meeting House in September 1833. She sought to inspire her female audience with examples of great women from the past, especially Christian martyrs, and recalled when "poor, despised Africa was once the resort of sages and legislators of other nations, was esteemed the school for learning, and the most illustrious men in Greece flocked thither for instruction." Stewart predicted that such times would come again because "the dark clouds of ignorance are dispersing. The light of science is bursting forth. Knowledge is beginning to flow." Stewart left Boston for New York, where she became an influential teacher. She issued no more jeremiads, but Stewart had set the precedent for other women to follow.

Democracy in America

Alexis de Tocqueville had never thought much about America. His situation in France as a young aristocrat on shifting political ground, however, suddenly made the idea of traveling to America attractive in 1831. Tocqueville and his equally aristocratic friend Gustave de Beaumont offered to tour the new penitentiaries of the United States on behalf of the French government, paying expenses from their own pockets. French officials, with no other use for the young men, agreed.

The two travelers, single and in their twenties, sailed from France with unclear purposes and weak English. They spent much of their time in Boston, where elite and elitist men persuaded Tocqueville and Beaumont that America was New England history writ large. By the time they returned to France nine months later, Tocqueville had sketched a vision of the new nation that would, for generations to come, define what America meant. He expressed his conclusions as maxims, stately judgments that read more like poetry than a travel account.[13]

Tocqueville titled his work *Democracy in America*, exploring what the new nation might foreshadow for France, for Europe, and the world. He published two volumes, one in 1835 and the other five years later. Tocqueville held up America as both an inspiration and a warning to his own countrymen. The United States showed France that democracy could work, that an enormous nation could be governed by its own people, that it need not slide into immorality or anarchy. But the young United States also demonstrated the risks and costs of democracy.

The engine behind America's barely governed social order, Tocqueville argued, was what he called "self-interest properly understood." Everyone looked out for themselves and thus created "a multitude of citizens who are disciplined, temperate, moderate, prudent, and self-controlled." Americans' comfort made them uniform and mediocre, their "tenacious, exclusive, universal" passion for economic gain ringing only in minor keys.[14]

As a result, Tocqueville concluded, "In America I saw the freest, most enlightened men living in the happiest circumstances to be found anywhere in the world, yet it seemed to me that their features were habitually veiled by a sort of cloud. They struck me as grave and almost sad even in their pleasures." Everyone worried about falling behind everyone else. The only grandeur in the United States lay in its landscape, and Americans voraciously attacked even that glory to turn it into property. With unimagined bounty stretching before him, the American "hurls himself" upon the land. "Ahead of him lies a continent virtually without limit, yet he seems already afraid that room may run out, and makes haste lest he arrive too late."

Tocqueville thought Americans' obsession with material gain

fed what he called "individualism," dangerous self-isolation. Americans were lonely, preoccupied with themselves. Fortunately, Tocqueville observed, Americans seemed taken with voluntary and spontaneous organizations devoted to causes, "some religious, some moral, some grave, some trivial, some quite general and others quite particular, some huge and others tiny." Such spontaneous and apparently leaderless associations spread through the democratic medium of the newspaper, which "can deposit the same thought in a thousand minds at once," an "advisor that comes every day unbidden to talk to you briefly about public affairs without disrupting your private pursuits."

Tocqueville arrived in the United States before political parties, the ad hoc machinery of democracy, had established themselves. The Frenchman absorbed the beliefs of his New England hosts that Andrew Jackson was an unfortunate mistake made by less enlightened voters in the West and South, a "tyranny of the majority." Visiting Jackson in the White House near the end of his journey, Tocqueville judged the president a "mediocre man."[15]

Soon after Tocqueville returned to France to write about the United States, a new political party began to organize itself from various opponents of Jackson. They called themselves Whigs, named after British critics of the king—in this case, King Andrew, and his unchecked power. Under the guidance of Henry Clay of Kentucky, the Whigs advocated a unified, intentional, and coherent vision of American development. They promoted a national banking system to stabilize the economy, a tariff to promote American manufacturers, and a coordinated network of internal improvements to knit the states together. The Whigs adopted Protestant campaigns for temperance and hostility to Catholic immigrants and the Masons. While antislavery advocates and opponents of Cherokee removal in the North were drawn to the Whigs, the party also attracted slaveholders from the South in support of its business principles. The coalition helped forge the national two-party system that would characterize the United States, but internal conflicts over slavery plagued the party.[16]

Tocqueville devoted the final, and longest, chapter of his 1835 volume to the problems of slavery and Native dispossession, but he profoundly misunderstood slavery and the South. He dismissed the full humanity of enslaved people, asserting that "the Negro scarcely feels his affliction" and "finds his joy and his pride in servile imitation of his oppressors." Judging the South by looking across the Ohio River to Kentucky, Tocqueville believed the South to be economically weak even as enslaved people hacked out vast plantations that would soon power much of the American economy. He asserted that almost all white people in the South owned enslaved people when in fact two-thirds did not.[17]

Tocqueville saw the situation of free Black people in the North more clearly. "Racial prejudice," he discovered, "seems to me stronger in the states that have abolished slavery than in those where slavery still exists." The tyranny of the majority hit the Black man with its full force: "If he goes to the polls, he puts his life at risk. He can complain that he is oppressed, but all his judges will be white." Despite the self-congratulation of his New England friends, Tocqueville came to understand that "slavery is being abolished in the United States not in the interest of the Negro but in that of the white man."

Tocqueville believed that American democracy would eventually destroy slavery. "No matter how hard southerners try to preserve slavery," he predicted, "they will not succeed indefinitely. Restricted to one part of the globe and attacked by Christianity as unjust and by political economy as disastrous, slavery is not an institution that can endure in an age of democratic liberty and enlightenment." Yet slavery and its power would expand voraciously for the next thirty years in the United States that Tocqueville held up as a the embodiment of democracy.[18]

Native Voices and Faces

The long-planned campaign to drive out the last Cherokees from the uplands and mountains of the East rose to a bitter conclusion in the 1830s. Beyond the sight of opponents, an ill-fated war against the Seminoles in Florida inflicted great suffering on the Natives and extracted enormous costs from the soldiers who fought against them. Struggles over Indigenous dispossession roiled the Great Lakes, the Arkansas Territory, and the Plains, as well as the Southeast. Some white authors and artists set out to record the words and images of people they believed would soon be destroyed by a flood of white settlers.

The Indigenous peoples living in the states of Ohio, Indiana, and Michigan—Cayuga, Delaware, Miami, Ojibwa, Ottawa, Potawatomi, Seneca, Shawnee, Winnebago, and Wyandot—occupied land that settlers wanted. They suffered from constant efforts at conversion, co-optation, and removal. As white settlement pushed Native peoples off their lands in the East, some moved into territories occupied by other Indigenous peoples. War and violence tore at the region. Conflict arose within Indian nations, as some leaders urged accommodation and adaptation while others called for the revitalization of ancient ways.

In Illinois in 1832, Black Hawk, a former ally of the British against the Americans, mobilized eleven hundred people from the Sauk and Fox tribes to resist their removal. In what white people decried as "Black Hawk's War," he led his people, mostly women and children, to an uncertain destination, skirmishing along the way. Black Hawk had hoped for help from the British in Canada or from other Native allies, but they held back from the fight.

The United States forces launched a confused and ineffectual effort against Black Hawk. Militia from Michigan and Illinois, supported by a United States gunboat and hundreds of Native allies from other tribes, caught up with the band at Bad Axe River in present-day Wisconsin. The militia detested the Indians who stood in their way and used the opportunity to kill, and scalp, about five hundred Natives, including women and children. Black Hawk surrendered to Lieutenant Jefferson Davis in August 1832.[19]

Black Hawk was taken, on the order of President Jackson, on a tour to demonstrate the immense power of the United States. People lined the streets of cities to see Black Hawk. Returning to his people, Black Hawk narrated the story of his life to white collaborators. To wide interest and strong sales, *Black Hawk's Autobiography* appeared in 1833. Black Hawk did not hide his disdain for Americans. "Why did the Great Spirit ever send the whites to this island, to drive us from our homes, and introduce among us poisonous liquors, disease and death?" he asked. And why were the white people so greedy? "If we have corn and meat, and know of a family that have none, we divide with them. If we have more blankets than sufficient, and others have not enough, we must give to them that want." But the white people demanded everything for themselves, no matter how much they already possessed. "What right had these people to our village, and our fields, which the Great Spirit had given us to live upon?"[20]

The federal government and freelance artists set out to document "whatever of the aboriginal man can be rescued from the destruction which awaits his race." An influential set of volumes published in Washington between 1836 and 1844 presented color lithographs and detailed biographies of American Indians from twenty tribes who visited Washington to negotiate treaties. The portraits included Tenskwatawa (the Prophet) and Sequoyah of the Cherokees, represented with his syllabary. The goal, the editor said, was to show white Americans that Native people should be "looked upon as human beings, having bodies and souls like ours."[21]

George Catlin, a young self-taught portrait painter from Pennsylvania, displayed an even more detailed and colorful "Indian Gallery." Inspired as a boy by a group of visiting American Indians, Catlin devoted himself to painting the Indigenous peoples of America. "If my life be spared, nothing shall stop me from visiting every nation of Indians on the Continent of North America," he declared. Starting in St. Louis, Catlin ventured on six journeys of thousands of miles between 1830 and 1836. He visited nearly seventy tribes, including the Pawnee, Omaha, Cheyenne, Crow, and Blackfeet. He painted Black Hawk during his imprisonment and traveled to Florida and the Great Lakes to paint others.[22]

Catlin gathered more than three hundred paintings and artifacts in his Indian Gallery and toured with them throughout the cities of the East in 1836. Catlin's portraits conveyed the individuality and dignity of Native men, women, and children, their distinct markings, clothing, names, and possessions. Catlin's subjects admired the portraits and eagerly sat for them. The paintings included no backgrounds showing the forts, trading posts, and prison cells where they were made. Catlin repeatedly lobbied Congress to buy his work, but he did not live to see that eventually come to pass.[23]

Washington Irving wanted to see the West and its Indians with his own eyes. By 1832, America's first famous author had been gone from the United States for seventeen years and yet remained popular. Upon his return Irving proclaimed, to cheers and toasts, that the United States would be his home for "as long as I live." The prodigal visited the Hudson River Valley he had made famous with "Rip Van Winkle" twelve years before, astounded by the speed of the steamboat that carried him upriver.

He admired the luxury hotel that overlooked the wilds where the ghosts of the Dutch bowled and Ichabod Crane had fled the headless horseman.[24]

Irving needed something American to write about to demonstrate his new loyalty. On a steamboat on Lake Erie, he made a fortunate acquaintance with a man who would soon be heading to Arkansas. The government agent invited Irving to accompany their band. "The offer was too tempting to be resisted," he gushed to his brother. "I should have an opportunity of seeing the remnants of those great Indian Tribes, which are now about to disappear as independent nations, or to be amalgamated under some new form of government." Irving longed to "see those fine countries of the 'far west,' while still in a state of pristine wildness, and behold herds of buffaloes scouring their native prairies, before they are driven beyond the reach of a civilized tourist."[25]

Disembarking at St. Louis and riding on horseback west to Fort Gibson, Irving saw little of the "pristine wildness" he had anticipated. He found instead that the "trackless wilds" of his imagination had been crossed by people for centuries. Determined to shoot a buffalo, Irving immediately regretted his triumph. The animal suffered long after Irving's shot, standing in the middle of a stream before collapsing. Irving felt "somewhat ashamed of the butchery."[26]

Irving expected Native peoples to be stoic and mysterious, but the Osages, sitting around a fire until late at night, "engaged in the most animated and lively conversation; and at times making the woods resound with peals of laughter." Famously reserved and taciturn in conversation with white men, "whose goodwill they distrust, and whose language they do not understand," among their fellow Osages "there cannot be greater gossips. Half their time is taken up in talking over their adventures in war and hunting, and in telling whimsical stories. They are great mimics and buffoons, also, and entertain themselves excessively at the expense of the whites with whom they have associated, and who have supposed them impressed with profound respect for their grandeur and dignity."[27]

Though Washington Irving found none of the things he expected to find in the West, he wrote about his experiences nevertheless, gently mocking his illusions and the expectations of the reader. The book, *A Tour on the Prairies*, despite its lack of drama, sold well in the United States and in Britain, judged by a reviewer as "a sentimental journey, a romantic excursion, in which nearly all the elements of several different kinds of writing are beautifully and gaily blended." Audiences in the East wanted to imagine the West as a mere excursion.[28]

In the meantime, the final removal of the Chickasaws, Choctaws, and Cherokees proceeded in the South. In the early 1830s, state militia and ungoverned vigilantes descended into violence, rape, and theft, driving people from their homes without time to gather belongings for the journey, pushing fifteen thousand Cherokees into camps in Tennessee and Alabama where large numbers died of disease and cold.[29]

White people bought, on the cheap, the things Cherokee families had been forced to leave behind: a bed or a spinning wheel, a fiddle or a horn. In 1838, a procession of the Cherokee removal passed within ten miles of Andrew Jackson's plantation as they walked the seven-hundred-mile, four-month journey to the lands beyond the Mississippi River. More than six hundred Cherokees died along the way, spurned by the white communities they passed and mistreated by agents who pocketed government funds for themselves. The suffering was immense and needless, the product of greed and incompetence.[30]

The United States sent a thousand troops to expel the Seminoles of Florida in 1835. The miserable US soldiers dragged heavy wagons through the swampy land of central Florida, their skin lacerated by the saw palmetto leaves. Steamboats and cannon were useless; new repeating rifles exploded; bloodhounds from Cuba proved a failure in the swamps. Seven commanding generals followed one another in failure over seven years. Malaria killed thousands of soldiers and rendered thousands more "enfeebled and destroyed" for life. Speculators followed the soldiers, eager to purchase enslaved people who lived in Seminole communities and their lands. One purchased an area more than twice the size of Connecticut.[31]

The United States ultimately dispossessed 3,824 Seminole people, at a cost of thirty to forty million dollars. Almost one white soldier died for every Native person deported. About a thousand Seminole people, a fifth of the population, died in the war. Osceola, the leader of the Seminoles, was imprisoned after he entered United States lines under a white flag. After Osceola fell sick and died, a doctor severed and embalmed the Seminole leader's skull as a specimen for a "cabinet of heads" in New York.

Andrew Jackson had prided himself on keeping the costs of government low. Under his leadership, however, the federal government spent $75 million to drive Native people out of their homes—in today's currency, a trillion dollars. About 40 percent of all government expenditures in the years between 1836 and 1838 went to the dispossession of Native people, mainly to government contractors who grew rich on the suffering.

William Apess ridiculed Andrew Jackson. Caricaturing the pretended language of paternalism in which the president often indulged, Apess's Jackson lectured his "red children." Because "we have now become rich and powerful; and we have a right to do with you just as we please; we claim to be your fathers." The whites "shall do you a great favor, my dear sons and daughters," by driving Natives off their lands, "to get you away out of the reach of our civilized people, who are cheating you." The lesson was clear: "So it is no use, you need not cry, you must go, even if the lions devour you, for we promised your land to somebody else long ago, perhaps twenty or thirty years; and we did it without your permission, it is true. But this has been the way our fathers first brought us up, and it is hard to depart from it; therefore, you shall have no protection from us."[32]

Both Alexis de Tocqueville and Washington Irving happened to meet Sam Houston during their travels in the west. Irving described Houston—former governor of Tennessee, husband of a Native woman, hard drinker, and friend of Andrew Jackson—as a large and flamboyant man "given to grand eloquence." Houston traveled to Texas at the end of 1832 to visit Stephen F. Austin. Austin had worked for more than a decade to populate the Mexican province of Coahuila y Tejas with white Americans and the enslaved Black Americans they brought with them. Austin labored, and often failed, to balance fragile relationships among shifting Mexican governments, a flood of American expatriates, and the *Tejano* farmers and planters among whom they lived.

Sam Houston received a huge grant of land from Austin and rose to quick prominence among the thousands of American settlers moving to Texas. Tocqueville thought the Anglo Americans were "gradually founding the empire of their own language and their own manners." The Americans resisted the Catholicism of Mexico, resented the Mexican government, feared the Comanches and other Native peoples, and determined to maintain chattel slavery even though it had been outlawed in Mexico. Enslaved people regularly fled from American enslavers into Mexico, finding refuge and infuriating slaveholders. Anglo Americans called for Texas to become its own nation, defending its borders and protecting slavery.

The conflict between the Anglo-American settlers and the Mexican government burst into open warfare in 1835. A Mexican commander sought to recover a small bronze cannon lent to the Anglo colonists of Gonzales to protect themselves against Comanches. A hundred and fifty Americans refused to give up the gun. Flying a six-foot white banner emblazoned with the outline of a cannon and words of defiance—"Come and Take It"—the Americans confronted the Mexican troops.

Sam Houston immediately called for volunteers from the United States with a tempting vision: "War in defence of our rights, our oaths, and our constitutions is inevitable, in Texas!" Volunteers from the United States "would receive liberal bounties of land. We have millions of acres of our best lands unchosen and unappropriated. Let each man come with a good rifle, and one hundred rounds of ammunition, and come soon." Within days, newspapers across the United States spread the call. "The work of liberty has begun," Houston proclaimed, as volunteers from slave states rushed to join the Texas Revolution and confront the armies of Mexico.[33]

Women in Public

Raised in Maine in a working-class family, Lydia Maria Francis was only twenty when she wrote an anonymous novel about early New England, *Hobomok*, written by "An American," in 1824. Meeting with unexpected success, Maria (as she preferred to be called, with a long "i"), founded a magazine for children, *The Juvenile Miscellany*, which quickly gained grateful audiences across the United States. She married David Child in 1828. While striking and idealistic, David was also impractical; he carried an enormous debt into the marriage. Eager to bring in money for the household, Maria authored an influential book that would go through thirty-three editions, *The Frugal Housewife, Dedicated to Those Who Are Not Ashamed of Economy*. It was a book for practical women, without servants, who wanted to conduct their households in responsible and thoughtful ways. Child soon published *The Girl's Own*

Book and *The Mother's Book* while her husband served six months in jail for libelous statements in the newspaper he edited.[34]

Maria and David Child became abolitionists in 1831 after reading the *Liberator* and meeting William Lloyd Garrison. "It is of no use to imagine what might have been, if I had never met him," Child recalled. "Old dreams vanished, old associates departed, and all things became new." While her husband helped Garrison found the New England Anti-Slavery Society, Maria Child, an accomplished author at the age of twenty-eight, wrote a comprehensive attack on slavery and defense of Black people. She read widely, confronting her own prejudices and assumptions. In the meantime, unaware of her book in progress, the influential and sedate *North American Review* proclaimed Child "the first woman of the republic," for she had contributed "the most useful books" to the new nation. "We trust that Mrs. Child will continue her useful labors, and have no doubt that they will be received with constantly increasing favor."[35]

Instead, in 1833 Child published *An Appeal in Favor of That Class of Americans Called Africans.* Child knew that many readers of her earlier works, beloved across the country including the South, would reject the new book. She challenged those readers "not to throw down this volume as soon as you have glanced at the title." Read it, she challenged, "if your prejudices will allow," if "merely to find fresh occasion to sneer." Read it "for an hour's amusement to yourself, or to benefit your children." Read it "from sheer curiosity to see what a woman (who had much better attend to her household concerns) will say upon such a subject."[36]

Child warned her fellow northerners that they could "not flatter ourselves that we are in reality any better than our brethren of the South." The "soil and climate" of the North prevented slavery from taking deeper root there, "but the very spirit of the hateful and mischievous thing is here in all its strength." While a slaveowner might treat a favored slave with kindness, as he would "a favorite hound," "our cold-hearted, ignoble prejudice admits of no exception—no intermission."

Child scoffed at the fear of "social intercourse between the different colored races." Black men, she assured white men, had no interest in "marrying your daughters." Should white people, she asked sarcastically, "keep this class of people in everlasting degradation, for fear one of their descendants may marry our great-great-great-great-grandchild?" The word *prejudice* was critical for Child. She put it succinctly: "We made slavery, and slavery makes the prejudice. No Christian, who questions his own conscience, can justify himself in indulging the feeling. The removal of this prejudice is not a matter of opinion—it is a matter of duty."

Family and friends abandoned Child, the Boston Athenaeum removed her library privileges, and parents canceled their subscriptions to the *Juvenile Miscellany*, which soon ceased to publish. Child's calm, systematic, well-researched argument appealed to those who found Garrison's sermon-like writing off-putting. Leaders of the fight against slavery and against discrimination in the North found this first book-length explanation of slavery's evils the best that would ever be written. Despite the praise and gratitude Child won with her book, however, she and her husband would struggle with debt and even poverty for years to come. She had sacrificed her hard-won reputation and prosperity to tell the truth.

Angelina and Sarah Grimké followed a different path to abolition, long and unlikely. The sisters grew up in Charleston, South Carolina, where their family commanded dozens of enslaved people, most laboring in distant fields but others in the intimacies of the home. Sarah, thirteen years older and a surrogate mother to her sister, had seen horrifying scenes of torture and decapitation of enslaved people. Angelina grew up in Charleston, where much of the violence of slavery was hidden by the high walls around mansions, but where she saw their own brother routinely beat enslaved people for amusement.[37]

Sarah, disgusted with slavery and the world it created, became a Quaker and moved to Philadelphia; Angelina followed in 1829. In that city's Quaker community, the Grimké sisters learned little of abolitionist ferment, for the community they joined disapproved of abolition and of outspoken women. The Grimké sisters knew little of the vibrant and determined Black community in Philadelphia and made no note of a brutal riot against Black Philadelphians in which bodies, including of an infant, were ripped from coffins and thrown down stairs.[38]

The Grimké sisters eventually came to understand the abolitionist movement that Black people had been waging for more than three decades. They began to attend the lectures at the biracial Philadelphia Female Anti-Slavery Society and to develop relationships with Black women. Sarah Douglass, a fellow Quaker, patiently explained the indignities and injustices she experienced as a Black woman. As Sarah Grimké recalled, "Before her wisdom, I was as a sheep in the wilderness, braying at the altar of selfishness." Sarah Douglass "selflessly taught me to see the error of color prejudice, of the sin that I had so long abided." The sisters read the *Liberator* and grew to understand the breadth and depth of Black determination to fight slavery in the South and prejudice in the North.[39]

The Grimkés' native Charleston was swept up in the national struggle over slavery in 1835. Abolitionists launched a print campaign to persuade enslavers of the sins of bondage, sending 175,000 publications from New York to the South. Alerted to the arrival of the steamship bearing the mailings, a mob in Charleston calling themselves the Lynch Men broke into the post office to seize the dangerous words. The next evening, at the parade ground of the citadel, two thousand people cheered as the abolitionist mailings burned, along with effigies of William Lloyd Garrison and Arthur Tappan, the wealthy New York merchant who funded the mailings.[40]

Riots against abolitionists broke out in cities across the North in the summer of 1835. Garrison was dragged through the streets of Boston by a rope, jailed for his own safety, and forced to leave the city. Abolitionist speakers confronted riots in towns and cities across the Northeast, from Philadelphia into Connecticut and along the Erie Canal. City leaders in business and politics joined with white workingmen to stone, tar, and feather abolitionists.[41]

Angelina Grimké read of the violence against white abolitionists with dismay and anger. She wrote William Lloyd Garrison a letter in August 1835, even though she had never met him. "I can hardly express to thee the deep and solemn interest with which I have viewed the violent proceedings of the last few weeks." She assured Garrison that "the ground upon which you stand is holy ground: never—never surrender it," Grimké wrote. "It is my deep, solemn deliberate conviction, that this is a cause worth dying for." Garrison published Grimké's letter, bearing her name, without permission. Grimké's fellow Quakers condemned the letter and urged her to retract it, but she refused.[42]

Instead, Angelina Grimké reached out to the women of her own race, class, and region, women who, she knew from harsh experience, despised her as a traitor. Grimké composed her *Appeal to the Christian Women of the Southern States* in 1836 because she felt "a deep and tender interest in your present and eternal welfare" for those who "have loved me as a relative" or were "bound to me in Christian sympathy, and Gospel fellowship." Grimké wrote not "in the heat of passion or prejudice, but in that solemn calmness which is the result of conviction and duty. It is true, I am going to tell you unwelcome truths, but I mean to speak those *truths in love*."[43]

Grimké offered Christ's fundamental teaching: "Whatsoever ye would that men should do to you, do ye even so to them." Grimké then asked "every slaveholder" to "apply these queries to his own heart": "Am I willing to be a slave—Am I willing to see my wife the slave of another—Am I willing to see my mother a slave, or my father, my sister or my brother? If not, then in holding others as slaves, I am doing what I would not wish to be done to me or any relative I have; and thus have I broken this golden rule which was given me to walk by."

The antislavery women in the North, Grimké assured her southern readers, "feel no hostility to you, no bitterness or wrath; they rather sympathize in your trials and difficulties." The abolitionist women recognized that the white women of the South "must work out your own deliverance with fear and trembling, and with the direction and blessing of God." It had become clear "to every reflecting mind, that slavery must be abolished; the era in which we live, and the light which is overspreading the whole world on this subject, clearly show that the time cannot be distant when it will be done." The only question was how slavery would end, "by moral power or physical force." It was up to the white South "to choose which of these you prefer." When Grimké's *Appeal* reached Charleston, city officials burned it publicly. Grimké's mother was warned that her daughter must never visit Charleston again.

White Men in Blackface

While controversies over slavery and abolitionism tore at the United States, blackface minstrelsy—white men covering their faces in burnt cork—rose as the most popular form of entertainment across the United States. White men began to pride themselves on their skill on the banjo, an instrument known for its association with Africa but developed and manufactured in the United States.[44]

A character named "Jim Crow" made his first appearance in 1832 at New York's Bowery Theater. Thomas Dartmouth Rice, a white twenty-four-year-old performer from New York City, had developed the character as part of a traveling theater troupe in Ohio and Kentucky. White entertainers had been appearing in blackface for decades, and looking for a way to enliven the show, Rice converted familiar parodies of the Irish to a Black man. Rice tried out different versions of the character on audiences in smaller cities in the North before unveiling "Jim Crow" in New York. Jim Crow would be clever though uneducated, happy though dressed in rags. The song, "Jump Jim Crow," claimed the *Spirit of the Times*, was soon "on everybody's tongue."

The Black men and women caricatured in minstrelsy knew no suffering, only crude sexual rivalry. They cared not that they wore patched clothes, though they dressed in ridiculous finery when they could. They never worked, though they showed energy and ingenuity avoiding work. Black minstrelsy turned slavery inside out, turning forced bondage into cultural freedom.[45]

Jim Crow immediately drew competitors. A white actor named George Washington Dixon had sung "Coal Black Rose," a love song performed in the guise of "Sambo" from South Carolina, several years before. After Rice's sensation, Dixon invented a new character, "Zip Coon." Zip Coon combined two stereotypes: the Black man filled with an exaggerated sense of his own worth and an overdressed dandy, effeminate yet assertive. White working-class men laughed at both kinds of threats, one a Black man of pretentious refinement and the other an example of soft men who worked in offices and shops rather than with their hands.

The audience for the minstrel shows included businessmen, editors, and politicians in private boxes as well as those in the raucous and promiscuous sections on the floor and in the balconies. Many of these men shared an aversion to, a contempt for, the culture of gentility preached at them by preachers, reformers, and perhaps their wives. The minstrel show, with its bawdy songs, transgressive humor, and parody of refined standards of taste, united white men otherwise divided by position or wealth. The minstrel show proved especially attractive to northern followers of Andrew Jackson, defenders of slavery and proud in their contempt for Black people.

The minstrel show pretended that Black people were in on the fun, that they laughed at themselves and their predicaments along with white people. The white men who invented the American blackface tradition claimed their admiration for, even their indebtedness to, those who shared gifts of song and laughter with them. The music and skits expressed fascination with, envy for, the imagined freedom of Black people to drink, gamble, sing, and have sex without guilt or apparent consequences. African Americans in the North deplored the minstrel shows as yet another assault on their dignity and striving, on their work ethic, religious faith, and moral rectitude.

Chapter Four

REFLECTIONS

1836–1848

Transcendence

A group of young people near Boston arose in the 1830s to challenge the authority of the churches and universities in which they had been raised. Their original concerns grew out of doctrinal conflicts few Americans knew or cared about, and their ideas were nourished by German and English thinkers who thought little about the new United States. Despite these unpromising sources, the vision of spiritual and intellectual freedom promulgated by the young dissidents eventually spread far beyond New England, their visions coming to seem particularly and peculiarly American.

Ralph Waldo Emerson, the son of a well-respected Unitarian minister, seemed an unlikely dissident. After his father died, leaving a wife and five sons, Emerson came of age in a bookish but straitened atmosphere in Boston. He expected to become a minister as well and prepared for the profession as a work-study student at Harvard, and yet Emerson drifted when he graduated from college in 1821 at the age of eighteen.[1]

Emerson accepted the junior ministry of a Boston church and became engaged to a young woman suffering from tuberculosis. He proved to be an excellent preacher but could not bring himself to preside over Communion, which he considered an empty, distasteful relic of a superstitious era. His wife's health steadily worsened until she died in 1831, at the age of nineteen. At twenty-seven, Emerson found himself widowed and divorced from the church. At a loss, he abruptly decided to catch a ship leaving Boston for Europe on Christmas Day 1832.

In Britain, Emerson sought out his heroes—Samuel Taylor Coleridge and William Wordsworth—but discovered them to be disappointing old men who had said what they had to say. He traveled into the Scottish countryside to meet someone else he had admired, Thomas Carlyle. Only thirty-seven, Carlyle had, unlike Emerson, distinguished himself as a writer. "There is a Divine Idea pervading the visible universe," Carlyle wrote, "which visible universe is indeed but a symbol and sensible manifestation."

Emerson returned to the United States in 1833, spiritually heartened but without a home, a profession, or a position. For a year he cast about, deciding that the lyceum offered a way to make a living while remaining true to himself and his powerful if inchoate convictions. Lyceums—local organizations for self-improvement, sometimes with their own buildings—were growing across the new nation, flourishing especially in New England. The new institutions offered platforms for all kinds of speakers, requiring only that they attract paying audiences.

Emerson could deploy his skills at public speaking, honed through two hundred sermons, without responsibility to Scripture, church, or faith. Instead, he would urge people to recognize the sacred within themselves. He would abandon argument in favor of aphorism. He would rely on no authority other than himself and his listeners' recognition of the truth he spoke. By translating prose into the spoken word, Emerson crafted a style that appealed in a lecture hall, alternately funny and oracular, down-to-earth and celestial, offering everyone a note that res-onated in their lives. Listeners remembered Emerson's turns of phrase even if they did not understand the larger consequences of all that he said.

Emerson fell in love again, married, and in 1835 moved to Concord, a town of two thousand, two hours outside of Boston, where he had spent time in his youth. The town embodied many of the transformations reshaping the nation. Its economy diversi-fied, its politicians jostled. Working people seldom stayed more than a few years, moving on to a mill town, a growing city, or some destination in the West. Residents heard traveling blackface minstrels, arcane lecturers, and temperance advocates. Newspa-pers, local and from Boston and beyond, arrived daily.[2]

Between lectures, Emerson pored over his journals and notes to compose a long essay he titled simply *Nature*. Steeped in the learning of the past, Emerson declared his independence from it. "Why should not we have a poetry and philosophy of insight and not of tradition," he asked, "and a religion by revelation to us, and not the history of theirs?" The answer, of course, was that there was no good reason, only timidity. "Why should we grope among the dry bones of the past?" he asked rhetorically. "The sun shines today also. There is more wool and flax in the fields. There are new lands, new men, new thoughts. Let us demand our own works and laws and worship." Emerson spoke of "we" and "us," seeking to persuade himself as well as anyone who might read his words. He offered a homely mysticism, a democratic spirit, a language available to all who would pay attention.[3]

Emerson's *Nature* had no obvious market, so he published it himself, anonymously, in the spring of 1836. Few would read the book at the time. In the meantime, Emerson joined a group of men and women who gathered in Boston to support one another in their fascination with German Romantic philosophy, new ways of educating children, and new ways of worshipping. They called themselves the Transcendental Club, and hosted gatherings where they encouraged and debated one another. The Transcendentalists found themselves ridiculed by conventional ministers and professors, criticism that only reinforced their iconoclasm.

Emerson unexpectedly confronted an important opportunity. After a local Episcopalian minister declined the honor, and impressed with Emerson's poem celebrating the anniversary of the Battles of Lexington and Concord and "the shot heard round the world," Harvard invited Emerson to deliver the Phi Beta Kappa address in 1837. Harvard dignitaries, including the college's president, attended, along with a United States Supreme Court justice and other influential men. Emerson's reputation as a dissident from orthodoxy helped attract an overflow crowd that gathered around the windows of the church near Harvard Yard where he spoke.[4]

Emerson titled his address "The American Scholar," a familiar theme on occasions to inspire new graduates. Despite its title, however, the lecture chastised rather than celebrated the United States, extolling the life of the mind in a land all too satisfied with commerce and mechanical skill. Emerson did not praise Harvard, nor did he celebrate the Christian faith or the Bible on which it rested. Instead, he criticized the very people who had invited him to speak, the authorities who taught young people to be obedient, the gatekeepers who rebuked those who dared teach school or preach sermons in ways that violated convention.

Bold young men, Emerson charged, were taught to be "decorous," to be "complaisant," even though "public and private avarice make the air we breathe thick and fat." The spirit of American politics stripped away individuality, reducing men into units "reckoned in the gross, in the hundred, or the thousand, of the party, the section, to which we belong; and our opinion predicted geographically, as the north, or the south."

The time had come, Emerson proclaimed, to set aside complacency and passivity. "We will walk on our own feet; we will work with our own hands; we will speak our own minds." All people—the tradesman, the farmer, and the scholar—should learn equally from nature, from books, and from action. "The literature of the poor, the feelings of the child, the philosophy of the street, the meaning of household life, are the topics of the time." Americans should feel the "currents of warm life run into the hands and the feet." Though his sponsors expressed discomfort from such proclamations, young members of his audience thrilled to the bold admonitions.[5]

Henry David Thoreau had addressed a different Harvard audience the day before, on his graduation day, as part of a program devoted to "The Commercial Spirit of Modern Times." One of his fellow students offered the Democratic perspective, attacking speculation, while another praised commerce as the engine of progress. But Thoreau challenged commerce altogether. From "an observatory in the stars," he told the hundreds gathered there, America's "beehive" of commercial activity bore little resemblance to freedom. A distant observer would see "hammering and chipping, baking and brewing, in one quarter," Thoreau noted, "buying and selling, money-changing and speech making, in another." None of that feverish activity fostered freedom. Thoreau did not deem the "commercial spirit" worth celebrating, especially as the prospects of the graduating students had evaporated in an economic panic then spreading across the country. Thoreau would not join the beehive.[6]

Thoreau had struggled to pay his bills at Harvard. Taking time away from college to teach school, Thoreau met people who read books that did not have a place on Harvard syllabi, books such as Emerson's new *Nature*. Emerson had written in support of Thoreau at Harvard, urging honors for the young man he had come to know as a neighbor in Concord and a kindred spirit. Soon, Thoreau would become a fixture at Emerson's home, helping take care of the children, doting on Mrs. Emerson, and meeting an array of Transcendentalists.

Emerson broke his ties with Harvard in an address to its Divinity School in 1838, declaring that the "word Miracle, as pronounced by Christian churches, gives a false impression; it is Monster. It is not one with the blowing clover and the falling rain." Instead, "one mind" united everything and lived "everywhere, in each ray of the star, in each wavelet of the pool, active; and whatever opposes that will, is everywhere baulked and baffled, because things are made so, and not otherwise. Good is positive. Evil is merely private, not absolute." There was no original sin, no limit to the unity of the universe, no need to be constrained in imagining ways to glimpse and represent that unity. For expressing such possibilities, Emerson would not be invited back to his alma mater, defender of conservative Christianity, for forty years.[7]

Together, the addresses of Emerson and Thoreau marked an outcropping of a strange but powerful critique of America by a new generation of young white Americans in what seemed the most American of places. Emerson wrote *Nature* within sight of the battlefields of Concord and Lexington. Thoreau had been one of a tiny number of young men able to attend college, much less Harvard. Yet, disdainful of business and politics, ignoring Christian orthodoxy and the Constitution, these young men appealed to a democracy of spirit independent of any church or creed. In their vision, all people held capacities denied by the common preoccupations of the new nation.

Emerson and Thoreau did not set themselves above or apart from their listeners, but invited all to recognize the divinity within themselves and the nature that surrounded them. Their message was alternately admonishing and encouraging, chiding and elevating. It did not draw from distinctly American sources and yet spoke a practical American vocabulary. It tapped a spiritual connection to nature and to one another that otherwise found no voice.

Emerson, still in his mid-thirties, became an icon for restless, educated young people in New England. Searchers, reformers, and eccentrics came to the Emerson home in Concord, invited and uninvited, to meet him in person, finding him intellectually engaged but personally diffident. Emerson's wife, Lydian, sometimes exasperated by the unannounced visitors, nevertheless made them feel welcome.[8]

Margaret Fuller proved herself the visitor most interesting to the Emersons. Universally described as a brilliant conversationalist, Fuller struggled to find a role as an erudite and confident woman. Born in 1810, trained by an intense father in multiple languages and literature, Fuller watched as her brothers went off to Harvard and professional careers while she devoted herself, willingly and unwillingly, to the care of younger siblings and her mother. When her father died unexpectedly at a young age, Fuller's dreams of traveling to Europe vanished. Needing to support the family, she taught in two experimental schools, both of which failed to pay her for months of labor. "A man's ambition with a woman's heart.—'Tis an accursed lot," she lamented in her journal in 1839. Emerson invited Fuller to the Transcendental Club, where her learning and sophistication impressed everyone.[9]

Fuller decided to host a series of subscribed "conversations" among women who wanted to discuss "the great questions. What were we born to do? How shall we do it?" The conversations celebrated strong women from the classics of Greece and Rome who confronted great challenges, inspiring the "woman's heart" with examples of bravery and victory. Fuller encouraged members of the class to "state their doubts and difficulties with hope of gaining aid from the experience or aspirations of others." She encouraged women to speak with conviction, to develop "a precision in which our sex are so deficient." Twenty-five women paid ten dollars each for a series of thirteen conversations.[10]

In 1840 the Transcendentalists, excluded from many publications, decided to launch their own journal, the *Dial*. Emerson thought it a perfect opportunity for Margaret Fuller. She agreed to take on the job of editor, both for its mission and for its potential salary. Fuller sought to stir an American culture mired in "sluggishness," to create an "everlasting yes" that would celebrate art, music, and literature. She struggled against the lethargy of her male Transcendentalist friends, however, who seldom offered their best writing for the new publication, even with her persistent encouragement. For two years, Fuller strained to produce the *Dial*, virtually on her own and without payment for her work. She sometimes composed half the content, unsigned to disguise its origin. The magazine won admirers, but few subscribers. Some of its poems and articles appeared in newspapers that spread influence but not profit. Fuller, at the age of thirty-two with no home of her own, moved among friends. She reluctantly resigned the editorship, which Emerson assumed with equal reluctance.[11]

Emerson, in the meantime, achieved growing success by carefully trading on his notoriety. His most popular lecture, "Self-Reliance," from 1841, wove his philosophical idealism into a secular idiom, a practical American vein. Listeners heard Emerson tell them that "to believe your own thought, to believe that what is true for you in your private heart, is true for all men,— that is genius." Those who came to hear Emerson assured others that his lectures contained nothing dangerous, simply combining "humor, truth, and common sense."[12]

The loss of his beloved five-year-old son, Waldo, from scarlet fever, in January 1842, shattered Emerson, his wife, and his circle. "I have no key, and no consolation, nothing but oblivion and diversion," Emerson wrote, but he searched for ways to move forward, to find strength. He finished a powerful and influential essay, "The Poet," in these terrible months. There, Emerson insisted that poetry was everywhere, in everything. "The people fancy they hate poetry," he noted, yet "they are all poets and mystics." American politics was filled with metaphors and signs; their sermons abounded with parables and images of heaven. The American landscape, vast and varied, barely contained its restless people. "America is a poem in our eyes," Emerson proclaimed; "its ample geography dazzles the imagination and will not wait long for metres."[13]

Margaret Fuller went in search of that poetry in America's "ample geography." She was "tired of books and pens and thought," she wrote Emerson, and longed to "take wing for an idle outdoors life, mere sight and emotion." Friends invited her on the first long trip of her life, to the western United States. Fuller wished she had grown up "amid the sources of the streams, where the voice of the hidden torrent is heard by night, where the eagle soars, and the thunder resounds." She found inspiration in the American landscape, but not where or how she had expected. The obligatory visit to Niagara Falls disappointed her because she had already experienced it through other people's words and pictures. She finally experienced the power of the falls at night, when she returned alone, where "the river below the falls was black as night" and where "no gaping tourists loitered." Then Fuller sensed "how here mutability and unchangeableness were united," and felt "a humble adoration of the Being who was the architect of this and of all."[14]

Launching out on the Great Lakes, Fuller at first felt deflated because the "people on the boat were almost all New Englanders, seeking their fortunes. They had brought with them their habits of calculation, their cautious manners, their love of polemics." It grieved Fuller to hear the immigrants talk not of what they would *do* in their new homes but what they would *get*. Suspecting she would view the "mushroom growth" of the West with "distaste," Fuller was determined to comprehend "the law by which a new order, a new poetry is to be evoked from this chaos."

Chicago, a place founded solely "for business and for nothing else," did not appeal to Fuller but she came to admire the people's frank pursuit of "material realities." The prairies also at first disappointed her, but after she had ridden out in the country on a wagon, "and seen the flowers and seen the sun set with that calmness seen only in the prairies, and the cattle winding slowly home to their homes," she "began to love because I began to know the scene." Fuller exclaimed that "I had never felt so happy I was born in America" than when she looked out over the Rock River and saw pastures "decked with great bunches of a scarlet variety of milkweed, like cut coral."

Just as she struggled to overcome the expectations and prejudices she brought to the landscape and its New England settlers, Fuller struggled to see Indigenous people without stereotypical disdain or romance. Visiting a Native camp, she and her fellow female tourists were welcomed into a woman's tent during a thunderstorm. The woman impressed Fuller with her "sweet melancholy eye" and a "delicacy of manners." Fuller considered the Indigenous people the "rightful lords" of the magnificent landscape of the West, which they had protected since the days of ancient Greece and Rome. Now, white settlers seemed determined to "obliterate the natural expression of the country" as quickly as they could.

Returning to Massachusetts, Fuller persuaded Harvard to allow her research privileges to flesh out the memoir she was turning into a book called *Summer on the Lakes, in 1843*. She was the first woman granted access to the library's riches. Fuller worked to convert her letters and notes into a meditation on what she had seen of America, amplified by her erudite understanding of other places and times. She received a contract from a Boston publisher, with a generous royalty of ten cents a copy, but the resulting book, with genres and styles mixed in profusion, confused readers who expected a conventional travel account. Fuller searched for elusive meaning in travel, America, nature, Native peoples, women, or even writing itself. Fuller would keep searching.

School Wars

The new United States had been built with the assumption that its citizens would be virtuous and civic-minded, but no mechanisms for public education had been devised to foster those traits. The two states where industry, commerce, and immigration had made the greatest inroads by the 1830s—Massachusetts and New York—became laboratories for education in America's future. Struggles in those places showed that schools, precisely because Americans invested so much faith in them, exposed fault lines opening in the new nation.

Horace Mann, trained in the law, was elected to the Massachusetts General Assembly at the age of thirty-one and began work on reforming the state's treatment of the insane. The promising young man married a woman of a prominent family, but she died just a year later at twenty-three. Bereft, Mann threw himself into politics, though he found the compromises of political life unworthy of his deceased wife's memory.

In 1837, Mann found a suitable purpose. The state formed a new board of education and looked for a secretary to lead the effort to improve the schools of Massachusetts. Mann accepted the poorly paid position though he had no experience with or commitment to education. He set about learning all he could. Mann prepared to visit, on horseback, every county in Massachusetts. He advertised his arrival in local papers and held "conventions" in churches and courthouses to build support for schools. He rode more than five hundred miles in his first year.[15]

Mann was appalled by what he found. Teachers, usually young men without better prospects, made little and lived with neighborhood families a week at a time, eating what they had and sleeping wherever there might be a bed. Schools were ramshackle, often without a privy. Every school, it seemed, forced students to sit on hard wooden benches without backs. Teachers taught with whatever books they had, which were often worn and outdated. While some communities prided themselves on their schools, others neglected theirs and resented the taxes that sustained them.[16]

Mann called for a system of education adequate to the challenges facing the state. Massachusetts was changing as factories grew along rivers and young women left home to live in dormitories in textile towns, as railroads connected farms with Boston and immigrants from Ireland and Canada arrived. Mann implored citizens to commit to pay higher taxes, to submit uniform reports about their schools, and to support state normal schools to educate teachers. He criticized private academies as competitors for students, teachers, and funding.

Mann envisioned the common schools as the very foundation of democracy, though the democracy he saw in the communities of Massachusetts made him question the capacity of people to make the best decisions for themselves and their children. He met too many parents who saw no need to educate their children; he met too many wealthy men who saw no need to pay for the education of someone else's children. For twelve years, Mann, in one annual report after another, chronicled the failings of Massachusetts' democracy and championed schools as the only solution.

In his final report, in 1848, Mann proclaimed, "Education, then, beyond all other devices of human origin, is the great equalizer of the conditions of men—the balance wheel of the social machinery." A truly public school system "knows no distinction of rich and poor, of bond and free." Mann celebrated an institution that "throws open its doors, and spreads the table of its bounty, for all the children of the State." Mann, satisfied with his labors, was elected to replace John Quincy Adams in the United States House of Representatives in 1848.

Horace Mann's emphasis on the common good of education inspired other states to establish their own systems and schools for teachers. The same emphasis, however, also led to a uniformity in the early common schools and their successors that made school stultifying for many students. Required to fill reports, teachers took less time to deviate from what was measured. Art, music, and literature, as well as practical crafts and skills, were set aside. Students who did not excel at spelling and mathematics felt themselves failures at an early age. "Men are cast-iron; but children are wax," Mann wrote, but American schools often sought to form that wax into a single shape.[17]

As Mann's experience showed, debates over schools divided communities. Caroline Kirkland wrote a humorous account of fights over a new schoolhouse on the Michigan frontier where she and her family moved from New York City. "The new schoolhouse, a gigantic step in the march of improvement," she sarcastically noted, "has caused an infinity of feuds, made mortal enemies of two brothers, and obliterated at least one pair of partners." She thought of telling the story of the school "for the benefit of all future school committees and their constituency," but despaired at untangling the complexities of the tale.[18]

In cities, as well as on the frontier, efforts to standardize schools led to the very political conflicts they were designed to transcend. Bishop John Hughes returned from a trip across Europe in 1840 to find his New York City diocese in turmoil over schools. Catholic leaders had requested funds from the city's leadership to help sustain the parochial schools, which were being taught in church basements and rented spaces for three thousand students. Those students did not attend the city's schools because they faced flagrant discrimination there. They were forced to hear and participate in daily readings from the King James Bible, overseen by Protestant teachers who made no secrets of their disdain for their Irish Catholic students and their religion. Textbooks described opulent priests and overbearing popes as characteristic of a corrupt Catholic faith.

New York Catholics were ignored in their pleas until Governor William Seward, in 1840, suggested that public funds be set aside for Catholic schools taught by Catholic teachers. Like Horace Mann, Seward saw the schools as essential to the civic health of the nation. "I desire to see children of Catholics educated as well as those of Protestants, not because I want them to be Catholics but because I want them to become good citizens," he announced to critics. Voters inclined to nativism and Protestantism attacked Seward, and Democrats accused him of duplicity. Some Catholics called for secular schools, with the Bible left out altogether.

Bishop Hughes called on the city's Catholics to translate their concerns to politics by supporting a slate of candidates favorable to their demands, and they won. Protestants proclaimed such actions the very embodiment of Catholic arrogance. In 1842 riots broke out in New York City. Gangs rushed into Catholic neighborhoods and threw bricks through the windows of diocese buildings as Irish women gathered around their church to prevent its destruction. After years of conflict, Catholic schools received none of the funding they had requested.[19]

The effort to create and sustain public schools would continue for generations to come. Americans made impossible demands on the schools, counting on them to serve, as Horace Mann said, as the "balance wheel of the social machinery" of the new nation. But the schools could not overcome constant imbalances of shifting demography, immigration, and religion, of parsimonious taxpayers and opportunistic politicians, of racism and nativism. While teachers performed everyday miracles for grateful students, the schools themselves suffered alternating bouts of neglect and intrusion.

Living by the Pen and Brush

Cheap daily newspapers burst into prominence in the cities of the Northeast in the early 1830s. The new "penny press" produced newspapers that working men and women could afford and want to read. Hawked by newsboys crying out from street corners, the papers bragged that advertising rather than the patronage of political parties or wealthy merchants guaranteed their independence. Depending on sensation to grab attention, New York's *Sun* and *Herald* competed for gossip, scandal, and readers. The *Sun* launched a popular series based on the discovery of strange beings on the moon, seen through a powerful new telescope in South Africa. Man-bats flew around temples, surrounded by unicorns and talking monkeys. The hoax, increasingly outrageous in its claims, ran for weeks, until its true nature was gleefully revealed by the paper. For its part, the *Herald* built popularity on the story of a young prostitute and a young businessman accused of her murder, culminating in his sensational trial.[20]

Newspapers and magazines took whatever they wished from one another. Authors might or might not be identified, the original source cited or not. Authorship had few boundaries; American or English, young or old, female or male, famous or unknown—anything that would help fill pages might be clipped and copied.

Most writing remained local in inspiration and in distribution, brief and anonymous, but reprinting could give a story or poem an audience far removed from its origin. The culture of reprinting, cheap and democratic, created a tumultuous market for authors and publishers, full of promise and disappointment. Books, for their part, enjoyed only regional markets. The few families that purchased books usually bought Bibles, almanacs, and school-books. Many books appeared first as periodicals that could be sent through the mail and then stitched together by the purchaser. The most widely distributed novels came from England, published cheaply because the pirated editions of authors such as Charles Dickens paid no royalties.[21]

The most profitable American publishing appeared in the form of elaborate "gift books," lavish volumes that interleaved images with poems and stories. In a time when few mass-produced goods had established a place in the distended American mar-ket, gift books pioneered. Produced annually for Christmas giv-ing and offering steel-engraved prints of fine quality, the books became popular everywhere in the country. By the end of the 1830s, thirteen different publishers issued gift books each year, in editions of up to ten thousand. The publisher of the most pop-ular annual gift book, *The Token*, prided itself on presenting only American authors and painters; Thomas Cole's scene from *The Last of the Mohicans* appeared as a print in its pages. Publishers sought out female authors and editors as gift books became cov-eted symbols of gentility and refinement, suitable for display on tables in parlors that bridged the outside world and the sanctuary of the home.[22]

Sarah Hale, widowed with five children, rose to become edi-tor of the most popular magazine in the United States for decades to come—*Godey's Lady's Book*. Reaching forty thousand subscrib-ers across the country, including the South, Hale's periodical featured engraved plates, hand-colored by 150 women, that featured scenes of female companionship. Women in the latest dresses and bonnets held books and flowers in postures of gentility.

Hale relegated the production of those engravings to her male partner in the business, for she focused her attention on the words among the illustrations. There, she advocated for women's intellectual independence and proclaimed their moral superiority. "The strength of man's character is in his physical propensities," Hale counseled, "the strength of woman lies in her moral sentiments." In the *Lady's Book*, women held a particular kind of authority, embodied in their character and deportment. The magazine's alluring pages provided guidance as women navigated ever-shifting demands of respectability.[23]

Nathaniel Hawthorne, a young man trying to make a living as an author while staying at home with his mother and sisters, wrote a series of anonymous stories for gift books. Many of those scenes were light and cheerful, as readers expected in such places, with titles such as "The Gentle Boy" and "Little Annie's Ramble." But others, such as "The Minister's Black Veil," struck darker notes. In tales inspired by Hawthorne's home in Salem, Massachusetts, and his family history of witch-prosecuting judges, New England appeared not as town greens and white church steeples but as cowering villages surrounded by dark woods and fearful visions.

An old college friend offered to underwrite the publishing of a collection of Hawthorne's stories as *Twice-Told Tales*. On its publication in 1837, when Hawthorne was thirty-three, a Boston newspaper noted that the book seemed to be "the production of 'Nathaniel Hawthorne'—whether a true or fictitious name, we know not—probably the latter." A few reviewers noted the collection, praising its charm. Few purchased the collection, and the stationery company that published the book went bankrupt.

The book disappeared after selling six or seven hundred copies. Hawthorne despaired of making a living as an author.[24]

Edgar Allan Poe, born in 1809, enjoyed a privileged upbringing in Richmond, Virginia, tended by enslaved servants, attending school from ages six to eleven in London, and expecting to inherit considerable wealth. Instead, Poe's adopted father disinherited him. Poe dropped out of the new University of Virginia after he could not pay his bills, his debts made heavier by desperate gambling. He then served in the United States Army for four years. Poe won admission to West Point and did well for a semester until he decided not to attend lectures or chapel; he was dismissed from service.[25]

Poe dreamed of editing his own magazine. He was alert to the trends and fashions in Britain and Europe, attuned to the complexities of publishing, skilled in foreign languages, sophisticated in his understanding of poetry and prose, willing to experiment with form and genre, and fearless in expressing his many opinions. He explored and excelled in every genre available in the early 1830s. He wrote poetry inspired by ancient ideals of beauty and by astronomical discoveries. He composed elaborate narratives of exploration of Antarctica concocted from his imagination and text borrowed from actual expeditions. He authored a successful textbook on shells—conchology—that helped readers understand the emerging science of geology. Much of his work appeared anonymously and circulated without attribution; some stories were reprinted in Britain and then reprinted yet again in the United States as products of a British author.[26]

Poe won a prize from a newspaper in Baltimore for his story "MS. Found in a Bottle" in 1833, published a story in *Godey's Lady's Book* in 1834, and accepted a position at the *Southern Literary Messenger* in Richmond in 1835. There, he wrote more than eighty reviews (many of them harsh), contributed stories, and began a long narrative inspired by the hoax of creatures on the moon in the New York *Sun*. The *Messenger* flourished and Poe was promoted to editor.

In 1836, Poe married his consumptive thirteen-year-old cousin, Virginia, and moved her and her mother to live with him in Richmond. After disagreements over salary and editorial independence, Poe resigned from the *Messenger* and relocated his small family to New York in early 1837 in hopes of finding another post. For more than a year, he found nothing and so moved to Philadelphia. Poe barely supported his wife and mother-in-law with borrowed money and spotty freelance work.[27]

In 1839, after two years lost to empty struggle and poverty, Edgar Allan Poe talked himself into a position as editor of a "gentleman's" magazine based in Philadelphia that offered literary writing and reviews alongside articles on sailing and cricket. Finally enjoying a modicum of financial stability, seeking to reach the widest audience and impatient with regional parochialism, Poe produced stories of startling range, of exotic locations and timeless settings. Aware of readers' hunger for novelty and sensation, Poe crafted shocking stories of people buried alive and of an escaped orangutan killing a mother and daughter in a city apartment. Poe's "The Fall of the House of Usher" charged familiar gothic scenes with a psychological depth and elegant style uniquely his own. Poe embraced the heterogeneity of magazines and newspapers, the mixing and invention of genres. More than any other American writer, Poe seemed equipped for the new era of publishing. His career over the next few years revealed the potential and risks of the volatile industry.[28]

In contrast to Poe, fellow southerner William Gilmore Simms rose from a poor background in Charleston to become the most popular American novelist of the 1830s. He published in quick succession a series of novels about the South set during the colonial and Revolutionary era, not unlike those of James Fenimore Cooper, and then an unending stream of fiction, history, and opinion. His 1835 novel, *The Yemassee*, which sold out in thirty-six hours and soon went into German and British editions, depicted enslaved people as loyal and helpless. After marrying an eighteen-year-old heiress in South Carolina, Simms found himself presiding over a four-thousand-acre estate and seventy enslaved people. He became a leading defender of slavery and of southern interests, his interest in fiction falling aside.[29]

Augustus Baldwin Longstreet brought a different southern element to national literature. His *Georgia Scenes*, published first by a small firm in Georgia in 1835 and then in New York to large sales, introduced an array of characters that would populate American fiction and film for generations to follow. Educated at Yale before returning to the South, Longstreet viewed the common people around him with amusement and friendly condescension. He converted their speech into dialect, portrayed political differences as personal feuds, and laughed at the trivial bases for the violence they inflicted on one another. The demand for this "southwestern humor" would grow for decades, often written in northern cities and spread through New York's *Spirit of the Times* and other popular magazines, parodying a South where slavery played little role.[30]

Artists, like authors, navigated an unmapped professional terrain. While the publishing of gift books offered occasional compensation for reproductions, artists painted first for patrons, men of wealth who wanted particular kinds of pictures. Thomas Cole had negotiated these complexities as a young man, grateful for the support of New York patrons who admired the same landscapes of nearby scenes that Cole loved. After travel and study in Europe, however, Cole found himself harboring visions of America that not everyone shared.

Thomas Cole returned to the United States in 1832 after two

years in Europe, fired with the excitement of creating a unique American idiom. "The painter of American scenery has indeed privileges superior to any other; all nature here is new to Art," he wrote in his journal. No tired scenes of European painting, "hackneyed and worn by the daily pencils of hundreds, but virgin forests, lakes & waterfalls feast his eyes with new delights."[31]

And yet Cole lamented the America he found on his return, for "the ravages of the axe are daily increasing—the most noble scenes are made desolate, and oftentimes with a wantonness and barbarism scarcely credible in a civilized nation." The devastation spread even in the Hudson River Valley he had helped make famous, for "the copper-hearted barbarians are cutting all the trees down in the beautiful valley on which I have looked so often with a loving eye." Cole was appalled at the United States that Andrew Jackson presided over, in which "the Freedom of the Individual Man" had been perverted into "vice, profligacy, irreligion and anarchy."

Cole portrayed the story of decline in a series of allegorical paintings, *The Course of Empire*, in which the cycles of history afflicted a landscape composed of Roman and Greek models that prefigured the United States. Securing a patron, Cole labored for years over the complex paintings, demanding a range of skills he had never before revealed. A New York critic praised Cole's craft but scoffed at the artist's implied warning to the new nation. While the decline and collapse of empires was indeed "*that* which *has been*," the United States would escape the cycles of history. America did not rely on the "usurpation of the strong over the weak," like all previous empires, but built on the immovable foundations of "political equality; the rights of man; the democratick principle; *the sovereignty of the people*." Those traits would allow the United States to escape, to transcend, the history of every other nation. The critic failed to note America's dispossession of a continent from its original inhabitants and the creation of a diabolical system of racial slavery.[32]

Cole struggled for more than a year to complete the *Course of Empire* series in his home in the Catskills. Discouraged, he wrote his patron to ask if he might be able to set that painting aside temporarily for another, more concentrated project. Cole had not displayed a painting in two years. He worried that the public and critics would forget him, and he needed the money. His patron accepted the diversion, and Cole had the perfect subject in mind: "a view from Mt. Holyoke," a nearby site and "the finest scene I have in my sketchbook." The painting would be a landscape, and thus more salable than the "fancy" historical works on which he had labored. Like allegorical works, but in the subtle forms of nature, this portrait of a landscape would "tell a tale." It would become known as *The Oxbow*, completed in 1836.

Cole's tale unfolded across a wide vista. On the left roiled wilderness and storm, shattered trees and lightning; on the right, in the valley far below, lay a scene of sunlit cultivation. The scenery on the left bore thick paints of dramatic dark purple and green; the pastures on the right carried thin paint in light green and yellow. The wilderness appeared dramatic and alive, the valley ordered and regimented. In the center of the painting, a river carved a giant question mark, echoed by the pattern of birds in the sky. In the distance, deforested areas formed Hebraic letter-like shapes on a mountainside, evoking biblical warnings. Seated on the boundary between the two, Cole painted himself, bearing a brush before an easel, looking at the viewer, as if awaiting a response to the question: Could the United States possess both God's nature and human progress?[33]

Escaping Slavery

In the mid-1830s, violence over slavery and race broke out across the United States. Abolitionists confronted brutal opposition even in states where the movement was strong, such as Massachusetts and New York, as well as in states of the Midwest where they found few allies. Black people created pockets of refuge in places such as New Bedford, Massachusetts, and Rochester, New York. Black men and women never abandoned their determination to exert political influence, and they created alliances with a shifting array of white compatriots, but Black rights remained tenuous in the face of hostile state legislatures and violent mobs fed by racist newspapers and cynical politicians.[34]

A meeting in St. Louis, for example, passed a resolution attacking abolitionism in any form, for slavery was "too nearly allied to the vital interests of the slaveholding States" to be discussed "either orally or through the medium of the press." The self-appointed group denounced "amalgamation," the "union of black and white," as "repugnant to judgment and science as it is degrading to the feelings of all sensitive minds." The claim that slavery was unchristian violated Scripture, for "our Saviour recognised the relation between master and slave, and deprecated it not." A Committee of Vigilance would enforce the pronouncements.

Elijah Lovejoy, who published an abolitionist newspaper in St. Louis, responded with defiance: "I am threatened with violence and death because I dare to advocate, in any way, the cause of the oppressed. Under a deep sense of my obligations to my country, the church and my God, I declare it to be my fixed purpose to submit to no such dictation. And I am prepared to abide the consequences." The fight between Lovejoy and the defenders of slavery in St. Louis exploded in early 1836, when a free Black cook on a steamboat was tortured and burned to death. The victim begged someone to shoot him, but none did; he sang hymns and prayed until he finally died. The mob left his remains hanging all night. "Our hand trembles as we record the story," Lovejoy wrote. "We stood and gazed for a moment or two, upon the blackened and mutilated trunk—for that was all which remained—of McIntosh before us, and as we turned away, in bitterness of heart we prayed that we might not live."[35]

Lovejoy moved across the Mississippi River to publish his newspaper in Alton, Illinois, a flourishing community. A drunken mob attacked the stone warehouse where a new press had been taken. Lovejoy, trying to save the building from burning, with a gun in his hand, was shot and killed. No one was convicted of the murder, though several men claimed the honor of firing the shot. Fury against Lovejoy's murder swept across the North.

In the midst of this violence, Angelina and Sarah Grimké began to speak across the North on behalf of the American Anti-Slavery Society. As word spread, their audiences grew from small gatherings of women in parlors to lecture halls and churches. Men as well as women began to attend. The Congregational Ministers of Massachusetts chastised female activists for violating "the appropriate duties and influence of women" defined in the New Testament, for yielding "the power which God has given her for her protection," for making her character "unnatural."

To confront the challenge, Sarah wrote a series of letters to the *New England Spectator* on the "Province of Women." Grimké defended "the simple moral truth, that God had made no distinction between men and women as moral beings." Speaking from her Quaker faith, she told female readers that instead of "puzzling themselves" with the "unnecessary inquiry, how far they may go without overstepping the bounds of propriety," they need only inquire "Lord, what wilt thou have me do?" To prove her point, Sarah Grimké documented the condition of women around the world, exposed inequities in law and employment in the United States, and portrayed the vulnerability of enslaved women in the South.

William Lloyd Garrison reprinted the letters in the *Liberator* and Grimké gathered them into a book, *Letters on the Equality of the Sexes*, in 1838, the first extended exploration of women's status in the United States. She ended with an admonition of fearlessness: "If they strike at some of our bosom sins, our deep-rooted prejudices, our long cherished opinions, let us not condemn them on that account, but investigate them fearlessly and prayerfully, and not shrink from the examination; because, if they are true, they place heavy responsibility upon women." Grimké saw "a root of bitterness continually springing up in families and troubling the repose of both men and women." That bitter root, she believed, was "the mistaken notion of the inequality of the sexes."[36]

Angelina Grimké addressed the Massachusetts General Assembly in February 1838, the first woman in history to do so. Lydia Maria Child, accompanying the Grimké sisters, described the event as "a spectacle of the greatest moral sublimity I ever witnessed." Angelina also spoke to three thousand people at Boston's Odeon Theater for two hours; the audience, Child wrote in wonder, seemed "to hang on her every word." Hostile newspapers ridiculed the speakers as "a parcel of silly women" and "petticoat philanthropists." One Boston paper expressed mock dismay: That "our females should have come forth from their retirement—from the holiness of the fireside, the protection of their household gods—to mingle in scenes like this, it is, it must be, but a dream. Oh deliver me from its agony."[37]

Later in 1838, Angelina Grimké married fellow abolitionist Theodore Dwight Weld in a ceremony attended by both Black and white people. The bride and groom dressed in plain brown homespun rather than fabrics with origins in slavery. Two days later, Grimké spoke before a convention in Philadelphia's brand new Pennsylvania Hall, built through contributions to create a fitting place for abolitionist speakers. As bricks, thrown by a mob outraged by rumors of an "amalgamation" wedding, crashed through the windows, Grimké spoke as a southerner who knew slavery firsthand. "I have seen it! I have seen it! I know it has horrors that can never be described. I was brought up under its wing. I witnessed for many years its demoralizing influences and its destructiveness to human happiness." To those who imagined that the songs of the minstrel show testified to slaves' content, she testified that "I have *never* seen a happy slave. I have seen him dance in his chains, it is true, but he was not happy."

As the windows shattered and the audience flinched, Grimké defied the violence: "What is a mob? What would the breaking of every window be? Any evidence that we are wrong, or that slavery is a good and wholesome institution?" She spoke for an hour. The next night, a mob burned the building and everything within, including the publications of the antislavery office. The following night, another mob set fire to the Shelter for Colored Orphans. A few months later, Pennsylvania disenfranchised Black voters. No Black person would vote in Pennsylvania for the next twenty-two years.[38]

Thousands of women across the North solicited names for antislavery petitions. The Anti-Slavery Convention of American Women aimed for a million signatures before the next Congress convened. Women, it turned out, enjoyed much greater success than men in persuading people to sign petitions; teenage girls proved adept at the task. But the work, even its advocates admitted, was not easy. Sarah Grimké, going door to door in a New Jersey town, met resistance "almost everywhere." One woman told Sarah that "she had rather see the slaves all shot than liberated, another said she would sooner sign a petition to have them all hung, than set free." Despite such struggles, the petitions grew. By April 1838, the petitions sent to Congress filled a room twenty by thirty by fourteen feet, all the way to the ceiling.[39]

After repeated and bitter votes, Congress "gagged" the petitions that flooded in from across the North, tabling them without debate. The gag had to be renewed in each new Congressional session, and for years the former president, now congressman, John Quincy Adams seized on each opportunity to challenge the rule and the violation of democracy it represented. He goaded the South and the Democrats with procedural strategies and defiance of the Speaker's pounding gavel; he spoke of sexual violence by slaveholders and the physical resemblance of many enslaved children to their enslavers. Adams called slavery "a slow poison to the morals of any community infected with it," and charged that the United States was "infected with it to the vitals."[40]

Angelina Grimké, her new husband Theodore Dwight Weld, and her sister Sarah devoted themselves to producing a factual account of slavery from the discarded files of a reading room in New York, which had received papers from major southern cities. The three editors clipped articles from twenty thousand pages of newspapers, working for six months to gather what became *Slavery As It Is*, published in 1839 by the American Anti-Slavery Society under Weld's name.

The book laid out, in hundreds of verifiable charges, the terrible deeds and injustices inflicted not "in corners, but before the sun; not in one of the slave states, but in all of them; not perpetrated by brutal overseers and drivers merely, but by magistrates, by legislators, by professors of religion, by preachers of the gospel, by governors of states, by 'gentlemen of property and standing,' and by delicate females moving in the 'highest circles of society.'" The book's catalog of inhumanity became the most important abolitionist book ever before published. Over a hundred thousand copies would be distributed. The Grimkés and Weld, exhausted by the battles of the preceding decade, moved to a farm and focused their energies on their growing family.[41]

The antislavery movement drew from multiple, and often

conflicting, sources of energy. Quakers shared inspiration and resources with coreligionists in Britain. Their belief in the inherent equality of people sustained the Quakers' dedication to antislavery when other motivations might have faded. The wealth they built from global trade and whaling poured into reform efforts, their anxiety about that wealth encouraging them to seek redeeming uses for their profits. The Quakers had little faith in secular politics.

Quaker women such as Lucretia Mott played especially important roles in the antislavery movement, for they challenged constraints of gender as well as race to speak in public. Black women joined them in boldly recruiting for the abolitionist cause. In the 1830s, Black and white women formed organizations in Philadelphia, Boston, and other places where they mobilized themselves and others for the antislavery cause. As teachers and preachers, Black women such as the Forten sisters of Philadelphia, Jarena Lee, and Zilpha Elaw sold newspaper subscriptions and raised money, formed dozens of female auxiliaries from Massachusetts to Ohio, and supported one another.[42]

The Garrisonians, advocates of emancipation without compensation to the enslavers, argued that the issues of women's voice, of nonviolence, and of abolition must all be pursued together "because everything in God's universe is linked with every other thing." Many male abolitionists, however, disagreed. They argued that only partisan political engagement would gain the rights of free Black people in the North and challenge slavery in the South. Black men who held the right to vote in their cities and states used the franchise to establish alliances and reward allies. Black and white male political abolitionists appreciated the work women did in building revivals, sustaining churches, teaching Sunday schools, and gathering petitions, but thought that votes by men would be essential. The men who led the American Anti-Slavery

Society in New York argued that only electoral politics could end the scourge of slavery, and only through a party dedicated to abolition. They broke from Garrison in 1840 to form their own society. They would challenge no social convention other than slavery, hoping to separate themselves from the "ultraism" of the Garrisonians to recruit more voters to fight slavery with the power of the ballot box.[43]

A young Black man emerged amid this struggle, navigating among the conflicts of white abolitionists to speak in his own voice. Frederick Bailey had, in his brief life, experienced the bewildering power and chaos of American slavery. Born in Maryland in 1818, Bailey as a child endured separation from his mother, hunger, near nakedness, and random cruelty. Told he was the son of his white owner and yet unacknowledged by any father, Frederick found himself given away, loaned, and hired from a ragged farm to an opulent plantation to a bustling city and then back to a ragged farm and then back to the city—all before he was twenty years old. The boy watched slave traders carry away his brothers and sisters to feed the endless hunger for labor on the cotton plantations of the South. He saw Christian faith ennoble and empower him and others, and yet he heard the words of the Bible used to excuse unspeakable violence. He had been whipped, and had beaten a white man who tried to whip him. He learned to read and write in stolen moments and rare moments of white indulgence. The young man carried with him an old textbook, *The Columbian Orator*, that spoke with transfixing words of freedom.[44]

In 1838, with the aid of a free Black woman, Anna Murray, Frederick Bailey determined to escape from Baltimore. A sailor loaned him clothes and papers to claim a false identity. He boarded a train in the city, then a steam ferry, then another train, then a steamboat, then another train and ferry, heading north through Wilmington and Philadelphia. Frederick made it to New

York, where a Black abolitionist, David Ruggles, provided shelter, money, and advice. He immediately sent for Anna, and they married in the Ruggles home three days after her arrival. New York was dangerous for an escaped enslaved person, its streets haunted by kidnappers and slave catchers, so the young couple, calling themselves Johnson, pushed northward to the whaling town of New Bedford, Massachusetts, where allies awaited. There, in the care of another Black abolitionist couple, Frederick Johnson became Frederick Douglass, the name inspired by a bold character in a poem by Sir Walter Scott. The young man added an "s" to make the name his own.[45]

For three years, Douglass and his wife struggled in New Bedford. Denied skilled labor on the ships by white workers who threatened to walk off if he was hired as a caulker, Douglass took whatever work he could find. He found his greatest strength and solace in a small African Methodist Episcopal Zion church, where the young man taught Sunday school and served as sexton and occasional preacher. Educating himself and finding allies, Douglass's confidence and determination grew. He paid his poll tax so he could vote.

Douglass subscribed to William Lloyd Garrison's *Liberator*, where Douglass found a voice raging against the sin of slavery and demanding its immediate destruction, a voice from a white man proudly in alliance with Black men and women. Douglass heard Garrison speak in New Bedford in 1839, thrilling to his words. Douglass learned from other ministers and speakers who came through New Bedford as well, watching how they moved people with their words and personas.

Douglass particularly admired Black men such as the Reverend Henry Highland Garnet, a Presbyterian minister, a temperance advocate, an ally of escaped enslaved people, a gifted speaker, and an editor of an abolitionist newspaper. In 1840, Garnet—himself only twenty-four years old—authored a statement for a convention "of the Colored Inhabitants of the State of New York." At that convention, 134 men from thirty-three counties issued an unequivocal demand for their political rights: "We are Americans. We were born in no foreign clime. . . . We have not been brought up under the influence of other, strange, aristocratic, and uncongenial political relations." These men declared themselves "to be American and republican."

The Black Americans at this political convention—one of many, in several northern states—understood and embraced "the nature, features and operations of our government." And they knew the nation's history. "We lift up our voices for the restored spirit of the first days of the republic—for the great Principles then maintained, and that regard for man which revered the characteristic features of his nature, as of more honor and worth than the form and color of the body in which they dwell." These Black citizens asked "for no vested rights, for no peculiar privileges, for no extraordinary prerogatives." Instead, they appealed for a "republican birthright" that had been stolen from them in 1821, when a property qualification disfranchised most Black men.[46]

Black abolitionists fought on multiple fronts at once, never sacrificing claims for political representation while recognizing that the white political parties of the time were, more often than not, enemies rather than their allies. In 1841, Douglass began to speak with his own voice. Douglass seized the opportunity when a white abolitionist, struck by the young man's eloquence and presence at local meetings, invited him to join a delegation of the Massachusetts Anti-Slavery Society at their convention on Nantucket. Douglass and his wife boarded a steamship for the exciting event only for the captain to relegate them and other Black delegates to an exposed area. Their white compatriots joined them in the discomfort of rain and sun, drafting a resolution of protest against the steamship company on the journey.

At the convention, Douglass rose on the third day to take the podium before a thousand people. The handsome and athletic young man deployed skills he had learned from years of preaching and studying. His speech astounded his listeners. "Flinty hearts were pierced, and cold ones melted by his eloquence," wrote one in attendance. "Our best pleaders for the slave held their breath for fear of interrupting him." William Lloyd Garrison himself testified that "I think I never hated slavery so intensely at that moment." The abolitionists had found an ally "in intellect richly endowed—in natural eloquence a prodigy." Exactly what Douglass said in that address, which stories he shared from his "fresh recollection of the scenes through which I had passed as a slave," no one recorded. But everyone who heard Frederick Douglass at Nantucket in 1841 knew they had heard someone remarkable.

Immediately, the abolitionists invited Douglass to join them on their lecture circuit through Massachusetts and New Hampshire. He remained vulnerable as a self-professed runaway, naming his enslavers to prove his story, and he met with contempt and violence as well as adulation. In places grand and humble, Douglass told the stories of his enslavement in "indignant and terrible speech," in terms "sterner, darker, deeper" than mere eloquence. An awed editor in New Hampshire described how the powerful young man strode back and forth, "lion-like" on the platform, "taking hold of the right of speech, and charging on his tyrants the bondage of his race."

Most churches closed their doors to Douglass and the rest of the traveling band, for Garrison attacked the ministry for complicity in slavery. Because the churches of the North refused to break from the churches of the South, Douglass chastised his audiences, and in Concord said, "You are yourselves our enslavers." Douglass told bitter and sarcastic stories about the racism he had found in the churches of the North, even among Christians who proclaimed themselves enemies of slavery. At one revival, he said, a young white woman, in the paroxysms of salvation, had fallen into a trance. Awakening, she declared that she had been to heaven and described the wonders she had witnessed there. One listener asked if she had seen any Black people in heaven. Surprised, the young woman replied, "Oh! I didn't go into the kitchen!"[47]

Douglass saved his strongest performance for the "Slaveholder's Sermon." He delivered a famous version of it early in his crusade. In January 1842, in Boston's Faneuil Hall, four thousand people gathered to hear the young speaker. Douglass attacked the "mockery" of Christianity "preached at the South." He mimicked white ministers, ridiculing their mock humility and erudition as they addressed the enslaved people in the South's churches. "Oh, consider the wonderful goodness of God!" Douglass intoned. "Look at your hard, horny hands, your strong muscular frames, and see how mercifully he has adapted you to the duties you are to fulfill." God's goodness appeared alike in the bodies of "your masters, who have slender frames and long delicate fingers," to whom "he has given brilliant intellects, that they may do the thinking, while you do the working." Audiences laughed at the absurdity and audacity.

Douglass's parody of southern ministers was blackface in reverse, an exaggeration and ridicule of traits of which the object was foolishly proud. As they laughed at the parody, though, Douglass turned on his self-satisfied listeners, the white northern Christians complicit in ecclesiastical union with such hypocrites. They tolerated in their denominational alliances the perverted gospel preached to the enslaved, a message that "more than chains, or whips, or thumb-screws, gives perpetuity to this horrible system." Some of his listeners "gnashed their teeth" when confronted with such charges. Douglass found himself "constantly interrupted, in an indecent, profane and mobocratic manner, by a considerable number of rowdies, who piously came to rescue the clergy and the church." The mob swore that they would not "stand such damned nonsense" and such "'rascally charges' to be brought against the divine order."

The young abolitionist delivered such speeches night after night through the early 1840s. He spoke throughout New England and ventured into Pennsylvania, New York, Ohio, and Indiana, traveling on every means of conveyance, confronting prejudice and violence at every turn. Frederick Douglass stood as "a living, speaking, startling proof of the folly, absurdity, and inconsistency" of slavery, one admirer wrote, speaking for many.[48]

Douglass found himself disagreeing with Henry Highland Garnet in 1843 when, at a convention in Buffalo, the powerful speaker dismissed Garrisonian ideas of nonresistance. While Garnet proclaimed that enslaved people should fight back in every way they could, including violence, Douglass raised his voice to warn that such admonitions to enslaved people were unrealistic and dangerous. He persuaded the delegates not to endorse Garnet's speech as an official statement of the convention.[49]

Enslaved people in the South did not have access to lecture halls, conventions, and newspapers. Their visions had to be enacted in the face of death. The 1840s saw two desperate efforts to escape slavery on the ships that carried enslaved people along the coasts of the United States. In 1841, the *Creole* left Richmond for New Orleans, destined for faraway plantations in Mississippi, Louisiana, and Texas. The ship carried 135 enslaved people as well as a crew of 13 and 6 white passengers. As the craft passed through the northern Bahamas, 19 of the captives, under the leadership of a man named Madison Washington—who had earlier escaped to Canada but returned to free his wife—took control of the ship and forced it to sail to Nassau, where thousands of formerly enslaved people lived, liberated under Britain's Slavery

Abolition Act of 1833. The British freed the ship's enslaved people and allowed it to proceed to New Orleans.

The revolt, thanks to the leniency of Madison Washington, had taken only the lives of one slave trader and two enslaved people. Southerners were furious about the loss, which followed the *Amistad* case of 1841, in which the United States Supreme Court freed enslaved people from Africa who had risen against their captors on a Spanish ship. Rebellions on the seas testified to the fragile international standing of slavery.[50]

In 1848, enslaved people in Washington, DC, sought to escape from the nation's capital to New Jersey, about two hundred miles away. Seventy-seven people joined in the attempt. Members of the Bell, Ducket, and Queen families, who had fought for their freedom in the courts for years, were desperate to flee Washington before they could be sold if a legal decision went against them. They recruited a sympathetic white captain and spread word among others that the ship would leave Washington during a raucous celebration of Napoleon's fall in France. "Shortly after dark the expected passengers began to arrive," their white ally recalled, "coming stealthily across the fields, and gliding silently aboard the vessel." The families included children and teenagers, whom their parents sought to protect from the slave trade.

A hundred miles after their departure, a posse on a steamboat captured their ship, the *Pearl*, and dragged the fugitives back to shore, where a proslavery mob rioted. The furious slaveowners sold the captives, at below-market rates, to traders who took them to Georgia and Louisiana. The enslavers intentionally separated families to punish them and to warn others. The two white allies were sent to prison. Abolitionists in Boston raised funds to purchase two of the women on board, but the rest were separated forever.[51]

In one facet of life after another, then, Americans sought a language adequate to the possibilities of the new nation. Rejecting the strictures and sacraments of Protestant Christianity, men and women sought unmediated connection with the sacred. Rejecting standards of art and literature inherited from Europe, Americans sought a language adequate to the astonishing new nation surging around them. Rejecting new boundaries of political control imposed by those in power, men and women demanded a fuller democracy.

Chapter Five

EXPLORATIONS

1832–1848

Go Ahead!

The United States became a giant venture in the 1830s and 1840s, a series of bets on where a farm might flourish, a town might take root, or a city prosper. "Every body is speculating, and every thing has become an object of speculation," a foreign visitor heard throughout the new nation. "All here is circulation, motion, and boiling agitation," he exclaimed. The nation's motto rang everywhere: "*Go Ahead!*"[1]

Capital touched everything in America but reached beyond the control of the United States. The supplies of gold and silver that underpinned the money supply of the nation rose and fell in response to a war over opium in China, struggles at silver mines in Mexico, and decisions made by bankers in London. State debts soared as agents borrowed more than $90 million from British investors.[2]

American cotton powered much of the accelerating trade across the Atlantic. By the 1830s the plantations of the United States produced more than eight hundred million pounds of raw cotton, two-thirds of it going to England, where it provided more than 80 percent of Britain's supply. The textile factories of Britain employed over three hundred thousand people working a hundred thousand power looms, turning American cotton into cloth of every grade and style, sold all over the world. Some southern cotton stayed in the United States, where it fed new mills opening along the rivers of New England. In Lowell, Massachusetts, young women worked in mills that wove southern cotton into cloth, much of it sold back to the South for its enslaved population. New Orleans rose to become the greatest export city in the United States, shipping cotton and sugar, trading in enslaved people and bills of credit, extending the reach of produce from farms north along the Mississippi, Ohio, and Missouri Rivers. Thousands of steamboats and sailing ships crowded around New Orleans, pausing on their journeys around the world.

The Black Belt stretching from South Carolina to the Mississippi River grew ever more densely populated with enslaved people. A sophisticated and lucrative trade in human property sped the forced migration of American slavery, as brokers and bankers financed men who gathered Black people from farms into pens and then marched them to railroad cars and steamboats for transport to New Orleans, Mobile, Natchez, and Galveston.[3]

The western half of the continent underwent deep and widespread change. The American Fur Company monopolized the trade from the Great Lakes to the Rocky Mountains with a network of agents and traders. John Jacob Astor, a German immigrant based in New York who oversaw the fur empire, became the richest man in America. The Lakota, with their horses, dominated the upper Missouri River basin and expanded west to control the buffalo trade. In the Southwest, the Cheyenne and Arapaho traded in bison furs and hides, competing with Comanches, Pawnees, and Sioux for hunting grounds and trading partners. Santa Fe, for more than two hundred years a trading center, grew with an enlarged fur trade. The Cherokees, Choctaws, Chickasaws,

Creeks, and Seminoles arrived in the Indian Territory impoverished and ill. Struggling to constitute new governments and institutions, the "civilized tribes" viewed the "wild Indians" of the West with fear and disdain.[4]

A Search for Heroes

Andrew Jackson remained popular through much of the South and the West, as well as among workingmen in the cities of the Northeast. Immigrants and Catholics embraced the Democrats' defense of religious freedom and attacks on government efforts to police morality. To the delight of many white men, the Democrats disdained the participatory democracy of reform organizations, local mobilization, and grassroots revolts of women, Black citizens, and churches.[5]

Many Americans, on the other hand, had only contempt for Andrew Jackson. Practical businessmen despaired at Jackson's imperious attacks on the national bank, his denunciation of bankers and capitalists, his manipulation of the money supply, and his vetoes of internal improvements. Educated people, especially women, disdained Jackson's crudeness and the Democrats' lack of support for public investment in institutions, schools, and improvement. Abolitionists and other reformers saw an unchristian spirit behind Jackson's brazen and unctuous treatment of Native people and the Democrats' sanction of violence against Black people and their allies. Protestants attacked the Democrats for their embrace of immigrants, especially Catholics.[6]

Andrew Jackson's opponents determined that they could not defeat the Democrats with appeals to cultivation, collaboration, and restraint—tactics that had failed in 1832, when Henry Clay lost to Jackson—and so they thought they might have the answer in David Crockett. Crockett, a congressman from Tennessee, was an actual frontiersman, squatter, and bear hunter, not the wealthy lawyer, slaveowner, judge, investor, and churchgoer Andrew Jackson had become. Elected to Congress from his west Tennessee district in 1827, Crockett championed the right of squatters to earn ownership of the land they worked, celebrating the families who "entered the country when it lay in cane, and opened in the wilderness a home for their wives and children."[7]

Crockett refused to support Jackson's Indian Removal Act of 1830 and found himself under attack by fellow Tennesseans. "This was considered the unpardonable sin. I was hunted down like a wild varment, and in this hunt every little newspaper in the district, and every little pin-hook lawyer was engaged." Crockett lost reelection in 1830 but regained his seat in 1832. His victory over Jacksonian opposition, in Jackson's own Tennessee, emboldened some in the new Whig Party to think they had found in David Crockett a winning candidate for the looming 1836 election, when Jackson would finally be gone.[8]

Crockett and a ghostwriter assembled an autobiography in 1834. The book told no tall tales but told of struggle and hardship in self-deprecating, deadpan humor. Crockett did not "know of any thing in my book to be criticised on by honourable men. Is it on my spelling?—that's not my trade. Is it on my grammar?—I hadn't time to learn it, and make no pretensions to it. Is it on the order and arrangement of my book?—I never wrote one before, and never read very many." Crockett's greatest claim was to have killed 105 bears in one year, sharing the meat with those in need.

Newspapers on both sides of the political spectrum began to pay attention to David Crockett in 1834. His handlers took Crockett for a tour of eastern cities between Baltimore and Providence. Along the way, crowds gathered to applaud him; wealthy hosts sponsored banquets and offered gifts. Alexis de Tocqueville described Crockett as an unfortunate example of democracy's weakness: "When the right of suffrage is *universal*, and representatives are *paid* by the state, it is striking to discover how low the people's choice may go, and how far astray."[9]

The tour of the Northeast, unfortunately for Crockett and the Whigs, proved to be the highlight of Crockett's political career. He lost his seat in his home district in 1835 and thus disappeared as a presidential candidate. Crockett told his Tennessee constituents that "you may all go to hell and I will go to Texas." He departed, heading down the Mississippi to Arkansas, and ultimately to Texas, where he entered into a new kind of legend.[10]

David Crockett arrived in Texas in late 1835, along with thousands of other disgruntled, indebted, and sometimes indicted white men who fled family and obligation to the Mexican colony. Crockett found himself carried along by the currents of a Texas rebellion against the Mexican government and its army of six thousand Mexican soldiers under the command of General Antonio López de Santa Anna. Only four months after his arrival in Texas, Crockett joined a band of Anglo American rebels at a mission at the Alamo in San Antonio de Béxar in March 1836. The Mexican army killed everyone in the Alamo except an enslaved man and a white woman and child.

Texas soldiers, under the command of Sam Houston, rallied to defeat Santa Anna at the Battle of San Jacinto in April. They then founded the independent Republic of Texas. Native Mexicans, including many who had supported the revolution, found themselves hounded by vigilantes hungry for their land. Texas portrayed itself as a safe haven for slaveholders under assault from abolitionists in the United States. Free Black people were ordered to leave. Texas established the most consistent and thorough slave regime on the continent.[11]

David Crockett became a useful legend. "Davy Crockett's Almanacs," illustrated with garish and crude drawings, clattered from printing presses in Boston, New York, Philadelphia, Detroit, and Albany long after Crockett's martyrdom. Begun as a hoax, the almanacs became a self-perpetuating mythology, ever more extreme. Crockett's colloquial language became a morass of an invented frontier dialect and hyperbole. The actual Crockett never wore a coonskin hat; the fictional one always did. The hack authors of these almanacs pushed beyond conventional limits of violence, genocide, racism, environmental destruction, and scatology. The almanacs spoke in the voice of white male adolescents, chortling when an Indian invited Crockett to kiss his "posterum" or when an attractive young woman freed Crockett by climbing above him and pushing trees apart with her legs.[12]

The almanacs adapted to current events, moving Crockett onto an ever-renewed frontier, replaying the story of white America's triumph over nature and Indians. Reformers and preachers appeared ridiculous in their priggish efforts to contain the anarchy. The America of the Crockett almanacs made a mockery of solemn stories of progress. The awkward woodcuts showed the course of American history running backward and sideways, the blessings and guidance of Providence nowhere in evidence.

The Whigs, disappointed in their loss of Crockett as an antidote to Jackson, searched for the next best thing for the 1836 election. Some settled on William Henry Harrison, the once-famous warrior against Tecumseh at Tippecanoe more than a quarter century before, now sixty-four years old. The Whigs divided their votes, however, unable to persuade southerners to support Harrison, and so they ran two candidates against Martin Van Buren, Jackson's vice president.[13] Van Buren entered the White House with a narrow victory, a fragile coalition, and an opposition gaining in strength and cohesion.

The foundations of American prosperity crumbled even as Van

Buren delivered his inaugural address in early 1837. Just hours before his speech, a prominent cotton brokerage firm in New Orleans went under. Financial disaster quickly spread to New York, the center of American trade and banking. "All is still as death; no business is transacted; no bargains made; no negotiations made," one prominent New Yorker wrote. Nine out of ten American banks failed. With imports plummeting, so did revenue from tariffs. The post office fell into deficit and required subsidy. The Army struggled to sustain West Point; the Navy languished. One state after another defaulted on its payments to foreign creditors, shattering visions of canals and railroads.[14]

No one at the time could see or comprehend the complex circuits of finance, manufacturing, and agriculture that brought on the economic crisis. People did not have a word for what they were experiencing, but settled on "panic," emphasizing the apparently irrational causes and consequences of the disorder. The Democrats blamed the crisis on the speculation of unprincipled businessmen, the behavior Jackson had tried to check with his anti-bank policies. The Whigs pointed at Jackson himself, who had interfered with the natural working of markets to demand payment for government land in gold and silver, causing a severe contraction.[15]

The panic turned into deep economic depression without apparent end. Those who labored on docks and in warehouses for a daily wage found no work. Artisans and seamstresses found no customers. Factories closed, throwing women and girls out of work. Work on canals and railroads halted, taking away the day labor on which unskilled men relied. Workingmen's organizations and unions collapsed. Children went hungry. Those who lived on farms counted themselves lucky to have ways to feed themselves as financial panic grew into desperation.

Across the country, voters turned against "Martin Van Ruin." In one state election after another the Whigs turned out in large numbers to defeat the Democrat voters blamed for the hard times. The Whigs looked forward to the presidential election of 1840 as a chance to take the prize they always thought they deserved. Henry Clay, the leader of the party, expected to be nominated, but instead delegates turned again to William Henry Harrison, who had done well across the North in the previous election.

The Democrats viewed Harrison's nomination as a gift. They called him "Granny Harrison" to emphasize his supposed physical weakness and to counter the effeminate reputation of Van Buren. One Democratic editor in Baltimore sneered that if the lazy and inert Harrison would only be promised a barrel of hard cider and a pension, he would gladly "sit for the remainder of his days in his log cabin." The sneer quickly turned into a Whig asset, however, for it replaced Harrison's actual background as a scion of the Virginia gentry and major Ohio landowner with with the persona of a frontiersman. Whigs seized on the image and made it their own. Soon, log cabins became ubiquitous in campaign celebrations, along with generous servings of hard cider. A portrait of a younger Harrison appeared on clothing, snuffboxes, hairbrushes, and razors; images of log cabins were inscribed on whiskey flasks and earrings. Coonskin caps became popular sights.[16]

Hard cider flowed at Whig events just as whiskey did at Democrats' gatherings, along with ridicule, sexual innuendo, and boasting. In cities, gangs based in fire houses bullied and intimidated opponents; in the countryside, men who dared vote against the spirit of the neighborhood, or simply not vote at all, risked ridicule and ostracism. Politics inflamed ethnic, denominational, and class differences. Even political editors wearied of such contests. "It is not very agreeable to be compelled to wallow in politics day and night, for months together," admitted one Whig editor. In the popular vote, Harrison won by 6 percentage points, making the election of 1840 the closest since 1800. Eight of ten eligible voters went to the polls, a leap of nine hundred thousand voters from the preceding presidential election.[17]

The high turnout reflected the economic depression but also the increasing power of print communication. The influence of newspapers accounted for the strange emergence of what would become the most widely spoken or written word in the world for generations to follow. The phrase "OK" first appeared in print in a Boston newspaper in 1838, an example of a national fad for intentionally misspelled abbreviations—in this case, "oll korrect." Others of those abbreviations quickly disappeared, but "OK" was picked up by the Democrats in 1840 as an abbreviation for "Old Kinderhook," the birthplace of Martin Van Buren. The Whigs spread the novelty by claiming that the false abbreviation represented the ignorance of the Democrats.

The convenient abbreviation stuck, long outliving the election that created it, demonstrating lowered boundaries among places, classes, dialects, and regions. As with Davy Crockett's almanacs, Americans created and consumed an informal culture that parodied its own crudeness, that played with convention and respectability, that demanded invention and moved with unprecedented speed.[18]

William Henry Harrison fell ill at the end of his first month in office. Treated with enemas, blistered with a hot cup, and dosed with opium, castor oil, and brandy, Harrison died after ten days, probably from septic shock. He was the first president to die in office.

Vice President John Tyler, a Virginian and a Whig in name only, became president. Made Harrison's running mate to attract southern voters, upon his ascension to the presidency Tyler ignored the Whig platform to proclaim that territorial expansion would "reclaim our almost illimitable wildernesses and introduce into their depths the lights of civilization." Tyler quickly resolved Maine's border with Canada, agreed that the United States and

Britain would share the Great Lakes, confirmed the 49th parallel as the northern boundary of the United States to the Rocky Mountains, and determined to add Texas as a new slave state. Tyler, the unexpected president, promoted American trade and military presence around the world with a new boldness and purpose.[19]

Atlantic and Pacific

The early 1840s saw the American whaling fleet at its pinnacle. More than seven hundred ships—three-fourths of those in the world—embarked from the coast of the Northeast to hunt the oceans of the globe. Whaling flourished as cities, towns, factories, and homes demanded better light. Unlike the flickering, dim, and smelly light from tallow candles made from the fat of barnyard animals, illumination from the highly refined oil of whales provided superior luminosity and a pleasant scent in lamps and candles. Whale oil cost more, but increasing numbers of customers were willing and able to pay.[20]

The whaling industry was lucrative and risky. Of the 750 ships that sailed out of New Bedford, Massachusetts, in the decades of whaling's ascendancy, 231 were lost. Others returned without having taken a single whale, representing great losses of money and opportunity. The ships that did return bearing barrels of oil, however, provided a return on investment of up to 45 percent.

Building, equipping, supplying, and repairing the ships employed thousands of workers of all skill levels. The Starbuck family of Nantucket owned the largest of the dozens of works that refined the "black, greasy, bulging casks" of oil from the ships, pulled by horses along cobblestone streets to factories. In the works, laborers emptied the barrels into giant receptacles to be boiled off, the heat "intense as the oil bubbled and seethed in the kettles, throwing off steam and sending particles of blubber and other impurities to the surface to be skimmed and fed to the fire." The oil thus refined waited for winter, when the cold congealed it into cakes to be refined once again into a product that would not freeze in the long New England nights. Factories produced candles by adding potash to the oil, pressing the mixture into molds, and inserting cotton wicks. Other processes extracted lubricants essential for textile mills and locomotives.[21]

The whaling industry pulled thousands of men to the docks. The crews of whaling ships were often young and inexperienced, for voyages lasted years and offered little financial reward for common crewmen. About a third of the sailors were Black men. The conditions on the ships were notoriously harsh, with inadequate food, rampant disease, voracious vermin, dubious crewmates, and tyrannical captains. The work of capturing, killing, dismembering, boiling, storing, and conveying the remains of the enormous mammals offered little romance.

Whaling ships, however, did provide room and board during the hard times of the 1840s. The ships plied the South Seas, famous for the beauty of its landscapes and of the people who lived on its thousands of islands. About two-thirds of the sailors on a typical whaling ship deserted at some point, eager to explore exotic lands and confident they could join another ship after exhausting the charms of a port's taverns and brothels.[22]

The largest ports lay in Hawai'i, an improbable outpost of the United States. Hawai'i—the Sandwich Islands, the British and Americans called them—first came into contact with Europeans in 1778, with the arrival of British captain James Cook, who was killed by the Indigenous people on his third visit to the islands. Discovering a Chinese demand for aromatic sandalwood that grew in Hawai'i and elsewhere in the South Pacific, American sailing ships arrived early in the nineteenth century. Even as disease killed many in the rural populations of the islands, native leaders made great profits from the sandalwood trade and purchased western goods and weapons to consolidate their power. Three villages—Oahu, Lahaina, and Hilo—grew on the three major islands.

Several Hawaiian boys were brought to Connecticut for schooling in the 1810s, their talent and devotion inspiring New England Protestants to launch an effort to convert the people of the islands. Missionaries from the United States arrived in 1820, built churches and schools, became advisors to the royal family, and helped develop a written version of the Hawaiian language that quickly spread through the islands along with newspapers. When the trade in sandalwood collapsed in the 1820s after overharvesting, the American-dominated whaling trade took its place.[23]

The New England merchants and Protestant missionaries in Hawai'i found eager support from John Tyler, who read their dispatches and encouragements with growing enthusiasm. King Kamehameha III sent a delegation to visit with Tyler in 1842, led by Timoteo Haalilio, a handsome and polished young prince, and William Richards, a prominent white American missionary who had inspired the Hawaiian monarchy to adopt a constitution and bill of rights. The emissaries planned to visit London, Brussels, and Paris after Washington, seeking acknowledgment of Hawaiian independence and sovereignty. Haalilio, despite his dark skin ("about as dark as a negro, but with Indian hair," judged the young woman who would soon be President Tyler's wife), quickly became popular at the soirees of the Washington social season.[24]

President Tyler and his secretary of state, Daniel Webster, granted the Hawaiian visitors' request for independence, for that would suit the interests of the United States. Not only did five out of every six ships visiting Honolulu fly under American flags, Tyler noted, but the Hawaiian government was eager "to improve the condition of its people by the introduction of knowledge, of religious and moral institutions, means of education, and the arts of civilized life." Americans believed they were uniquely qualified to supply those arts. Even the Whig enemies of President Tyler cheered what became known as the Tyler Doctrine to protect Hawaiian independence, and abolitionists praised its "liberal and philanthropic" tone and purpose.

Merchants applauded Tyler's determination to maintain access to the markets of China. They agreed with the president that the debilitating economic depression of the United States showed that Americans needed access to markets beyond the bounds of the nation. In 1843, Tyler and Webster sent a legation to China, carrying with them two pistols, a model steamship, and "a Globe, that the Celestials may see they are not the 'Central Kingdom.'" A flotilla of four ships sailed to Macao in the South China Sea, where the delegation patiently awaited a meeting with the Chinese imperial commissioner. The United States received trading privileges equal to those the British had won in their defeat of the Chinese in the first Opium War that had only just concluded. The US Senate immediately and unanimously approved the treaty in 1844. Trade between the United States and China more than doubled over the next fifteen years, to more than $22 million.

Growing Pacific trade required better understanding of the world's largest ocean, which retained vast uncharted areas. The United States had fallen far behind other seagoing nations in exploration; Britain had sent twenty-eight expeditions throughout the world's oceans; France, seventeen. After years of planning and vacillation, in 1838 the United States launched its own Exploring Expedition "to extend the empire of commerce and science." Through the early 1840s, the Americans traveled on six sailing ships carrying 346 men, one of the largest expeditions launched by any nation.[25]

The Exploring Expedition ranged south to Cape Horn and then west to Sydney, explored the Fiji Islands and other islands of the South Pacific, and then sailed to the Pacific Northwest of North America. There, it charted the Columbia River and the coast of California to the Mexican port of San Francisco. Over the four years of its journey, the expedition traveled 87,000 miles, surveyed 280 islands, produced 180 charts, mapped 800 miles of North America's coastline, and, remarkably, 1,500 miles of the coast of a previously undiscovered continent: Antarctica. Along the way, the expedition lost two ships and twenty-eight men. The United States Exploring Expedition proved to be the last group of sailing ships to circumnavigate the globe.[26]

The head of the expedition, Charles Wilkes, expected his report of the adventure to win fanfare when he arrived in Washington in 1842. But Tyler and Webster, negotiating with Britain over the future of Oregon at the time, would not release Wilkes's report while those sensitive conversations were underway. Though the specimens from the ships drew large audiences in Washington's Patent Office, Wilkes found himself court-martialed for erratic leadership at sea. He oversaw a multivolume report on the expedition, elaborately illustrated, that came out a few years later. Without a popular narrative to capture attention in the moment of return, however, the accomplishments of the United States Exploring Expedition were slowly forgotten.

The Exploring Expedition left an enduring legacy in the forty tons of specimens and artifacts that became the basis for the Smithsonian Institution. James Smithson, a British scientist who admired but had never been to the United States, had left an estate to his nephew. When that nephew died in 1835, the Americans sent a diplomat to England to gather the money willed to the United States by Smithson "for the increase and diffusion of knowledge." The representative returned with 105 sacks containing nearly 105,000 gold sovereigns, worth about half a million dollars at the time (and about twenty times that amount now). When the Smithsonian Institution, chartered in 1848, opened in 1855 in an impressive "castle" in Washington between the White House and the Capitol, the specimens and artifacts of the Exploring Expedition formed the heart of its collection. Other government-sponsored bodies contributed to the Smithsonian as they gathered Native materials from the West.[27]

In the meantime, it fell to fiction to give Americans a tantalizing portrait of the Pacific. Herman Melville came to New Bedford in the winter of 1840–1841, when Frederick Douglass lived there, to find a whaling voyage. From a prominent but reduced family in New York City, Melville had a difficult time establishing himself. He had already sailed to Liverpool and back as a cabin boy and then journeyed across the Great Lakes, down the Mississippi, and back up the Ohio on an adventure with a friend, but the twenty-two-year-old had never been on a whaling ship. He signed on to the *Acushnet* and sailed south in January 1841. Six months later, he deserted in the Marquesas Islands in the middle of the South Pacific, a popular stop for American whaling ships.[28]

With an injured leg, the young sailor spent several weeks in the Typee Valley, whose people bore elaborate tattoos and were rumored to be cannibals. Native women ministered to Melville until he recovered and descended from the valley to find a place on an Australian ship. Six weeks later, Melville was jailed in Tahiti for his role in a mutiny on his new ship. Upon his release, he worked as a field hand, growing sweet potatoes to sell to crews hoping to avoid scurvy. Soon tiring of that unadventurous work, Melville caught a Nantucket whaler to Honolulu, a town of ten thousand, where he worked as a bowling pinsetter and at other mundane tasks. Finally, Melville joined the Navy frigate the *United States* and eventually returned to Boston in 1844.

As Melville told his mother and sisters of his adventures, they encouraged him to write them down. With no better prospects, he described his sojourn with the people of Typee, charging the story with (a possibly imagined) risk of cannibalism and (strongly implied) sexual experience with the young women who cared for him, especially the alluring Fayaway. The largest New York publishing firm turned down Melville's narrative because "it was impossible that it could be true." Melville's brother, however, a prominent Democratic politician with a new appointment in London, shared the manuscript with the English publisher of Washington Irving. Irving happened to be visiting that publisher, who read Irving portions of the story over breakfast. Impressed, Irving told his New York publisher of the promising manuscript. Entranced by the passages he read, the American editor sought out its young author.

Typee won strong reviews when it appeared in 1846, and controversies helped it reach strong sales as well. Christian newspapers protested Melville's portrayal of missionaries in the South Seas islands, some reviewers objected to the voluptuousness of the rendition of Fayaway and the other women, and others protested that such an improbable story could not be true. Melville's comrade Toby Green offered confirmation of Melville's tale, published as an appendix to a second edition, where Melville deleted disparaging comments about missionaries. Melville quickly followed with a companion novel, *Omoo*, which also met a warm reception. Melville both relished and resented his sudden fame as a purveyor of adventure stories. He longed for stranger shores.[29]

Overland

The American West had been traversed by Indigenous peoples for all memory and crossed by trappers and merchants for generations. The United States government sent an expedition to the West, as it did to the Pacific, to create texts, maps, charts, and narratives to help guide settlement of the region.[30]

John C. Frémont led the expedition to the West thanks to a combination of surveying skills and a fortunate marriage. Through the help of influential men impressed with him as a youth, Frémont had secured positions as a mathematician on a United States Navy ship sailing to South America, a surveyor in Cherokee lands in South Carolina, and then in the Army Corps of Engineers on an assignment to help map portions of the Louisiana Purchase.[31]

Working in a Washington office in 1841 to translate figures from his Louisiana notebooks into maps, Frémont was visited by Senator Thomas Hart Benton of Missouri, a Democrat and leading proponent of western exploration and expansion to the Pacific. Impressed with the charming young man, Benton invited him to his home for dinner. There, Frémont met Benton's daughter Jessie, a student at a Washington boarding school. Though only sixteen, Jessie soon secretly married Frémont, eleven years her senior, and the couple moved into her room in the Benton home.

The senator, furious at first, reconciled himself to the marriage and arranged for his new son-in-law to lead an expedition to the South Pass of the Rocky Mountains. The goal was to inspire migrants and build political will for the expansion of the United States to the Pacific. Frémont would be accompanied by a skilled German mapmaker and a young American mountain man named Kit Carson, who had married a Native woman in Taos and spoke several Indian languages.

Americans knew more about the distant Pacific coast than they did about the land between. Like Hawai'i, Oregon had attracted Protestant missionaries who lived among the British, French Canadians, and Native peoples near an encampment of the Hudson's Bay Company, close to where the city of Portland would grow. The missionaries, arriving in the 1830s, failed to convert many Native people, and so, like their counterparts in Hawai'i, turned their energies toward promoting the region to the government in Washington. A hundred migrants followed an overland route to Oregon in 1842, led by guides who knew the land from experience, so the Frémont expedition often followed the prosaic paths carved by heavy wagons pulled by oxen.[32]

Frémont returned to Jessie in time for the birth of a child in October. Jessie Frémont saw that her husband had difficulty composing a narrative of his expedition, so she pitched in. As John paced the room, glancing at his notes, he narrated as Jessie helped shape a compelling story; he watched her face as he spoke, alert to "slight dissent" or "pleased expression." Together, they created a stirring narrative, sometimes poetic, as when they evoked an image of peaks "cut clear against the glowing sky." The couple also offered reassurance to prospective migrants. The fabled South Pass turned out to be no steeper than a Washington street, they told readers, rising so gradually that the expedition crossed the pass without realizing it. The Frémonts often turned to familiar vocabularies and analogies to describe a scene as "picturesque" or in relation to the Alps, for Americans had no language to describe the novelty and immensity of the West. Frémont deemed some areas beautiful and fertile, others barren wastes of no use or interest. His words, reinforced by writers and painters who followed, would define American understanding of the West for the next half century and beyond.[33]

Frémont prepared for a second, longer, and more challenging expedition, crossing the Rockies to the Columbia River. The large expedition moved slowly, in part because Frémont insisted on dragging a heavy howitzer despite orders not to do so. His superiors feared that the weapon sent the wrong signal to the

Natives through whose territory it passed, but Frémont relished that very effect. The expedition passed near the Great Salt Lake and clambered through the Rockies. Arriving at the Columbia River in winter, Frémont decided that rather than rest and replenish his exhausted men and animals, they would push across the Sierra Nevada mountains into California. The Paiute and Washoe people who lived nearby counseled against traveling during the winter through dangerous snow drifts, but Frémont persisted, reluctantly burying the howitzer along the way. After five weeks of misery, in which his men were reduced to eating their mules and a pet dog, they arrived in the Sacramento Valley at a place called Sutter's Fort.

Johann Sutter had fled Switzerland years before to avoid imprisonment for debt, leaving his wife and children behind. He had roamed through Santa Fe, Oregon, and Hawai'i, where he contracted eight Hawaiian laborers to come to California to develop forty-eight thousand acres he persuaded the Mexican government to grant him. Sutter also forced hundreds of Native people, weakened by disease, to labor for near-starvation rations. By the time the United States expedition arrived, Sutter's settlement included a gristmill, tannery, blacksmith shop, distillery, and an imposing house. "Captain" Sutter profitably resupplied Frémont's expedition, which passed through the valley of California south to the Old Spanish Trail that stretched from Los Angeles to Santa Fe. Heading east, the straggling force crossed the Mojave Desert and what would become known as the Great Basin. They finally arrived in St. Louis in August 1844, haggard and emaciated.[34]

Frémont set to work with Jessie to craft another report, filled with inspiring descriptions of Oregon, California, and the lands between. The expedition mapped interior mountains, rivers, vegetation, wildlife, as well as several routes to the west. The journey had also revealed knowledge of the diverse Native peoples who dwelled throughout the enormous region. The report became a publishing and public relations phenomenon, translated into multiple languages. A map ten feet long detailed watering places and salt licks for those who dreamed of making the journey. John Charles Frémont became famous as the Pathfinder, his charming young wife as his accomplice. Senator Thomas Hart Benton's power and influence increased. Oregon and California assumed a vivid place in American imaginations.

A thousand emigrants embarked on the Oregon Trail in 1843. Almost all were farmers, for the depression that had begun six years before still haunted the Midwest and Upper South, making families desperate enough to launch out on a treacherous journey. They abandoned Iowa, Illinois, Indiana, Missouri, Kentucky, and Tennessee, where they had struggled with debt, tenancy, and disease.

Migrant families sold all they possessed to purchase a trail wagon and six oxen to pull their heavy loads on the two-thousand mile, eight-month journey. The travel proved more tedious than dangerous, though disease and accidents took the lives of children and others along the way. The Native peoples, long accustomed to trading with people of European descent, seldom threatened the settlers. More commonly, the Indians supplied guidance, food, and assistance.

In 1844, more people traveled the Oregon Trail than in the preceding three years combined. Fueled by news that wagons could make it all the way to the Columbia River, 2,750 Americans migrated in 1845. One train of 460 wagons carried 850 men and twice as many women and children, accompanied by 400 horses and mules, 1,000 goats, and 7,000 cattle. Migrants to Oregon would eventually bring half a million cattle and as many sheep to their new homes.[35]

Oregon settlers arrived in the Willamette Valley, a place of astounding beauty and promise. Each family received 640 acres from the provisional government—320 acres to the husband and an equal number to his wife—after they lived on and improved the land for four years. Disease had greatly weakened the Native people, reducing their ability to negotiate with the influx of settlers from the United States. Laws enforced temperance and encouraged families rather than single men to migrate. Oregon outlawed slavery in 1844, but any Black person who arrived would be subject to a whipping of twenty to thirty-nine lashes. The early white settlers and lawmakers of Oregon had no idea of when, how, or whether the territory might enter the United States.[36]

Nauvoo

The twenty-three-year-old Joseph Smith, judging himself finally worthy of the task, translated the Book of Mormon in words biblical in tone and language. In 1830, he persuaded the publisher of a local newspaper to print the six-hundred-page book, guarding it from townspeople who threatened to destroy the work. Those who read the Book of Mormon found that it told of a civilization in the Western Hemisphere centuries before the birth of Christ. The book related the story of a people's decline, one prophet after another calling for a return to ancient values and warning of the consequences of their failure to do so. The Mormon gospel preached that Christ died to atone for the world's many sins, expanding the world's history to embrace the Americas and vast spans of time. The Church of Jesus Christ of Latter-day Saints dedicated itself to sharing the new gospel.

Guided by revelations, Smith drew a plan for Zion, a city arranged in grids around a large temple, where people from around the world would come for knowledge and training before spreading across the world to recruit yet more converts. Smith moved his family to Ohio and attracted a thousand converts. In 1832, persecuted and assaulted by a mob there, Smith and his allies moved to Missouri to build Zion, constructing a hundred buildings surrounded by two thousand farms. Such growth outraged other citizens of the county. More than two thousand militia took Smith prisoner and demanded that all Mormon property in the state be confiscated.

Escaping from prison, Smith and four allies fled to Illinois under false names to found a new Mormon city—Nauvoo—on a two-mile-long peninsula on the Mississippi River near Keokuk, Iowa. Nauvoo prospered and grew rapidly, outpacing a nearby rival called Chicago. Smith rose to national visibility in 1838 and 1839, as the church grew in New York City and Philadelphia, where the prophet "electrified" an audience of three thousand. The Mormon message, Smith told a reporter, was simple: "The first and fundamental principle of our holy religion is, that we believe that we have a right to embrace all, and every item of truth, without limitation or without being circumscribed or prohibited by the creeds or superstitious notions of men." The promise of new revelations brought the Latter-day Saints thousands of converts, eager to build a new Zion.[37]

Smith declared that in Nauvoo "we can enjoy peace, and can worship the God of heaven and earth without molestation." The Mormons' faith offered a mirror image of the America emerging around them. They emphasized community welfare rather than individual advancement, abstention rather than consumption, religious unity rather than competition among denominations. They welcomed people without property and immigrants into their communities. They resisted the conventional American boasting about the nation, understanding history on a longer and broader scale.

Across the landscape that would become the United States, people envisioned what the new nation might be. Their visions often endured for generations, speaking to those who glimpsed possibilities yet unfulfilled.

Indigenous leaders in every part of North America encountered the relentless claims for territory by the United States. Some fought back with violence against settlers and militia. Others accommodated by adopting Christianity, private property, and holding Black people in slavery. Tenskwatawa of the Shawnees called for all Native peoples to return to traditional ways and unite against the European Americans. Sequoyah of the Cherokees created a written language for his people, adopting a cultural technology of white Americans to help the Cherokee nation resist domination.

People of African descent challenged the new United States to live up to the ideals proclaimed in the Declaration of Independence and the Bible. Black people did not wait for rights and dignity to be bestowed upon them but labored to bring those ideals to fruition. Jarena Lee, like other Black women in the states where slavery had been gradually abolished, preached the gospel of Christian self-determination and self-respect. Paul Cuffe, a Quaker of Ashanti and Wampanoag ancestry, created a prosperous shipping business in Massachusetts. He used his wealth and status to foster alliances among Black people across the Atlantic and the Caribbean, transporting people at his own expense to Sierra Leone to found a new Black nation in Africa.

Protestant Christianity gained ever greater strength in the early nineteenth century, spreading along with settlement and the growth of cities. Dissidents frequently challenged clergy, denominations, sacraments, and articles of faith. Charles Grandison Finney, in the top image, sparked revivals across the North, creating converts and breeding dissension within and among congregations. Joseph Smith, disheartened by the competition among Protestant denominations, felt called to found a new faith, the Church of Jesus Christ of Latter-day Saints. That church faced repeated persecutions, but the Saints grew into a powerful presence in the United States and beyond.

Indigenous people who spoke boldly against the depredations they suffered sometimes found sympathetic audiences among white people. William Apess of the Pequot in Massachusetts, in the top image, wrote blistering and sarcastic critiques of Andrew Jackson's Native removal policies "through an Indian's looking glass." Black Hawk fought against intrusions on the lands of his people. After his defeat and capture, Black Hawk narrated a popular autobiography that attacked the greed of white settlers and the American government.

Debates that began in the rarefied realms of the churches and universities
of Massachusetts grew into a distinctively American intellectual movement.
Ralph Waldo Emerson, educated as a minister, found inspiration in nature
and in human possibility rather than in miracles and ritual. Margaret Fuller,
educated by her father for roles women were not permitted to fulfill, made
herself into a wide-ranging intellectual. After working with Emerson, Fuller
launched out to write bold books on women's capacities and the social landscape of the nation.

Opponents of slavery labored for decades to end American bondage. Black and white abolitionists, male and female, launched newspapers, wrote books, and spoke to audiences large and small, friendly and hostile. William Lloyd Garrison, following the example of Black abolitionists, founded the *Liberator* to demand the immediate end of slavery and other forms of injustice. Frederick Douglass was a leading voice in the antislavery movement for decades, his powerful narratives of his escape from slavery, uncompromising speeches, and bold newspaper challenging slavery's spread and power.

Thomas Cole, a self-taught painter, inspired Americans to embrace their landscape as worthy of great art. Distraught by the destruction of nature by thoughtless exploitation, Cole painted *The Oxbow* as a meditation on the consequences of settlement: the river carves a question mark on the land, a storm threatens, and cut-over forests present a mysterious script on a distant mountain.

Edgar Allan Poe and George Lippard wrote with imaginations that shocked and intrigued their contemporaries. Poe's work ranged across genres of prose and poetry, using horror, humor, crime, and science to explore unmeasured possibilities of human nature and the natural world. Lippard wrote best-selling fantasies of elite corruption and debauchery as well as patriotic stories of the emerging nation. Both men, who died young, pushed against boundaries of propriety and convention.

American music and dance grew from styles, rhythms, and traditions that spanned continents. William Henry Lane, calling himself Master Juba, astounded Black and white audiences with his ability to perform every kind of dance and to invent his own, drawing on African and Irish traditions. Stephen Foster appropriated Black dialect and personas to compose many of the most popular songs of the era. Seeking large audiences, Foster increasingly blurred racial identity in his lyrics to convey universal human emotions of joy, love, and loss.

Women seized public roles, uninvited and sometimes unwelcome. Dorothea Dix, in the first image, labored successfully across the nation for the humane treatment of people locked away with mental illness. Elizabeth Cady Stanton worked with allies for decades to demand political and legal rights for women.

American writers launched bold experiments in fiction. Herman Melville, in the first image, wrote *Moby-Dick*, a monumental novel at once richly metaphorical and starkly physical, along with subtle stories of false appearance and deception. Nathaniel Hawthorne created *The Scarlet Letter*, a reflection on guilt and responsibility driven by sexual longing and religious hypocrisy.

Two bold voices challenged conventional tastes and standards. Walt Whitman invented new poetic forms in *Leaves of Grass*, celebrating himself and all other people, glorying in the pleasures of the body and tumultuous democracy. Fanny Fern made herself into one of the most popular writers in the new nation by using humor to ridicule both the pompous and the timid. She welcomed Whitman's sensuous poetry even as other critics attacked it.

Free Black women advocated for their own rights and for those of enslaved people. They published poetry, wrote autobiographies, and spoke before audiences of men and women, Black people and white. Sojourner Truth emerged as a powerful speaker against slavery and for the power of women. Harriet Tubman led enslaved people to freedom in daring exploits, supporting her crusades with her own labor and donations won by speaking.

Several white artists portrayed Black people with respect and dignity, countering caricatures that proliferated in American culture. William Sidney Mount reflected his upbringing on Long Island, New York, and his friendship with Black musicians in *The Banjo Player* and *The Power of Music*. Such paintings, widely distributed as lithographs, carried quiet messages of shared humanity.

Some Americans voiced eloquent appreciation of the natural world. Susan Fenimore Cooper portrayed subtle changes and looming dangers in the New York landscape in *Rural Hours*. Henry David Thoreau composed an admonition and reflection on nature and social change from two years of living alone in a small house he built on the shore of Walden Pond in Massachusetts.

When the struggle over slavery exploded with John Brown's raid on the armory at Harpers Ferry, the writings of Frances E. Watkins, on the right, and Lydia Maria Child defined the moral issues at the heart of the conflict.

Nearly three thousand British immigrants came to Nauvoo in the early 1840s, traveling from Liverpool to New Orleans and then up the Mississippi, the result of missionary efforts by the Mormons. The immigrants were, by and large, poor people, dissatisfied with the religion and laboring conditions in Britain. Joseph Smith foresaw the arrival of "persons of all languages, and of every tongue, and of every color; who shall with us worship the Lord of Hosts in his holy temple." The laws of Nauvoo declared that "Catholics, Presbyterians, Methodists, Baptists, Latter-Day Saints, Quakers, Episcopalians, Universalists, Unitarians, Mohammedans, and all other religious sects, and denominations, whatever, shall have free toleration, and equal privileges, in this city."[38]

Smith sought to bind Nauvoo together through family connections conceived in bold new ways. The Mormons began to baptize the dead, symbolically bringing salvation to deceased ancestors who had not enjoyed the chance to accept the true gospel. "They without us, cannot be made perfect," Smith preached; "neither can we without our dead, be made perfect." Six thousand living people were dipped into the Mississippi River in baptism in 1841 as the Mormons sought to fulfill the prophecy of unifying humankind across time as well as space. They began construction of a massive temple that would preside over the raw but rapidly growing city. They wended their way through partisan politics as they rebutted attacks from a ceaseless round of hostile books and newspaper articles.

Despite the progress, a startling innovation created turmoil in Nauvoo. Smith believed an angel had revealed to him that families should be extended through plural marriage, in which priests "sealed" themselves to multiple wives. Smith resisted the revelation and kept it secret, even from his devoted spouse, Emma. He married a second wife in 1836. In the two years after 1841 Smith married thirty additional wives, ten of the weddings consented to by the women's husbands. To what extent the marriages were sexually consummated remains unknown. Women married to other men continued to live with their first husbands after their sealing with Smith, who did not accompany any wife in public other than Emma.

Smith understood how dangerous the revelation of plural marriage would be, but he told prospective wives—and their often-reluctant fathers and husbands—that marriage to him would "ensure your eternal salvation & exaltation and that of your father's household & all your kindred." Smith instructed the church's leaders of the vision in 1841 and they, too, began marrying other women. Twenty-nine Mormon men were "sealed" to at least one other wife over the next three years. Women without husbands, whether widows, abandoned, or never-married, may have found in the practice a stability and connection they did not find elsewhere in America. Those who accepted Smith's revelation believed it transcended secular life or personal affection. They married not for themselves but to save the world.[39]

Despite these understandings, the Latter-day Saints did not publicly acknowledge plural marriage. No matter its divine sanction and purpose, Smith knew, the practice would be considered bigamy in secular law and scandalous in traditional morality. Knowledge of plural wives would lend credence to those who attacked the Mormons as a cult rather than a religion, a concentration of power contrary to American principles, a sexual corruption Protestants saw in nunneries and monasteries. Emma Smith headed the Female Relief Society, with over a thousand members, which devoted much of its energies to combatting sexual impropriety. She struggled to understand and accept plural marriage, especially Joseph's involvement. He continued to take wives without her knowledge or agreement.

Even as controversy spun around Nauvoo, Smith formed an exploring expedition for a new Mormon settlement in Oregon,

California, or Texas. He created the Council of Fifty to begin preparations for a new base, a place that would be, as one council member put it, "a home where the saints can dwell in peace and health, and where they can erect the ensign & standard of liberty for the nations, and live by the laws of God without being oppressed and mobbed under a tyrannical government without protection from the laws." Their plan was to raise a force of a hundred thousand men to protect American settlers as they moved west, volunteers who would resist Native enemies, foreign powers, or criminals who would threaten the migrations.

Dissension continued to build within Nauvoo over plural marriage. Leading men turned against Smith. They published a newspaper, the *Nauvoo Expositor*, to urge a return to the religion "originally taught by Joseph Smith." They denounced the newer doctrines as "abominations and whoredoms." Smith ordered the press burned in the street. He considered the *Expositor* a pretense for outsiders to destroy Nauvoo, a tool to excite "suspicion, wrath, and indignation among a certain class of the less honorable portion of mankind, to commit acts of violence upon the innocent and unsuspecting." He put Nauvoo under martial law and prepared to defend against an attack.

The governor of Illinois attempted to control mobs and militia that were eager to attack Nauvoo and kill Smith, and so persuaded Smith to come to the town of Carthage to stand trial for the destruction of the press. There, in July 1844, a hundred men in blackface surrounded the jail and filled it with gunfire. Hit multiple times, once through the heart, Joseph Smith collapsed and died. The leaders of the Church of Jesus Christ of Latter-day Saints immediately began to plan for the future in the West their martyred prophet had envisioned.[40]

Another native-born American religion fell into crisis at the same time as the Mormons. The followers of William Miller had looked forward to the fall of 1844 for the long-awaited return of Jesus Christ. Fifty thousand Americans gathered outside in answer to "The Midnight Cry" of the Second Coming. Many had given away all they possessed in anticipation of the event. In their faith in the literal truth of the Bible and in the imminent arrival of the Millennium, the Millerites resembled many evangelicals. When the appointed day came and went without the expected arrival, however, skeptics were quick to ridicule those who believed. While some Millerites turned away from the faith after what they called "the Disappointment," others retained elements of the doctrine. Some believed that Miller had been right, that Jesus had indeed returned but He did so in heaven, where He was reunited with the Father.

Ellen G. White of Maine received visions as a young woman soon after the Disappointment. "While praying, the thick darkness that had enveloped me was scattered, a bright light, like a ball of fire, came towards me, and as it fell upon me, my strength was taken away," she testified. "I seemed to be in the presence of Jesus and the angels. Again it was repeated, 'Make known to others what I have revealed to you.'" Published in Millerite papers, White's visions spread through the late 1840s and early 1850s. White and her followers believed that worship should take place on Saturdays rather than on Sundays. They later became known as Seventh-day Adventists, establishing a faith that in coming generations would spread to every part of the world.[41]

"The Sensorium of Communicated Intelligence"

Samuel F. B. Morse had cultivated plans for an electric telegraph since 1832, but had faced technological, financial, and political setbacks. Finally, in 1843, Congress grudgingly contributed funds to run a test line forty-four miles from Washington to Baltimore.

Morse rushed to gain allies for the trial. Partners buried wires in lead tubes and strung them on chestnut poles along the Baltimore & Ohio Railroad. Others took responsibility for digging trenches, making the pipes, and preparing the wire by wrapping it in colored cotton thread and coating it with varnish. Morse and his associates raced through the winter to finish the work, improvising and improving the batteries, machinery, and coding techniques as they progressed.

In May 1844, a colleague set up a station in Baltimore while Morse arranged a post in the chambers of the United States Supreme Court. He asked a young female friend to suggest the content of the first message and she in turn consulted her mother, who suggested "What hath God wrought!" Morse sent the message to Baltimore as a test, eliciting the less inspiring response of "yes." The original message, despite its biblical resonance and subsequent fame, received little attention at the time.[42]

Skeptics wondered whether, despite such tidy demonstrations, the telegraph could convey anything of value. Fortunately, the Democrats' national convention then underway in Baltimore offered a dramatic test. Torn over their nominee, the Democrats deadlocked. People filled the offices in Washington where Morse was stationed. They were astounded to learn the unlikely news from the dots and dashes: the Democrats had nominated James K. Polk of Tennessee, a virtual unknown. The news arrived in telegraphic brevity and cadence: "Illinois goes for Polk . . . Mich goes for Polk. . . . Intense anxiety prevails to . . . hear the result of last Balloting. . . . Polk is unanimously nom." Morse returned an exultant reply: "3 cheers have been given here for Polk and 3 for the Telegraph."[43]

The successes continued. Morse was able to alert Washington officials of a riot between Catholics and Protestants in Philadelphia and to convey the mayor's request for aid. A post office employee learned of the birth of his grandson. Chess club members in Washington and Baltimore played a telegraphic match "with the same ease as if the players were seated at the same table." Charles Wilkes of the Exploring Expedition used the telegraph to define latitude and longitude with a new precision, allowing more accurate mapping and timekeeping around the world.

Americans thrilled to consider what the telegraph might mean for the United States, a nation growing so rapidly, so fragmented and distended. The telegraph promised to unite Americans across space and in spirit. "The mother may, each day, renew her blessing upon her child a thousand leagues away," exulted one paper, "and the father, each hour, learn the health of those around his distant fireside." The nation would be made stronger and more prosperous by the new "sensorium of communicated intelligence," as the *Christian Observer* put it. "Steam and electricity, with the natural impulses of a free people, have made, and are making, this country the greatest, the most original, the most wonderful the sun ever shone upon."

Despite the success and excitement, the federal government showed little interest in sustaining its investment in the telegraph. Nor did Morse display the ability to convert his invention into a commercial enterprise. The telegraph, heralded as the harbinger of a new age, struggled for years, its meaning undirected and uncertain. It would require innovations in finance and technology to make the telegraph an effective system of communication.[44]

A Nation's Destiny

In 1845, Mexico watched the new president of the United States, James K. Polk, with distrust. Polk had defeated the prominent and popular Henry Clay on a platform advocating the annexation of Texas. Mexico was as large as the United States, and Mexico City dwarfed Washington in size and splendor, but Mexico had fallen behind its northern neighbor in growth and in stability. Mexicans fought the Comanches, Apaches, Kiowas, Navajos, and other Native peoples throughout their vast and thinly populated northern region. The Republic of Texas stood as a threat and a challenge, a slaveholding rival on Mexico's northern border.[45]

In the United States, by contrast, many dreamed of empire. The long wagon trains on the Oregon Trail, the exciting visions of Frémont's narrative, the ships departing the cities of the North for ports and oceans around the world, the new telegraph lines and railroads reaching ever farther, the states joining the Union, the recovering vitality of the economy after the long depression—all created the sense that America's time was imminent.

In early 1844, Ralph Waldo Emerson told an audience in Boston that "in every age of the world, there has been a leading nation." Guided by a "sublime and friendly Destiny," America stood as the "country of the Future." The United States had emerged as "a country of beginnings, of projects, of vast designs, and expectations. It has no past: all has an onward and prospective look." The nation had just begun to fulfill its destiny, for "the bountiful continent is ours, state on state, and territory on territory, to the waves of the Pacific."[46]

As a part of that vision, the influential *Democratic Review*, under its young editor John L. O'Sullivan, called for Texas to come immediately within the "dear and sacred designation of Our Country." Mexico, too "imbecile and distracted" to settle and control its distant provinces, had no right to Texas or California. England, "our old rival and enemy," threatened the United States on the new nation's own continent with its overtures to Mexico, "checking the fulfillment of our manifest destiny to overspread the continent allotted by Providence for the free development of our yearly multiplying millions."

Two words in O'Sullivan's declaration—"manifest destiny"—rose to become a national motto in 1845. Its internal rhyme made an audacious claim: God had given North America to the

United States. By "manifest," O'Sullivan meant "self-evident";
by "destiny," he meant that Providence would permit no other
course. War would be unnecessary to fill the continent, O'Sullivan declared, for "the advance guard of the irresistible army of
Anglo-Saxon emigration" would occupy it peacefully and inevitably. "Armed with the plough and the rifle, and marking its trail
with schools and colleges, courts and representative halls, mills
and meeting-houses," the Anglo-Saxon occupation of the western half of the continent would take place "without agency of our
government," the product of "the natural flow of events, the spontaneous working of principles."[47]

John L. O'Sullivan spoke in the voice of a group that called
itself Young America. They saw themselves as harbingers of
democracy and enlightenment, proclaiming the United States
the leading edge of a global movement toward freedom, original thinking, and innovative literature. They identified with the
bold Democrats rather than what they saw as the stodgy and self-
satisfied Whigs. Embedded in the optimism of Young America
was the modern belief that "*Race* is the key to much that seems
obscure in the history of nations." History repeatedly showed, the
Democratic Review proclaimed, "the whiter race ruling the less
white, through all gradations of color, from the fairest European
down to the darkest African."

This notion of "race," gaining power in scientific circles and
the popular imagination in Europe and Britain, claimed that
character, intelligence, and independence circulated, somehow, in
the very "blood" of people who shared skin color and hair texture. Scientists measured cranial capacities of skulls to "prove"
that people of European ancestry possessed understanding and
logic that "lesser" people did not. Manifest destiny stood as the
natural, beneficial result of the superiority of the "Anglo-Saxon"
race. It was up to the United States to enact the next stage in an

ancient and global drama of progress, inevitably sweeping to the West. Mexico violated the drama of progress in its devotion to Catholicism and its population of the mixed ancestry of Native peoples and Europeans.[48]

Critics blasted the absurdity of such claims. The *National Intelligencer* sneered at "such political 'Clap-Trap' as 'our *Manifest Destiny*,' along with the second word-snare, *'Anglo-Saxonism.'*" "If anything was wanting to prove that this age is an age of imbecility and false philosophy, it is furnished in this drivel about races," raged a senator from Illinois. "The Anglo-Saxon race and the Celtic race, and this race and that race, seem to be the latest discovery of the present time to account for all moral, social, and political phenomena. This new theory is founded neither on Christianity nor philosophy."

Albert Gallatin, the elderly former advisor to Thomas Jefferson and other presidents, warned against the "extraordinary assertion" that "the people of the United States have an hereditary superiority of race over the Mexicans, which gives them the right to subjugate and keep in bondage the inferior nation." The United States, he reminded Americans, had been founded as a "model republic" based on the truth that all people had the capacity for self-government. The new nation had adapted ideas and institutions from the English because the "English" had been created by waves of invasion and immigration, not because they belonged to an imaginary "Anglo-Saxon" race. "Allegations of superiority of race and destiny," Gallatin bitterly warned, "are but pretences under which to disguise ambition, cupidity, or silly vanity."

George Catlin, who had traveled throughout the West to make his paintings of Native peoples, understood the situation better than most. With disgust, he had witnessed "the bustling, busy, talking, whistling, hopping, elated and exulting white man, with the first dip of the ploughshare, making sacrilegious trespass on the bones of the valiant dead." Catlin had seen "the skull, the pipe, and the tomahawk rise from the ground together." He had witnessed the "splendid juggernaut" of white settlement sweep across the land, and "no one but God knows where the voracity of the one is to stop, short of the acquisition of everything that is desirable to money-making man in the Indian's country." The United States had compiled "an unrequited account of sin and injustice"; Americans had become "cruel dispossessors."[49]

The North American continent offered threat as well as promise in 1845. Recent settlers to Arkansas, Missouri, and the Iowa Territory found that the best free land had been taken and they were ready to move again. Florida, after the debacle of the Seminole Wars, entered the Union in 1845 but remained tumultuous and thinly populated. Native peoples of the Southeast, forcibly removed only a decade before, now seemed an impediment to white settlers in Indian Territory. The unconquered peoples of the Great Plains posed an unmeasured threat to American expansion. The Pacific Coast remained remote and tenuous, vulnerable to invasion from within and without. And the Republic of Texas, bold but weak, demanded attention if it was not to fall to the British. Whatever destiny the United States held would not arrive without a trial.[50]

War

In May 1845, word arrived in Washington of failed diplomacy in Mexico, almost immediately followed by news of eleven American lives lost on the north side of the Rio Grande. James K. Polk, ready to declare war even before the news, seized on the report to send a war message to Congress. Two days later, large majorities in both houses, supported by both parties, approved funding for a war against Mexico. More men rushed to volunteer than the United States Army could absorb.

The American public learned of the war in Mexico in pieces. The emerging telegraph network brought news of distant battles after delays of two weeks to two months. Reports had to be conveyed by courier from the sites of the battles, through territory populated by the enemy, to a Mexican port, to the Mississippi River, and then to New Orleans. Nine newspapers in New Orleans competed for the best dispatches, establishing the first American foreign war correspondents. From New Orleans, steamboats, stages, and trains carried the news to telegraph stations, first in Petersburg, Virginia, just below Richmond, and by February 1848 to Charleston, South Carolina.

Despite complaints that reporters revealed more about the army's movements and morale than appropriate, they faced few constraints on their movements or their words. As a result, one paper observed, the events of the war and the experiences of its participants were "more thoroughly known by mankind, than those of any war that has ever taken place."[51]

The war also unleashed an explosion of paperback books, costing only twelve and a half cents, bound in bright yellow and featuring martial woodcuts, fewer than a hundred pages for quick reading. Harper & Brothers in New York ran twenty-two presses, driven by steam, printing over thirty-three thousand sheets a day. Some books reached a hundred thousand readers. Soldiers carried books with them, reading of fictional wartime adventures even as they embarked on actual ones. The lead character often resembled Natty Bumppo of James Fenimore Cooper's popular Leatherstocking novels—a man of pure heart and purpose, sympathetic to the people he fought against. Often, the soldiers in the novels fell in love with Mexican women, finding shared humanity amid the suffering.

A firm in New York churned out more than seventy inexpensive print illustrations of the war, featuring victories at exotic places called Resaca de Palma, Buena Vista, and Veracruz, as well as triumph at a nonexistent battle at Matamoros. The company, led by Nathaniel Currier and James Ives, employed engravers for different components of each scene, some focused on soldiers and others on landscapes imagined from sketchy reports from the field. The prints bore little resemblance to reality, often presenting massed identical soldiers charging at one another. But the prints conveyed what Americans wanted to see: a war of gallantry, purpose, and victory over determined foes on striking landscapes. The most popular prints, including those of the death of Henry Clay's son, portrayed fighting at close quarters to show the expressions on the faces of the dead and wounded. Currier and Ives emerged from the war as a leading chronicler of American life. Over decades to come, they would complement scenes of battle with dogs and horses, ships and landscapes, children and beauties, sleighs and holidays.[52]

In the midst of the war, Sarah Hale, editor of *Godey's Lady's Book*, called for a new American holiday: Thanksgiving. She sought, home by home, table by table, to "unite our great nation" from the Atlantic to the Pacific. In a war opposed by much of New England, Hale sought to extend a New England holiday—without Native peoples—to the entire country, a white holiday bathed in nostalgia. She had recently printed a poem by Lydia Maria Child, later set to music, that evoked a New England scene: "Over the river, and through the woods / to Grandfather's house we go / the horse knows the way to carry the sleigh / through the white and drifted snow." Hale's campaign would continue for years, until Thanksgiving finally became a national holiday during the heartbreak of the Civil War.[53]

Despite the profusion of print and image, Americans grew weary of the war they had thrilled to a year earlier. Most volunteers went home rather than reenlist when their terms of service ended. Exhausted soldiers looked in vain for reinforcements. Desertion from the ranks became widespread. More than a hundred recent Irish immigrants responded to Santa Anna's call to join their fellow Catholics in the Mexican ranks rather than fight for the United States.

The Mexicans, furious at the "devastation, ruin, conflagration, death, and other depredations" inflicted on the "inoffensive inhabitants" of their nation, refused to negotiate even as the war bred chaos within the Mexican government. Months dragged by with no new victories for Americans to celebrate. Finally, in February 1848, diplomats agreed in the Treaty of Guadalupe Hidalgo for the United States to acquire California and New Mexico for fifteen million dollars. Seventeen days later, the proposed treaty arrived in Washington. Polk, though disappointed that the treaty did not grant Baja California and more of northern Mexico, felt compelled to accept the terms. Whigs thought the document too demanding of Mexico, Democrats considered it too lenient, but both ratified the treaty to end the war.[54]

Between 1845 and 1848, in fewer than a thousand days, the United States had acquired more than half a million square miles of territory, more than half of Mexico. "The United States are now estimated to be nearly as large as the whole of Europe," Polk proclaimed in his annual message of 1848. With control of Oregon and California, the United States could command "the rich commerce of China, of Asia, of the islands of the Pacific, of western Mexico, of Central America, the South American States, and the Russian possessions bordering on that ocean." The new nation, despite its small and poorly funded army and navy, had proved surprisingly adept at war.[55]

A young American artist, Richard Caton Woodville, captured the contradictions of the Mexican War in a popular painting. Woodville had left the United States in 1845, at the age of twenty, to study in Düsseldorf, Germany. There, he worked to master techniques of genre painting that had been popular in Europe for centuries. From abroad, Woodville painted American scenes that appeared conventional on the surface—men telling stories to one another, waiting for a stagecoach or train—but on closer observation revealed that cardplayers cheated, that men harangued one another with tiresome politics.

Reading of the war in Europe, Woodville imagined how a paper bearing news of the war might be received in some out-of-the-way place in the United States. In *War News from Mexico*, an excited white man reads the latest reports aloud from a crowded front porch at the rustic American Hotel. It is not clear whether the news is good or bad. A Black man sits on a step, a little girl standing close at his side; together they are dressed in red, white, and blue, the girl's dress a mere rag, the man's face inscrutable.

The American Art-Union of New York, despite the painting's foreign origins and ambiguous political message, declared the piece "strictly AMERICAN" and commissioned an engraving for the Union's subscribers. Woodville would not live long to enjoy the renown, for he died of a morphine overdose in London in 1855 at the age of thirty, never having returned to the United States.[56]

Many New Englanders resented the war, though few went as far as Henry David Thoreau. He refused to pay his poll tax because, he proclaimed, the war with Mexico was "the work of comparatively a few individuals using the standing government as their tool." He blamed the "State" for demanding "blind reverence" even when engaged in the crime of an unjust and unprovoked war. Individuals must resist a government engaged in such a wrong, Thoreau argued, using whatever means they possessed, even if that meant arrest. He spent one night in jail before someone paid his fine. Thoreau delivered a lecture in Concord on "The

Rights and Duties of the Individual in Relation to Government," explaining his actions, and in 1849 the essay was published in an obscure collection. It would be discovered generations later, inspiring men and women who fought against colonialism, segregation, and other wrongs.[57]

The war against Mexico changed the tenor of American life. While the victorious war enacted notions of providential design, the violence and brutality belied the rhetoric of innocence, peace, and progress in which Americans indulged. Few doubted that the United States had provoked the war against a fellow republic. Scenes of heroism proved to be fewer than scenes of barbarism. Even officers in the United States Army admitted, as Ulysses S. Grant later put it, that the nation had waged a "wicked war." The United States prepared to expand slavery with the annexation of Texas and perhaps other territories taken from Mexico. The country descended into a divisive reckoning.

The war with Mexico also inaugurated a new era of firearms in American life. For generations, most people bought the single rifle a family owned from a local gunsmith, each weapon made by hand. Pistols found little demand. Samuel Colt of Connecticut had invented guns in the 1830s that could fire five shots without having to reload. He adapted the principles of interchangeable parts, developed in the federal armories in Massachusetts and Virginia, that allowed the components of one gun to work equally well in another.

In the absence of a civilian market, Colt sought a military contract. He was told his revolving-chamber guns were too complicated for the average soldier in the field, so Colt encouraged friends in the United States Army, fighting against the Seminoles in Florida, to try his guns and demonstrate otherwise; he traveled there personally to deliver them. The repeating weapons proved effective against Seminole ambushes, but without a large and guaranteed military market, Colt's firm shut down in the depression of the early 1840s.

The Republic of Texas enabled Colt's revival. A veteran of Florida's Seminole Wars, Samuel H. Walker, joined the fighting of the Texas Rangers against Mexicans and Comanches in Texas. Walker and fourteen allies used Colt's guns in 1844 to overwhelm eighty Comanche warriors. When Walker enlisted to fight the Mexicans, he traveled to Washington in 1846 to recruit men and to visit with Colt. Walker suggested several changes to make the revolver pistol more effective for military use, including adding another chamber to make the gun a six-shooter. Colt won an order for a thousand of the improved weapons for the fighting in Mexico, the pistols engraved with inspiring images of the triumph over the Comanches.

Colt shipped the guns to Mexico in August 1847, making special gifts to Generals Zachary Taylor, Winfield Scott, and other influential United States officers who might offer testimonials. Colt's pistols, along with other American innovations in artillery, won credit for battlefield victories. Colt leveraged his battlefield success to reach new markets. The United States War Department decided that it would need at least a million arms to protect the new territories it had taken from Mexico, for troops would be "almost constantly in the field" to protect migrants to Oregon, New Mexico, and California. Guidebooks told immigrants they needed to spend almost a fifth of the total cost of their trip on a rifle and a pistol, and so they purchased many guns. Assured by Zachary Taylor's testimony that Colt's guns "may be relied upon under all circumstances," many of those weapons were of his manufacture. As his expanding New England factories turned out thousands of weapons, Colt traveled to England, the first of many trips that would secure lucrative contracts with governments around the world eager to purchase the ingenious American technology.[58]

The new United States acknowledged no boundaries to its ambitions. Justified by the rationales of natural progress, limitless wealth, and providential destiny, the leaders of the country imposed their will on any who might oppose them. They pushed into lands possessed by Indigenous peoples and claimed outposts across distant seas. They launched a war against a neighboring republic and seized a vast new domain for slavery. Commanding the power of political parties, print, and the telegraph, those who controlled the United States confronted few who could constrain their desires.

Chapter Six

BOUNDARIES

1840–1845

The Body

As young men and women moved beyond the advice of family, books on sexual relations and contraception sold in increasing numbers. A popular guide to family limitation bore the decorous and deceptive title *The Fruits of Philosophy*—followed by the slightly more descriptive subtitle *The Private Companion of Young Married People*. The small book was written by a youthful father and physician from Massachusetts, Charles Knowlton. Despite centuries of admonitions in Christian culture for men and women not to engage in sexual relations except for procreation, Knowlton frankly acknowledged that those same centuries revealed that "mankind *will not so* abstain." People sought sex not only for procreation but also for pleasure, which Knowlton praised as healthful for both women and men. The denial of natural desire, he warned, led to "peevishness, restlessness, vague longings, and instability of character."[1]

Knowlton risked censure when he instructed couples that they could avoid having children if the female partner douched after sex with a syringe containing "any salt that acts chemically upon the semen, and at the same time produces no unfavorable effect on the female." While it was true that the woman had to leave bed "for a few moments," the method's advantages were clear: "It requires no sacrifice of pleasure; it is in the hands of the female; it is to be used after, instead of before connexion." Syringes were inexpensive, widely available, and carried no stigma.[2]

Despite his calm assurances, Massachusetts courts prosecuted Knowlton twice in a campaign against "licentiousness," the second time with three months of hard labor. The physician persisted, however, and released a second edition of his book that defended, with scientific and practical grounding, the necessity of discussing reproduction. This time, a Massachusetts jury failed to convict him. Knowlton went on to publish editions through the 1840s, each more frank than the last. His medical practice flourished as he and his wife, Tabita, spaced children as they thought appropriate. A critic of Knowlton acknowledged that his book is "in nearly every part of our widespread country," its advice "highly prized."

Frederick Hollick, another young physician, published in 1845 his popular illustrated *The Origin of Life*. It offered advice about birth control along with other topics related to reproduction. A young married immigrant from Britain, a follower of Robert Owen and his idealistic community of New Harmony, Hollick told readers that sexual intercourse provided "the deepest and most sacred, moral, and social interests and obligations! Sexual desire originates the holy feeling of *love*, the great tamer of mere brute passion, and the great sweetener of life." Hollick counseled that women naturally experienced sexual pleasure and "*it ought to be so always*." His book went through multiple editions, each of two to ten thousand copies. Hollick lectured on the lyceum circuit, before audiences containing both women and men, with a papier-mâché model of a female body from which he removed layers to reveal the workings of its reproductive organs.

A district attorney in Philadelphia charged Hollick with

obscenity in 1846 and the city's newspapers covered the trial in detail, one attacking Hollick and another defending him. Women, especially those who were married, professed themselves grateful for the information and the capacity it offered to better control their bodies; they presented Hollick a gold medal and an endorsement signed by thirty women, most of middle- or lower-class standing. Acquitted after much free publicity, Hollick continued to publish popular books and market contraceptive devices and aphrodisiacs through the next decade.[3]

Couples, especially those able to purchase books and the aids they described, apparently followed the advice they offered about birth control. With women as "the final umpire" in the bedroom, the number of children per family in the United States began gradually to decline from its average of seven to about half that by the end of the century, slowing first in towns and cities where access to information about family planning was most available and where children were an expense rather than inexpensive labor. The 1840s saw the largest percentage decrease in birth rates in the century.[4]

Abortion played a role in that declining birth rate. Laws did not prohibit the inducement of miscarriage, as it was understood, in the first trimester of a pregnancy, or "quickening," when the fetus could be felt to move. Pills to end pregnancy were widely advertised and available through the mail, as were other means to terminate an unwanted pregnancy. In the 1840s, some physicians charged that increasing numbers of married women, including those of the upper class, requested abortions. Some nativists worried that the decisions of Protestant women to limit their family size in this way would permit Irish Catholics, who did not regularly use abortion, to overwhelm Protestants in numbers. Some states passed antiabortion laws to punish those who injured women with drugs and poison after the first trimester, though they did not punish women who sought abortions.[5]

While any physician could legally administer an abortion, many women sought out females to perform the work in private. Female abortionists promoted their services in city newspapers, though physicians increasingly attacked female practitioners as the medical profession sought to professionalize. The so-called sporting press, based in New York, waged campaigns against the women who performed abortions. The campaigns offered an opportunity for discussions of sexual practice even as they criticized women who sought control of their sexuality beyond the sight of men. One cartoon portrayed Madame Restell, the most prominent and prosperous abortionist, the target of repeated criminal prosecutions, with a flying devil biting into the flesh of an infant. Despite, or even thanks to, such campaigns, the marketing of books, devices, pills, techniques, and services to control reproduction continued to grow.[6]

In contrast to the practical representations of sex in the books by Knowlton and Hollick, Sylvester Graham railed against "the convulsive paroxysms attending venereal indulgence," as he called sexual intercourse, because it leads to "the most intense excitement and causes the most powerful agitation to the whole system." In what he meant as a warning, Graham described how the "brain, stomach, heart, lungs, liver, skin—and the other organs—feel it sweeping over them, with the tremendous violence of a tornado . . . and this violent paroxysm is generally succeeded by great exhaustion, relaxation, lassitude, and even prostration." The body should experience such excitement only when absolutely necessary, Graham warned.

Masturbation posed a particular threat, turning young men toward a morbid fixation on themselves and enticing young women toward fornication and prostitution. Graham recommended cold water, unrefined grains, exercise, and loose clothing to reduce ardor. Those habits brought benefits other than those he espoused—his support of vegetarianism helped spread the practice—but his misguided physiology created unnecessary worry and guilt.[7]

Some of the same advocates who promulgated information regarding healthy sexual relations between men and women also advanced the campaign against masturbation. Young men had been warned for centuries against the practice, but in the 1830s and 1840s the warnings spread to women as well. Frederick Hollick attacked "the solitary vice," as it became known, and warned that Black women were particularly subject to sexual excess. African American female reformers vehemently denied such charges. They launched campaigns for sexual virtue within free Black communities, denying white claims for a purity unique to them. The same medicalization of sexual practice that enabled Knowlton and Hollick to speak and write in frank ways became a weapon against masturbation. Doctors and superintendents of institutions identified masturbation as a leading cause of insanity, a belief that gained increasing sanction among the general population. The fixation on masturbation helped label other forms of sexual expression deviant and dangerous as well.[8]

Phrenologists built upon the understanding of the body as a system whose impulses could be recognized and regulated. With ideas imported from Austria and Britain, phrenologists argued that the brain was controlled by twenty-seven to forty distinct elements—experts disagreed on the exact number—each of them located in a particular region of the head. The more developed the trait, the theory went, the more prominent its presence on the exterior of the skull.

The components of a person's character could be discerned by skilled phrenologists, they claimed, by consulting a detailed map of the skull, where scientific-sounding propensities such as "adhesiveness," "alimentiveness," "amativeness," or "acquisitiveness"—

just to cite the "a's"—were located. Fortunately, the brain also made room for "benevolence," "ideality," and "wonder," and other positive traits that phrenologists were certain to discover in their clients. "Practical phrenologists" toured the country to give lectures, hold demonstrations, and conduct examinations, teaching that a person who recognized his or her natural traits could work to enhance or mitigate their influence. Despite its demonstrated failures as science, phrenology grew into a popular pastime and a profitable business for publishers and lecturers. It also fed a belief that interior traits bore a physical origin and displayed legible markers on the body, such as skin color, a dangerous idea that would grow into an article of faith even as phrenology faded.[9]

Woman's Place

Contrasting visions of the nature and responsibility of women competed in the new American nation. While rural households maintained much of the patriarchal, hierarchical, and mutually dependent character inherited across many generations, households in towns and cities began to differentiate roles and divide spaces. Husbands went to work in offices or shops, wives made the home a shelter to nurture children, and children went to school. Households became smaller as the number of children declined. Women's roles became simultaneously constrained and elevated.[10]

Female authors sought to help other women navigate or resist changes in their households. Catharine Beecher became one of the most popular authors in America. After founding a school and helping initiate the Ladies' Circular against Native removal, in 1841 Beecher published *A Treatise on Domestic Economy for the Use of Young Ladies at Home and at School*, reprinted every year through the 1840s. In addition to instruction on calisthenics, the treatise offered practical guidance and inspiration for a modern American household, one that replaced servants with labor-saving devices and strategies, one that assumed that a woman could not rely on nearby relatives or friends to provide counsel and support. Beecher offered calm and confidence to young women overwhelmed with the lonely responsibilities of motherhood and housekeeping. Her fifty-cent book offered the first comprehensive advice on everything from health and childcare to the design of a kitchen.

Beecher presented up-to-date information on the working of the human body, based on the latest medical knowledge. She reflected, too, recent changes in philosophies of child-rearing, encouraging "rewards more than penalties," counseling patience for "children of active, heedless temperament, or those who are odd, awkward," who, "above all others, need tenderness and sympathy."[11]

Beecher reassured women that they held special authority in the household. Their work there, beyond the reach of profit-seeking or politics, allowed American democracy to survive "by carefully dividing the duties of man from those of woman, in order that the great work of society may be the better carried on." Citing Alexis de Tocqueville, Beecher acknowledged that Americans lived in a society where "every thing is moving and changing," where "persons in poverty, are rising to opulence, and persons of wealth, are sinking to poverty." In such turmoil, the home, and the respect justly afforded the women who presided there, offered the best hope for stability, the best chance to sustain common values that transcended region, class, and politics. All men, Beecher counseled, should respect all women, creating a sphere of safety when women and girls left their homes. The home, in its self-lessness and courtesy, offered a refuge from the rough tumult of American life.

Margaret Fuller, former editor of the *Dial* and author of *Summer on the Lakes*, held a vision unlike Beecher's, one that urged women to engage the world beyond the home. The editor of the the *New-York Tribune*, Horace Greeley, was a supporter of reform in many guises. After Greeley's wife told him of the inspiring young woman she had met leading a "conversation" in Boston, he hired Fuller as literary editor of the *Tribune*. Fuller was excited by what newspapers had to offer that magazines and books did not. "This mode of communication is susceptible of great excellence in the way of condensed essay, narrative, criticism, and is the natural receptacle for the lyrics of the day," she exulted. Newspapers promised an "infinite harvest," if the right seeds could be planted.

Fuller launched expeditions into places of misery in New York City. She described the "vagrant, degraded air" of the men at the almshouse. She told of a young girl, bearing a deformity and abandoned in the city by "some showman." The girl rushed to the front gate of the almshouse to greet each new visitor, in search of a friendly face. Fuller despaired at the sight of disturbed inmates who huddled in the corner of their rooms with "no eye for the stranger, no heart for hope." At a penitentiary, Fuller regretted that young mothers found themselves exposed to the "careless scrutiny of male visitors" as they nursed their babies. She raged at the condition of the seven hundred women, many accused of prostitution, locked up "simply as a social convenience," forced to "receive the punishment due to the vices" of men. Fuller broke through barriers of gentility and condescension to chronicle what others did not want to see.[12]

As Fuller began her work as a newspaper columnist in New York in 1845, she published a manifesto, *Woman in the Nineteenth Century*, a product of long labor. Fuller deployed her learning to argue, audaciously, that "there is no wholly masculine man, no purely feminine woman." Male and female "are perpetually passing into one another. Fluid hardens to solid, solid rushes to fluid." What it meant to be a man or a woman was, therefore, a social fiction, the product of particular times and places, and that was just as true in the United States of 1845 as in any other place or time. As a result, there should be no limits to women's ambitions. "If you ask me what offices they may fill; I reply—any. I do not care what case you put; let them be sea-captains, if you will." Fuller advocated chastity along with her championing of women's rights, avoiding attacks as a supposed proponent of "free love."[13]

Readers and reviewers responded warmly to Fuller's book. The first edition of fifteen hundred copies sold out in a week. Fuller wrote with satisfaction of seeing placards in New York's bookstore windows proclaiming hers the "Great Book of the Age." An advertisement claimed that "the thousands who have perused this book speak of it as being the only one which has been written, in which WOMAN is portrayed in her real and true character." Fuller introduced a bold new language of female independence into public discussions, taking women's personal fulfillment as the measure of their contributions to American society.[14]

Other women joined Margaret Fuller in making themselves heard. Dorothea Dix published *Remarks on Prisons and Prison Discipline in the United States* in 1845, culminating years of dedicated and disturbing work, confirming her position as one of the most important women in American public life. Without a secure home despite her education and circle of friends in Boston, Dix had finally discovered in her late thirties her great purpose: improving the condition of the insane and the imprisoned. On her own, she visited dozens of jails, homes, and poorhouses in Massachusetts, from Cape Cod in the east to the mountainous Berkshires in the west, and submitted a memorial to the state legislature to *"tell what I have seen!"*—"Insane Persons confined within this Commonwealth, in *cages, closets, cellars, stalls, pens! Chained, naked, beaten with rods,* and *lashed* into obedience!" Dix told of a tormented woman she had witnessed in "the horrid process of tearing off her skin by inches; her face, neck, and person." Dix told of "something I was told was a man, I could not tell, as likely it might have been a wild animal." His feet had frozen and been amputated.[15]

Dix did not moralize about the sources of insanity in victims' supposed drinking or prostitution. The state, she declared, had an obligation to those who suffered, regardless of the cause or whether they could be cured. By August 1845, Dix had traveled more than ten thousand miles, most by stagecoach, fired by what she called "a certain sort of obstinacy that some people make the blunder of calling zeal." She proclaimed herself "the voice of the maniac whose piercing cries from the dungeons of your jail penetrate not your Halls of Legislation. I am the Hope of the poor crazed beings who pine in the cells, and stalls, and cages, and waste-rooms of your poor-houses. I am the Revelation of hundreds of wailing, suffering creatures." Thanks to Dix's work, states across the nation built modern penitentiaries and facilities for those with mental illness. She lobbied successfully for a federal appropriation for "the Benefit of the Indigent Insane," paid for by sales of public lands in 1854, but the president of the United States vetoed it, arguing that such care was state responsibility. Disheartened, Dix left for Britain and Europe to extend her crusade there.[16]

Secret Chambers

George Lippard, a young crime reporter in Philadelphia, attacked the rich men who preyed on working people and the poor. A proud Democrat, Lippard detested the Whigs and their pretensions. In 1845, Lippard began to spin out a dark serialized novel in a Philadelphia paper, portraying a web of collusion and corruption among the city's elite in *The Quaker City; or, The Monks*

of Monk Hall: A Romance of Philadelphia Life, Mystery, and Crime.
The twenty-two-year-old Lippard dedicated the book to the
memory of another Philadelphian, the novelist Charles Brockden
Brown, dead thirty-five years now, whose gothic works had laid
"bare the secret springs of human action."[17]

In *The Quaker City*, Lippard claimed to unmask the lust, greed,
and corruption of an imaginary cabal. Hidden in an exclusive
club, privileged men in Lippard's tale indulged not only in seduction but also in incest and cannibalism, in opium and counterfeit-
ing. Lippard portrayed a society without a moral center, without
checks on the power of the wealthy and ruthless. "Woe to the
weak, the crippled, or the poor whom the locomotive of modern
civilization finds lingering in its way," he warned. "Why should it
care? Its work is to move onward and to cut down all whom poverty and misfortune have left in its path."

The Quaker City sold in enormous numbers—sixty thousand
copies in its first year and ten thousand copies each year for the
next decade. In fact, Lippard's book would be one of the most
popular of the century. Lippard imagined his novel as a work of
social reform, its exaggerated scenes building a sense of outrage
proportionate to the wrongs he saw around him. He spoke with
disgust of the serene literature of his age, suitable for Sunday
schools and tract societies, as "lollypopitude."

Lippard came to know Edgar Allan Poe in Philadelphia. Still
young at thirty-five, Poe had published thirty-one tales and stories in the preceding five years. The stories, austere and disturbing, had won him warm reviews and frequent reprints—three
hundred thousand copies of one story, he bragged—but little
money. Poe struggled to care for his young, tubercular wife, Virginia, as they moved with her mother among boardinghouses and
ramshackle rentals.[18]

Poe's tales of the gothic and the mysterious, boldly original
and expertly crafted, conveyed powerful scenes of dread or anxi-

ety. Some, like "The Pit and the Pendulum," told of horrific settings where rats nibbled on the quivering lips of a man unable to move. Others, like "The Tell-Tale Heart," evoked terror from within, from the torments of guilt and insanity. Others, such as "The Murders in the Rue Morgue"—a detective story, a genre Poe polished—showed cold logic triumphing over apparent mystery. Poe composed with an intensity both feverish and professional, producing fiction and poetry that seemed to come from somewhere other than the boardinghouses and back offices of American cities.

Poe had no patience for the Transcendentalists or the genteel poets of Boston and New York. He wrote in the spirit of Charles Brocken Brown and John Neal, telling hard truths about the darker capacities of the human spirit. Lippard judged Poe "the most original writer that ever existed in America. Delighting in the wild and visionary, his mind penetrates the inmost recesses of the human soul, creating vast and magnificent dreams, eloquent fancies, and terrible mysteries."

Poe achieved national fame in 1845 when a New York newspaper devoted nearly a full page to his new poem, "The Raven," warning that "it will stick to the memory of everybody who reads it." And it did, haunting with metronomic repetition. The narrator, torn between wanting to remember and desperately hoping to forget, implores an ominous and inscrutable black bird for reassurance but hears only "nevermore" in response. Poe, pressed to explain his intentions, said the raven was the embodiment of "mournful and never-ending remembrance."

Within two weeks, an observer noted, "everybody reads the Poem and praises it, justly we think, for it seems to us full of originality and power." Poe gloried in the long-denied attention brought by "The Raven," performing the poem for audiences to admiring response. But, desperate for funds, Poe had sold the rights to the poem for ten dollars, so that all the reprintings and performances by others returned nothing to its author. "I have made no money," he lamented; "I am as poor now as ever I was in my life."

Poe once again fell ill. He and his wife Virginia moved from New York City to the countryside, where a visitor found the pale young woman attacked by spasmodic coughing that threatened "to almost rend asunder her very body." Poe, invited to Boston to read a new poem, failed in his effort to compose one for the occasion and instead performed a long, strange piece he had written in his youth. People walked out of the hall before he performed "The Raven" to powerful effect; afterward, many attacked Poe's talents and character. Though revised editions of his tales and poems appeared in 1845 as the first publications of an ambitious Library of American Books published in New York, Poe grew ever more distracted and desperate, driven alternately by ambition and poverty.

The Guiding Clue

Ralph Waldo Emerson spoke to ever broader audiences in lectures and books made from those lectures. While he traveled through the United States and Britain, Henry David Thoreau remained behind to help Emerson's wife and to immerse himself in the local landscape, searching for direction. When Emerson finished his second book of essays in 1844 he celebrated by buying, on a whim, fourteen acres of briar patch and pine grove near Walden Pond in Concord. The next year, he bought forty more acres of the worn-out land. He thought of building a cottage, a "poet's lodge," for a retreat. The busy Emerson never got around to it, but Thoreau asked if he might build his own lodge on the land in return for the right to clear and plant there. The friends shook hands on the deal.[19]

The land around Walden Pond had been occupied before. As

Thoreau knew, Native people had long lived there. Later, so had Black people, such as Zilpah White, who supported herself by spinning and basket-making until her death at eighty-two; and Brister Freeman, a Black veteran of the American Revolution, who built a house he shared with his wife, Fenda, who was from Africa. Irish immigrants and poor white people had lived on this land, which other people had considered worthless, making lives out of little. Thoreau found the cellars they had dug, and he enjoyed apples—"wild and ciderish"—from the orchards they had left behind when they died or moved.

In March 1845, Thoreau cleared a spot for his house of ten feet by fifteen feet. Ice still floated in the water of the pond as he cut down several young pines and hewed them into studs, floor-boards, and rafters, fitting them together with mortises and ten-ons. Thoreau purchased a shanty from a departing Irish railroad worker for $4.25, carrying the boards to his site to allow them to bleach in the sun. Thoreau dug a deep cellar and recruited friends—including Emerson—to help raise the ridge pole. Tho-reau brought stones from the pond to build a chimney and used the boards from the shanty for the walls and roof.[20]

He hired a team of oxen and driver to plow through briars and stumps to clear two and a half acres for beans to sell at mar-ket, and potatoes and peas for himself. On the Fourth of July 1845, Thoreau, twenty-eight years old, moved into the small, snug house. He brought only a green writing desk and a table, three chairs and a bed, and a few books. There was no privy.

Thoreau began a new notebook on his first morning: "Yes-terday I came here to live." Thoreau had launched an interior adventure, simplifying his material life to see what his spiri-tual life might mean. "I wish to meet the facts of life—the vital facts . . . face to face, and so I came down here." Thoreau had many skills, interests, and friends but he had not been able to find, as Nathaniel Hawthorne noted sympathetically, "exactly the guiding clue." Thoreau came to Walden Pond to seek that clue, to watch and listen so intently that he would find truths hidden in plain sight. He did not flee society, for he visited often with family and friends. Instead, Thoreau used the little house as a meditative space, a metaphor for the solitary journey on which he embarked.

Thoreau dedicated himself to finishing a book he started the day he moved into his Walden home: *A Week on the Concord and Merrimack Rivers*. The 1839 trip had begun as a casual adventure with his beloved brother John. After John's accidental death in 1842, Thoreau gathered material for the book in his memory and for the memory of a New England passing away in the face of railroads, lumbering, and damming. Thoreau collected insights and inspirations wherever he found them, making what he called "the long book" ever longer and less marketable as he labored on it for the next two years.

In the meantime, Thoreau began composing a different kind of book, one that tried to explain to his neighbors, and to himself, why he would do such a strange, impractical thing as build a little house on Walden Pond and dwell on the inconsequential things that transpired there. "Life! who knows what it is—what it does?" he asked his journal. Thoreau, holding himself still and quiet, came to see the miraculous in the everyday. He looked for a new language to convey what he saw and heard. It would take years and many attempts to find that language.

Narrative of Freedom

Frederick Douglass quickly rose in the early 1840s to widespread recognition as the nation's most powerful spokesman against slavery. Douglass spoke hundreds of times after his startling debut in Nantucket in 1841, finding that episodes from his own life moved his listeners with a unique power. In late 1844, Douglass paused in his travels to translate his oratory into the *Narrative of the Life of Frederick Douglass, an American Slave, Written by Himself*. He knew which stories and characters would connect with readers, which words conveyed the anguish and heartbreak of enslaved people.

Narratives of escape from bondage had emerged as an American genre. At least a dozen men who had escaped from slavery wrote or dictated autobiographies in the 1840s, each of them telling of their sufferings and of the suffering of those left behind. Lunsford Lane, Moses Grandy, Lewis and Milton Clarke, William Hayden, William Wells Brown, Leonard Black, Henry Watson, Henry "Box" Brown, Henry Bibb, and Josiah Henson offered powerful accounts of their servitude and their escape.[21]

Douglass's experiences did not fit the stories most white northerners knew of slavery. They had heard of enslaved people laboring on cotton plantations in Alabama and Mississippi, but Douglass had lived in Maryland, even in a large city, and practiced a skilled craft as a ship caulker. White readers knew of illiterate enslaved people, kept in darkness, but Douglass had taught himself to read, write, and orate. They knew of shattered families and anguished mothers, but Douglass had escaped when he was twenty years old, encumbered by neither wife nor children. So impressive was Douglass's eloquence and bearing that many doubted that he had ever been enslaved at all.

Douglass's *Narrative* held many complexities, for so did American slavery. The story combined a literary style of refinement, sensibility, and poetic evocation with unblinking testimony about sex, violence, and greed. While staying close to Douglass's experience, the account allowed readers to see the human range of slavery: hiring, breeding, beating, hunger, sale, abandonment of the disabled, reading, friendship, folklore, singing, Christmas, drinking, solidarity, betrayal, failed escape, and conflict with white workingmen.

With economy and engagement, Douglass provided glimpses not only of the wrongs of slavery but also the strategies the enslaved used to survive those wrongs. Like Nat Turner, Frederick Douglass found himself shifted from one white employer, renter, or overseer to another. Demoted in work and autonomy, he maintained solidarity with fellow slaves even as he carried a sense of superiority born of literacy and initiative. While Turner was moved by religious prophecy of divine deliverance, Douglass found hope in a secular prophecy of freedom. Both turned to violence, Douglass humiliating his opponent with strength and skill.

Douglass charted his stumbling path through the darkness of slavery, and admitted his own doubts, fears, and failings. His narrative read much like a novel by Charles Dickens, the most popular author of the time. In the writing of both, innocent children suffer from the cruelty and neglect of adults. Mothers die and fathers disappear; children seek solace from one another and search for surrogate parents. Accident and luck move the stories into unexpected directions, threatening disaster and offering hope. Readers build empathy as interior worlds of dream and disappointment open before them. Douglass knew, on the other hand, that a true narrative would be more powerful than a fictional one, and so he published the names of his enslavers.

Douglass's greatest risk came in his portrayal of Christianity's influence on slaveholders. Repeatedly, he called out the hypocrisy of southern Christians and, as he had in his most popular lecture, the complicity of white northern Christians. Douglass charged with hypocrisy "the overwhelming mass of professed Christians in America" who by "the words, deeds, and actions, of those bodies, north and south, calling themselves Christian churches, and yet in union with slaveholders."

Margaret Fuller reviewed Douglass's *Narrative* for the *New-York Tribune* soon after it appeared. "Considered merely as a narrative," she judged, "we have never read one more simple, true, coherent, and warm with genuine feeling." Fuller, who in these same months expressed disappointment with the latest books of Emerson and Hawthorne, judged Douglass's story "an excellent piece of writing." It stood as "a specimen of the powers of the Black Race, which Prejudice persists in disputing. We prize highly all evidence of this kind, and it is becoming more abundant."

Fuller gave Douglass the last word, quoting at length his passage on slaves' singing. "They would sometimes sing the most pathetic sentiment in the most rapturous tone, and the most rapturous sentiment in the most pathetic tone," he wrote. Douglass admitted that he did not immediately understand the songs, "then altogether beyond my feeble comprehension; they were tones loud, long and deep; they breathed the prayer and complaint of souls boiling over with the bitterest anguish. Every tone was a testimony against Slavery, and a prayer to God for deliverance from chains. The hearing of those wild notes always depressed my spirit, and filled me with ineffable sadness."

Even now, in freedom and with his family in Massachusetts as Douglass wrote his narrative, "I have frequently found myself in tears while hearing them." The "songs still follow me, to deepen my hatred of Slavery, and quicken my sympathies for my brethren in bonds." In the North, some invoked the "singing among slaves as evidence of their contentment and happiness. It is impossible to conceive of a greater mistake. Slaves sing most when they are most unhappy. The songs of the slave represent the sorrows of his heart; and he is relieved by them, only as an aching heart is relieved by its tears." Fuller added nothing to Douglass's eloquence except to note that the book could be purchased at the *Tribune*'s office for fifty cents.[22]

The *Narrative* came out in May; by August, Douglass was on his way to Britain and Ireland for what would prove to be a twenty-month tour. Douglass was met with warm excitement wherever he went. As his trip drew to an end, supporters in England raised money to purchase Douglass's freedom and a steam printing press with which to publish his own paper when he returned to the United States. Frederick Douglass was now an international celebrity, his vision of freedom ennobled by his triumph over enslavement.

Minstrels of Slavery and Abolition

Blackface music had been popular since the 1830s, when "Jim Crow" and "Zip Coon" had bounded across New York stages. The performances—less a fixed genre than a permission to steal music and audiences—changed from one year to the next. The songs' structures were British, the lyrics white ventriloquism of imagined Black identity. Blackface depended on its obvious artifice, its transparent fakery. The burnt cork was a carnival mask, not a disguise. The audience was in on the joke, knowing that the makeup provided an excuse to say and sing things that could not be expressed otherwise, to ridicule the sentiment and sincerity that dominated much popular culture, to entertain with an identifiably American and male voice.[23]

Audiences for blackface, eager for something new, found it in the Virginia Minstrels in 1843. The four white men had nothing to do with Virginia; instead, they came together in New York, veterans of other shows in many places. They transformed the rough music of blackface into something more elaborate and flexible. Dan Emmett of Ohio played the banjo—learned from a white man three years before—and joined with an established performer, Frank Brower of Baltimore, who had developed the use of animal bones (ribs, generally) to make a kind of castanets. They added a fiddle and a tambourine. With "Mr. Tambo" at one end of a seated row and "Mr. Bones" at the other, an "interlocutor" served as master of ceremonies. The four men dubbed themselves "minstrels" to sound more genteel while acknowledging that they were not in fact typical concert hall fare. They published sheet music of their songs and advertised their theatrical performances in newspapers and on handbills and posters. They presented skits, parody speeches, and dance performances with the music in "negro extravaganzas" that paraded the "oddities, peculiarities, eccentricities, and comicalities" of Black humanity.[24]

Imitators proliferated in the mid-1840s, especially after the Virginia Minstrels broke apart under the pressure and allure of their sudden fame. Soon, about thirty "minstrel" troupes toured the United States. The longest-lived of these groups were Christy's Minstrels, who polished the formula to provide what one critic judged "very fine" music and "chaste, refined, and harmonious" singing—a far cry from the rambunctious yelling of the first "Jim Crow" and "Zip Coon" performances a decade before. Christy's Minstrels charged only twenty-five cents for adults and half that for children. They performed nearly 2,800 shows over seven years in New York. The troupe grew to seven men who staged a three-part show, featuring characters from the urban North and ending with a full-scale re-creation of an imagined plantation scene from the South. The band played marches and dances while the singers performed spirited sing-alongs, parlor songs, and even opera selections, all in blackface.[25]

While the music of blackface owed little to the music African American people sang and played among themselves, the dance performed in the shows does seem to have derived from Black forms. In 1844, Charles Dickens, visiting New York's Five Points, saw William Henry Lane, a teenage Black dancer from

Long Island who called himself Master Juba. "Single shuffle, double shuffle, cut and cross-cut; snapping his fingers, rolling his eyes, turning in on his knees, presenting the backs of his legs in front, spinning about on his toes and heels," there seemed to be nothing Lane could not perform, Dickens marveled. Lane's grand finale was a series of "correct Imitation Dances of all the principal Ethiopian Dancers in the United States." In other words, Lane imitated blackface dancers who imitated Black dancers. Lane concluded with "an imitation of himself."[26]

Blackface minstrelsy found new and unlikely competitors in the early 1840s: singers inspired by the traveling Tyrolese Minstrels, two men and two women dressed in traditional Swiss costume. Americans fell in love with the four-part harmonies and comic performances of the singers from the Tyrol, purchasing their sheet music and working up their own arrangements. The music from the Hutchinson Family, from New Hampshire—three brothers and their thirteen-year-old sister—adapted the styles to American audiences and traveled the Eastern Seaboard, performing for President Tyler in 1844. Accompanying themselves on violin, cello, harmonium, and guitar, the Hutchinsons played up their family relationships. Their music was "simple, sweet, and full of mountain melody."[27]

The Hutchinsons used their fame and family appeal to promote their political beliefs. They began with temperance but soon moved into antislavery. In 1843, they appeared in Faneuil Hall in Boston, performing alongside William Lloyd Garrison, leading abolitionist orator Wendell Phillips, and the emerging star, Frederick Douglass. One observer admitted that "speechifying, even of the better sort, did less to interest, purify and subdue minds, than this irresistible Anti-Slavery music."

The Hutchinsons adapted one of the most popular blackface songs to their own purpose. They turned "Old Dan Tucker" into "Get Off the Track!" Warning heedless listeners that the train of freedom was bearing down on them, the Hutchinsons pretended to be "an alarmed multitude of spectators, about to witness a terrible catastrophe," wrote one admiring review. Out of the cacophony, the Hutchinsons gently settled into a glorious harmony. "The multitude who heard them will bear me witness, that they had transcended the very province of mere music."

Christian against Christian

By the 1840s, the revivals and camp meetings of the preceding two decades had faded. Charles Grandison Finney's campaign to convert New York City had fallen to the effects of fire, financial depression, divisions over abolition, and schisms within the Presbyterian Church in which Finney had worked.[28]

Most evangelical Americans invested themselves instead in their national denominations. Methodists, Baptists, and Presbyterians competed for congregants with separate missions, colleges, seminaries, books, and newspapers. Each denomination raced to establish outposts in new communities and to build impressive edifices in cities across the eastern United States, boasting stained glass, lush carpets, and sonorous organs.

Christians in the South prided themselves on their participation in this denominational progress. Indeed, southern Christians bragged that they claimed a larger share of their states' white population than their coreligionists in the North. They pointed to new colleges in Virginia, North Carolina, South Carolina, and other southern states as evidence of their financial and cultural strength. Moreover, the churches of the South, they pointed out, strictly adhered to what the Bible said, not what self-appointed prophets and philosophers took it to mean. Southern evangelicals disdained the growth of Mormonism, Unitarianism, Transcendentalism, and the fervor of the Millerites as evidence of northern fanaticism and denominational failure.

God had allowed slavery to spread in the United States, white Christians in the South believed, to give white people the opportunity and the obligation to save Black people through conversion. White southern church leaders proudly listed the growing numbers of free and enslaved Black congregants in their denominations as testimony to the sincerity and success of their convictions. Protestants launched missionary efforts in Texas, reaching out to the growing number of enslaved people there before they could be pulled under the influence of the Catholic Church.[29]

To the frustration and anger of white southern Christians, national denominational organizations refused to allow slave-owning missionaries to minister beyond the South. Southern Methodists brought the conflict to a head in their General Conference of 1844, when they put forward a slaveholding minister as a national bishop. Northern Methodists, though recognizing the candidate as a good man who had become a slaveowner through marriage, rejected him for as long as he remained "connected with slavery." They judged slaveholding a sin, regardless of circumstance or intention. Facing this irreconcilable difference, the northern and southern delegates agreed to adopt a Plan of Separation to divide the resources of the national denomination.

Southern Methodists cheered the division, denouncing the action of northerners as "an outrage against our civil, social, and religious compact, to which we ought not, cannot, and will not submit!" Moderate antislavery advocates and militant abolitionists shared the blame, southerners charged, for they wielded "*ecclesiastical* weapons for extra-ecclesiastical purposes." Southerners who had seen fellow northern Methodists as allies against rabid abolitionists now saw them as one and the same, as "incendiaries" inflamed by "fanatical excitement."

In the North, some Methodists worried that the schism in their church broke the "golden chains" that helped bind the country "together in the bonds of love." Northern ministers divided almost equally when asked to vote on the Plan of Separation. A 1,200-mile line cut a ragged border through Virginia, Maryland, Kentucky, Arkansas, and Missouri, dividing congregations, triggering lawsuits, and feeding bitter charges of voter manipulation. The denomination completed the division the following year, creating the Methodist Episcopal Church, South. The Baptists soon followed, for identical reasons and with similar struggles, to create the Southern Baptist Convention in May 1845.

After the breaks of the mid-1840s, evangelical ministers in the South more tightly embraced the connection between slavery and Christianity, each sanctioning the other. Denominations strengthened themselves as churches promoted mission work among enslaved people. Baptists and Methodists developed bureaucracies to aid the mission, rivaling their northern counterparts in organizational strength and efficiency, expanding at twice the rate of population growth and increasing annual giving fivefold. A conference on "The Religious Instruction of the Negroes" convened in Charleston in 1845. One attendee enthused that "what is particularly a subject of gratitude is, that *all denominations* of Christians are entering the field. It is wide enough for all." Ministering to enslaved people was a severe obligation, for "it lies at our own doors, and God in his Providence and holy word, has laid the duty upon us to cultivate it. We can anticipate nothing but his displeasure, if we neglect it." As a committee of Virginia Baptists put it, "We support the gospel in foreign lands, at great expense of life and toil and treasure. Why should we not care for the souls that are found in our own houses—that understand our own language—that are accessible to our instructions?"[30]

White Christians recognized that Black people wanted their own churches. The Baptists of Virginia created quasi-independent Black churches, with white pastors but largely guided by Black deacons. The First African Baptist Church in Richmond grew into the largest congregation in the city—over two thousand members—under the eye of Robert Ryland, a white Baptist leader appointed to the position by the denomination. Ryland acknowledged that the Black people in the congregation did not think they needed his guidance, though they were required by the state to accept it. It was illegal for Black people to preach, but the deacons did deliver "some very long prayers," the white minister wryly observed. Black Christians in the cities of Virginia joined these churches by the thousands. They tolerated white pastors and their sermons so that they could hold their own classes, exert their own discipline, and foster their own spiritual lives.[31]

The North and the South became more opposed even as they became more alike in important ways. The South, contrary to the stereotypes of the North, was, by international standards, a literate and prosperous place for white people. Only a few European populations were more literate than the South—and England was not one of them. Southerners subscribed to the same magazines northerners read and purchased the same books—most of them by people other than Americans. They created temperance societies, fraternal organizations, and lyceums like those of the North. Moral, political, and economic differences generated by slavery, not free-floating cultural differences, drove the North and the South apart.[32]

Chapter Seven

VOYAGES

1845–1850

New Americans

More people moved to the United States between 1820 and 1860 than had lived in the country in 1790. The 150,000 immigrants of the 1820s grew to 600,000 in the 1830s to 1.4 million in the 1840s and then to 2.8 million in the 1850s, the pace of arrivals reaching its peak between 1845 and 1854.[1]

Tragedies in the potato fields of Ireland transformed lives on both sides of the Atlantic. The United States emerged as a refuge for millions of people starving in their beloved homeland. In July 1845, "there was a cry around that some blight had struck the potato stalks." The leaves blackened and then crumbled. Throughout Ireland, the very "air was laden with a sickly odor of decay, as if the hand of death had stricken the potato field, and . . . everything growing in it was rotten." Disease and even starvation afflicted the poorest people. Landlords removed hundreds of thousands of tenants from their lands to raise cattle and grain. As many as a million people died.[2]

More than 1.25 million Irish people left their homes over the next ten years. The Atlantic exodus began in 1846, doubled in 1847, briefly slowed and then reached a peak in 1851; it would not decline for another four years. Most emigrants gathered in Liverpool before heading to New York and Boston. They negotiated their moves with little assistance from the government or anyone else, surviving disease, neglect, and hunger on cramped and dirty ships. Those who had gone before offered advice and what financial help they could. "We hope that you will brace your nerves and steel your face and be nothing daunted and you will soon join with us on this Great Continent," a friend wrote on the back of tickets sent to a family coming to the United States with four daughters. "There will be dificultyes to meet with but then consider the object you have in view."[3]

Once in the United States, Irish women—who accounted for most of the migrants—worked as domestics. Men took whatever laboring jobs they could find. Those who arrived in winter found that construction work on railroads and canals in the Northeast slowed or stopped in the coldest months. The immigrants moved often, seeking comfort in the company of other Irish people. Their children had to go to work early in their lives and labor for long hours, missing education. Catholic churches were overwhelmed with need and numbers. The Irish organized clubs, fire companies, and charities. They recruited one another into labor unions and political clubs. Some native-born Americans offered help as well, though often tying their aid to efforts to convert Catholics to Protestantism. Male immigrants, eligible to vote soon after their arrival, found that the Democrats welcomed Irish voters into their ranks.[4]

Immigrants streamed to the United States from other places as well, for the potato famine assailed nearly all of Northern Europe. It afflicted the Low Countries and the Nordic countries; it ranged from Prussia into Spain and Portugal; landlords in Sweden and Germany paid tenants to leave. By the end of the 1850s, most immigrants came to the United States on steamships; a voyage that had been six or seven weeks by sail became a trip of six or seven days by steam. Arriving in America, those with the money to do so bought farms in the Midwest sold by American families moving farther west. People from Sweden and German-speaking areas of Europe settled near one another for companionship and support.

Jews from Europe accounted for a growing share of those immigrants. The two thousand Jews in the United States in 1820 grew tenfold by 1860. In contrast to the Irish, Jewish immigration began with young, single men. They worked as peddlers, starting in the cities of the East and then spreading into every part of the country. After they accumulated enough money to start a store of their own, they returned to Central Europe to find a wife, and often to bring the wife's sisters for bachelors remaining in the United States.

These Jewish immigrants met little organized opposition; nativists were obsessed with Catholics. The immigrants found few rabbis and so organized their own spiritual and collective lives, often in ways that Jewish leaders in Europe found alarming. Isaac Mayer Wise arrived in the 1840s and worked to shape Reform Judaism in America with newspapers and an American prayer book. Rebecca Gratz of Philadelphia organized Sunday schools for Jewish children, often taught by women, and produced English texts for Jewish students.[5]

Bolstered by immigrants and migrants from the hinterlands, urban populations ballooned. New York, in particular, surged from four hundred thousand people in 1840 to seven hundred thousand in 1850. By then, half of New Yorkers had been born abroad, up from only one in ten in 1830. Boardinghouses jammed five people to a room. Poor neighborhoods jostled against exclusive districts, shops and factories abutted tenements and stables. A cacophony of hooves on cobblestones, streetcars on iron rails, and whistles of boats on the river echoed throughout the city.[6]

The American West

After the war with Mexico, the United States struggled to incorporate the land and peoples the nation had suddenly acquired. The men in Congress, the White House, and government offices knew little about the lands they mapped and even less about the people who occupied those lands. They portrayed much of the West as land to cross as quickly as possible to get to the Pacific. For their part, the Native peoples of the West, diverse in languages, allies, and enemies, paid no attention to the lines the United States government drew on paper.

In the place they called Deseret, Mormon leaders sought to enter the United States as a distinct territory under their control. Their self-imposed exile at the Great Salt Lake had purchased Mormons a credibility and power unimaginable when Joseph Smith had been martyred in Illinois in 1844. The Saints built a prosperous settlement with startling speed, served the United States in the war with Mexico, and provisioned settlers bound for Oregon and California. Many Americans despised the Mormons for polygamy, but the United States was grateful for the Mormons' help in occupying the West. Though the Mormons advocated for an even larger territory, Congress approved an expanse that stretched between California's eastern border to the Colorado River.

Mormon men worked alongside Miwok people to build a sawmill at Sutter's Mill in the Sierra Nevada mountains of California. Sutter's Fort, the major outpost of white settlement in California's interior, was located about fifty miles away. At the mill, in January 1848, workers found that gold, gathered over millennia, pooled where the water did not move forcefully enough to dislodge the heavy, lustrous mineral. White men who owned large land grants in California moved Native laborers to the gold fields to claim larger areas than any individual could work. Mormons built a settlement around their diggings, pitching tents and putting up stores in shanties. Some Native families mined on their own but found themselves pushed aside if they succeeded too well. In December, emissaries of the United States military in California arrived in Washington with samples of rumored gold. Tests confirmed the mineral's purity, and samples went on display in the offices of the War Department. The news spread through papers across the nation, disbelief growing into gold fever.[7]

California sped through decades of history overnight. California applied for statehood without slavery. The white men who labored in California's gold fields refused to compete with Black people, and enslaved people brought to California in the late 1840s often escaped at the first opportunity. Trade across the limitless Pacific Ocean fed the economy of San Francisco, which claimed the most diverse population of any city in the nation. Newspapers, printing presses, daguerreotype studios, bookstores, and theaters emerged full-grown. Political parties arrived with principles, patronage, and enemies already in place. The federal government, army, and navy held a visible and valued presence from the outset.[8]

Gold seekers streamed into California from Australia, Hawai'i, Chile, Mexico, China, and every state in the East. People of Mexican or Spanish ancestry, in California for generations, were pushed aside by the Anglos. The Miwoks, living in villages among the rivers and streams flowing off the western slopes of the Sierra Nevada mountains, were overwhelmed by gangs of white prospectors. In 1850, the United States Army attacked Pomo men, women, and children trapped on an island at Clear Lake, north of San Francisco, clubbing, shooting, and burning hundreds of people. California newspapers and government up to the United States Senate condoned the killing as necessary to the peace and stability of the new state.[9]

In the early 1850s, gold that had been so plentiful and accessible only months before became ever harder to find, especially by the greenhorns who arrived by the thousands without equipment or money. The absence of white women spurred sexual violence against Mexican and Native women; drunkenness, assault, and gambling flourished. Men from China formed their own communities in California; they dressed, ate, spoke, and worked in ways that westerners found exotic, entertaining, and threatening. Forced labor of poor and defenseless people, whether Native, Mexican, or Chinese, haunted remote valleys and isolated mines.[10]

Rights

As Frederick Douglass prepared to return to America in 1847, he spoke to hundreds in London who gathered to wish him well. He voyaged back to the United States, he told them, with "no patriotic applause for America or her institutions," a nation of "inconsistencies, completely made up of inconsistencies." The country proclaimed its war with Mexico as a fight for democracy and civilization, but slavery remained "interwoven with the very texture—with the whole network" of the country. The proud and handsome man, just thirty years old, admitted that "I scarcely know what to say in America, when I hear men get up and deliberately assert a right to property in my limbs—my very body and soul; that they have a right to me! That I am in their hands . . . a thing to be bought and sold!" And yet he would return to the United States "to glory in the conflict." The crowd responded with wave after wave of cheering.

Douglass did not soften his language when he arrived in America. Speaking in New York only weeks after his return, Douglass proclaimed that "I have no love for America, as such. I have no patriotism. I have no country." He loved his family and the "three millions of my fellow creatures groaning beneath the iron rod," but as for the United States, Douglass declared, "I desire to see its overthrow as speedily as possible, and its Constitution shivered in a thousand fragments." He saw no hope in political parties, in the press, or in the pulpit.

Douglass's many enemies seized on the speech, even reprinting it as a pamphlet. As he traveled through the North and Midwest with William Lloyd Garrison, Douglass risked attack every time he spoke. In Harrisburg, Pennsylvania, a brick thrown through a window barely missed his face as men screamed, "Let the damned nigger have it!" A circle of Black allies surrounded Douglass and helped him escape the building. As Douglass traveled west by rail he went two days without food because no one would serve him, though large audiences came to hear him at night throughout Ohio.

Other fugitives from slavery seized the attention and admiration of allies in the North. The story of Ellen and William Craft delighted sympathizers with is audacity and guile. Ellen, three-fourths white and enslaved by her father, had been given as a gift to remove her from the household. William, a skilled carpenter, was permitted to work for wages on hire. He saved money to purchase fine clothes in which Ellen disguised herself as an enfeebled white man, wearing a sling so that he could not be asked to write, attended by William as a servant. They traveled in first-class cars and stayed in fine hotels, traveling from Macon, Georgia, to arrive in Philadelphia on Christmas Day 1848. Supported by abolitionists, the Crafts married and gave lectures about their bold escape, William talking and Ellen standing with him onstage at first, then speaking for herself. They sold a popular engraving of Ellen dressed in her disguise.[11]

In early 1848, Frederick Douglass moved his family to Rochester to launch his newspaper, the *North Star*. Upstate New York sustained a community of reformers engaged in interlocking crusades and Douglass found himself in alliance with a cause new for him: women's rights. Douglass supported the campaign from the outset, spreading word of a meeting to be held in Seneca Falls, New York, in July. Douglass looked forward to attending.

The idea of a convention devoted to women's rights had long appealed to female activists working from distinct but interrelated traditions. Women's efforts on behalf of the enslaved and the dispossessed had alerted them to their own power and powerlessness. Women had petitioned state and federal governments for more than two decades, declaring their role as citizens and exercising their eloquence on behalf of others. Even though they could not vote, women had attended political meetings, labored on campaigns, and supported those who shared their principles. They had worked on behalf of women's property rights lost upon marriage.[12]

Seneca Falls, a small town boasting several textile mills and a recent rail connection to New York City, seemed an unlikely place to hold any kind of convention. And Elizabeth Cady Stanton, a thirty-two-year-old mother of three boys and the wife of a political abolitionist, Henry, seemed an unlikely organizer. But the currents of reform ran through Upstate New York, connecting Seneca Falls with other towns where women devoted their energies to improving American life. Most important were those from Quaker families, especially the M'Clintock sisters of nearby Waterloo, and the prominent abolitionist Lucretia Mott, who visited her sister Martha Wright in Auburn, New York, each summer. The Quaker women valued the Inner Light of the Spirit in each person, and saw their support of women's rights as a natural extension of their faith.

Elizabeth Cady had been raised in a prosperous and important family. She was deeply influenced by her cousin, Gerrit Smith, an owner of nearly a million acres of land who supported reforms ranging from tract societies to abolition to debt reform to vegetarianism, all in a spirit of tolerance and welcome.

It was at the Smiths' home that she met her future husband. Elizabeth's father disapproved, for Henry Stanton had not proven himself capable of supporting a family, but she persisted and they married in 1840—just in time to travel to London for the World Anti-Slavery Convention. Along the way, they visited with Theodore Dwight Weld, Angelina Grimké Weld, and Sarah Grimké.

In London, a long-simmering debate over women's roles and rights in the movement divided the delegates. Female delegates from the United States were denied a place on the floor or the right to speak. The honeymooning young woman declared herself "humiliated and chagrined" by the "narrow-minded bigots" who championed the freedom of enslaved people but opposed the rights of women. Lucretia Mott described her new friend as a "bright, open, lovely" young woman, now devoted to women's rights. Returning to the United States, Elizabeth Cady Stanton threw herself into reforms.

In 1847, Stanton and her family moved from Boston to Seneca Falls, where her father provided a house as a gift to her, independent of her husband. New York was considering a constitutional revision—prompted by a petition from six women—to protect women's property, causing newspapers to fill with debates over the nature and rights of women. A group of Quaker women determined to make equality of the sexes a public issue. Stanton, among other non-Quakers, joined them. To call attention to their purpose, they crafted a Declaration of Sentiments based on the Declaration of Independence. The women searched through law books and statutes to find eighteen grievances that would correspond to the number in the original Declaration against King George III. Stanton added the right to vote to their demands.

The female authors began with a critical addition to the wording of the Declaration of Independence: "We hold these truths to be self-evident; that all men and women are created equal." Echoing the original Declaration, the new document proclaimed that "the history of mankind is a history of repeated injuries and usurpations on the part of man toward women, having in direct object the establishment of an absolute tyranny over her."

The grievances listed wrongs in legal rights, in work, in education, and in the church. A married American woman, the Declaration pointed out, had no rights to property, "even to the wages she earned." Husbands had the "power to deprive her of her liberty, and to administer chastisement," including physical punishment. Men "monopolized nearly all the profitable employments, and from those she is permitted to follow, she receives but a scanty remuneration." Man closed to woman "all avenues to wealth and distinction," including theology, medicine, law, and the ministry. Moral delinquencies "which exclude women from society, are not only tolerated but deemed of little account in man."

All in all, man "has endeavored" to diminish woman "in every way that he could to destroy her confidence in her own powers, to lessen her self-respect, and to make her willing to lead a dependent and abject life." The Declaration of Sentiments concluded with a defiant announcement: "Because women do feel themselves aggrieved, oppressed, and fraudulently deprived of their most sacred rights, we insist that they have immediate admission to all the rights and privileges which belong to them as citizens of these United States."

The women called a convention to meet in Seneca Falls to hear a reading of the Declaration of Sentiments. A hundred people gathered there on July 20, 1848, in the Wesleyan Chapel, where Elizabeth Cady Stanton read the document; sixty-eight women signed, while thirty-two men signed an accompanying endorsement. Most of the signers were women in their thirties and forties from nearby towns, of moderate wealth, a quarter of them Quakers. Frederick Douglass was the only Black signer of either sex.

Newspapers responded as the women's advocates had expected. Descriptions of the meeting ranged from "extremely dull and uninteresting" to "a most insane and ludicrous farce." One wit warned that if the women won their rights, men would have to "wash dishes, scour up, be put to the tub, handle the broom, darn stockings, patch breeches, scold the servants, dress in the latest fashion, wear trinkets, look beautiful, and be as fascinating as those blessed morsels of humanity whom God gave to preserve that rough animal man, in something like a reasonable civilization." Abolitionist papers endorsed the women's effort as an extension of their principles of equal justice and humanity. The influential *New York Herald*, which had hired Margaret Fuller three years before, offered a backhanded endorsement of the women's call for the vote: "However unwise and mistaken the demand, it is but the assertion of a natural right, and such must be conceded."

A few months later, at the National Convention of Colored Freedmen in Cleveland, Frederick Douglass and his ally on the *North Star*, Martin Delany, called for women to have the right to speak and vote as men did. After debate, the convention resolved, "We fully believe in the equality of the sexes, therefore, Resolved, That we hereby invite females hereafter to take part in our deliberations." Three cheers for women's right erupted. Efforts to secure those rights appeared in many facets of Black public life, for people who witnessed the injustice of arbitrary laws based on race clearly understood the injustice of laws based on sex. In churches, fraternal organizations, and reform bodies, Black women and male allies called for equality. The masthead of Douglass's *North Star* proclaimed that "Right is of no sex—Truth is of no color—God is the Father of us all—and all we are brethren."[13]

The Marble Slave

Hiram Powers had discovered a talent for sculpture as a youth in Cincinnati even though he had no training in the art. He perfected his skills in plaster, showing an ability to capture human individuality. Emboldened by the reception of his work in Ohio, Powers traveled to Washington in 1835 to make busts of politicians.[14]

Powers managed to secure a commission for Chief Justice John Marshall, and then, remarkably enough, President Andrew Jackson. Jackson told Powers to represent him just as he was: an old man with sunken mouth and lined face. Jackson was pleased with the results and Powers was on his way. He set up shop in the basement of the Capitol and sculpted Daniel Webster, John Quincy Adams, and other leading statesmen, along with their wives and daughters. Men of both parties liked and admired the American sculptor.

Powers, like other American artists before him, longed to master the highest levels of his art. He brought his family to Florence, Italy, where Powers saw that statues of the female form embodied the highest accomplishments of sculptors. He decided to attempt a full statue, his first, "something in the feminine way." He settled on a representation of Eve "just before eating the forbidden fruit," her face caught "in an expression of sorrow, reflection, and desire." A serpent twined about her feet, "his head brought in front just below the right thigh." Powers judged that "clothing would be preposterous for she was conscious she was naked only *after* she had fallen. History and nature both require entire nudity." He worked for two and a half years on the statue; visitors to the studio, American and Italian, were struck by its beauty and expressiveness. Powers refused offers to purchase *Eve Tempted*, intending to display it in the United States.

Powers searched for a theme worthy of his growing skill and

effort. White Americans had long identified with the ancient Greeks and extended their sympathies to their modern descendants. In the 1820s, the Greek War for Independence against the Turks had become well-known in the United States, carrying accounts of Greek women dragged into slavery and sold in markets in Constantinople. Powers decided to carve one of those white women, "too deeply concerned to be aware of her nakedness." The figure's expression would convey "scorn for all around." She would avert her eyes from the viewer. The dominant theme would be woman's faith in "Divine Providence for a future state of existence."

Chains bound his subject's hands, held before her; a cross and a locket, presumably stripped from her neck, lay nearby. By positioning the woman in the moment between her capture and violation, Powers evoked but evaded overt scenes of sexual violence. Powers gave no indication that he had America's millions of enslaved women in mind when he chose his subject and theme.[15]

In August 1847, the *Greek Slave* went on display in New York. Word spread immediately. "No modern statue ever awakened more interest or gained for its author such instant fame," an astounded critic remarked. "Orders flowed upon him from the English and the Italians, as well as Americans"—testimony, long craved, that an American artist enjoyed standing among those to whom the new nation still looked for approval. The statue toured twelve American cities and attracted more than a hundred thousand viewers. While sophisticates admired the nude form, other Americans declared the statue "indecent." Powers offered a Christian defense. A "pure heart" can "look upon the entire human form" without risk of "defilement." A pamphlet explained the political and religious story behind the statue, testified to its moral purpose, and offered testimonials from clergy to its worthiness.

The statue's tour took it to slaveholding New Orleans, Augusta, Charleston, Columbia, Louisville, and Washington, without protest. Proslavery papers lamely joked that the abolitionists, if they were so righteous, should set the statue's figure free when she visited their city. Antislavery papers offered more powerful lessons. The *Greek Slave*, charged one, "brings home to us the foulest feature of our National Sin; and forces upon us the humiliating consciousness that the slave market at Constantinople is not the only place where beings whose purity is still undefiled, are basely bought and sold for the vilest purposes." While slavery was being abolished throughout the world, bondage "still taints a portion of our Christian soil, and is at this very moment clamoring that it may pollute yet more."

Women recognized the figure's vulnerability, for she was stripped not only of clothing but of protection, of family, of children. As they viewed this art, an antislavery newspaper suggested, white mothers and daughters should "let the solemn lesson sink deep into the hearts of the fair women of the North and of the South! Waste not your sympathies on the senseless marble, but reserve some tears for the helpless humanity that lies quivering beneath the lash of *American freemen!*" The white stone ignored Black suffering so nearby.[16]

Science, Spirits, and Nature

Science achieved bold breakthroughs and public respect in the 1840s and 1850s. In an era before the institutionalization of scientific research, the public avidly followed debates in cosmology, geology, electromagnetism, chemistry, phrenology, and mesmerism. The boundaries between truth and blasphemy, proof and fraud, flickered in uncertainty.

As American culture extolled the stolid values of business,

party politics, and Protestant denominations, spiritualism testified to a yearning for deeper meaning. Spiritualism—the belief
that individual consciousness lived on and could communicate
after physical bodies had perished—seized attention across the
nation. Spiritualist events and publications explored profound
questions of human identity in a universe of unknown bounds.

Spiritualism grew from simultaneous origins, without organization and without leaders. Practitioners and prophets rose and
fell in popularity. Simple knocking in response to simple questions
in a farmhouse in Hydesville, New York, gave way to elaborate
séances in fashionable parlors. Young girls and women appeared
onstage in trances, able to speak with a fluency and sophistication that belied their age and gender. Some spirits spoke through
planchettes, heart-shaped pieces of wood that seemed to move
of their own accord to spell words and answer questions. Some
spirits appeared as apparitions, vaporous human forms visible in
the shadows, while others played musical instruments, wrote on
walls, or moved furniture.[17]

Mediums, most of them female, bypassed the authority of
ministers and professors to connect spirits with those desperate to hear from them. Spiritualism challenged, implicitly and
explicitly, precepts of original sin, hell, and final judgment even
as its practitioners prayed and sang Christian hymns. Spiritualism expressed female sentiment, emotion, and physical experience
in ways the culture encouraged, especially when the séance, held
for eight people in private parlors, offered alternatives to public
displays. The new faith afforded women prominent roles in every
aspect of its practice.[18]

The widespread appeal of spiritualism testified to the unset-
tled definition of science. Despite its mysterious-sounding name,
believers understood and portrayed spiritualism as scientific, as
a way to tap into aspects of nature not yet fully understood but

that were verifiable through experiment and testing. The ether, electricity, and magnetism appeared to be conductors of spiritual connection. Confident in their scientism, spiritualists submitted themselves to examination by skeptics. They emerged, at least in their own eyes, vindicated.

The leading spiritualist newspaper called itself the *Herald of Progress*; another, the *Spiritual Telegraph*. Andrew Jackson Davis, of Poughkeepsie, New York, defined spiritualism as a religion that brought people "into harmonial relations with each other," to create "one common brotherhood, where angelic wisdom and order can be freely unfolded." Jesus, Davis explained, had instituted an "era of Love," but modern days demanded a relation to "the faculty of REASON, which the Bible *does not* contain."[19]

People believed that spirits reached ever higher levels of perfection after death, gaining insight and comforting wisdom to share with the living. Young children, spiritualism taught, continued to mature after their passing, able to talk with and write to their parents. Spiritualists wore white at funerals, celebrating the ascent of their beloved to a higher level. Emanuel Swedenborg, the eighteenth-century mystic and polymath who had influenced Johnny Appleseed and the young Ralph Waldo Emerson, continued his influence in spiritualism.

Spiritualism especially appealed to people who sought to free themselves from other kinds of conventions and constraints. The practice won support among women's rights advocates, abolitionists, and advocates of health reform, though people of every political persuasion and inclination participated in spiritualism. Powerful shapers of public opinion such as Horace Greeley promoted spiritualism as he and his wife desperately longed to converse with the five young children they had lost.[20]

Many Americans denounced and ridiculed spiritualists; some paid a dollar to discover the fraudulence of the trance speakers and automatic writers. Spiritualists made little headway in the South, where the practice seemed akin to the other strange innovations of the North. Emerson, finding many of his neighbors taken with a spiritualism they imagined as an extension of Transcendentalism, attacked the practice as another example of the hollowness of American life: "I hate this shallow Americanism which hopes to get rich by credit, to get knowledge by raps on midnight tables, to learn the economy of the mind by phrenology, or skill without study."[21]

Science of an entirely different order flourished alongside spiritualism. Audiences streamed to talks on geology and chemistry, on astronomy and wildlife. The celebrity of science was embodied in Louis Agassiz, who became famous across the country upon his arrival from Switzerland in the 1840s. Popular as a speaker, Agassiz was also renowned as a researcher and writer. He soon occupied a prestigious post at Harvard College.

Agassiz engaged in scientific debates on relatively arcane subjects but won broad attention for his vigorous assertion that different "races" of humans had developed separately on separate continents, a notion called polygenesis. God had created nature just as it was, suited for its place, and it did not change. People were no different. Those who wanted to emphasize racial difference were tempted by the theory, though the Bible told of Adam and Eve as the progenitors of all people.[22]

Agassiz confronted the dilemma in Charleston, South Carolina. The scientist found a warm welcome there among those eager to prove the inferiority of Black people, but he also found a powerful enemy in John Bachman, a Lutheran pastor from the city. Bachman had collaborated with John James Audubon on *The Birds of America* and was now writing a companion work on the quadrupeds of North America. As a Christian, Bachman rejected polygenesis for its denial of Scripture; as a naturalist, he recognized the hollow evidence Agassiz claimed. Bachman, who defended slavery on Biblical grounds, published *The Doctrine of the Unity of the Human Race*. When Agassiz visited Charleston for a meeting of the new American Association for the Advancement of Science in 1850, he challenged Bachman, pronouncing that there was not a "particle of proof" of the common origin of all races. Adam and Eve were white, and their story was that of white people.[23]

After the Charleston meeting, a prominent scientist and planter offered Agassiz a tour of plantations to document the differences among people from various parts of Africa. Agassiz pronounced, on site, the supposed origins of the people he viewed; he could, he bragged, "readily to distinguish their nations, without being told whence they came, and even when they attempted to deceive him, he could determine their origin from their physical features." After Agassiz left, his host took several enslaved people, selected by Agassiz as "specimens," to a studio in Columbia, South Carolina, where they were stripped naked to be photographed. The images of Alfred, Fassena, and Jem, of Renty and his daughter Delia, and of Jack and his daughter Drana showed them from various angles, bodies held rigid by an iron brace. Their faces conveyed disgust and exhaustion. Fifteen wooden cases of portraits, lined with velvet, were shipped to Agassiz at Harvard. There, he used them for a lecture at the Cambridge Scientific Club to support his doctrine of racial difference.[24]

Agassiz eagerly contributed an essay to the imposing *Types of Mankind: Or, Ethnological Researches, Based Upon the Ancient Monuments, Paintings, Sculptures, and Crania of Races, and Upon Their Natural, Geographical, Philological, and Biblical History*, published in 1854, more than seven hundred pages long, richly illustrated, edited by Josiah Nott, a prominent collector and measurer of skulls. In that book, Agassiz proclaimed that "I am prepared to show that the differences existing between the races of men are of the same kind as the differences observed between the different families, genera, and species of monkeys or animals." More than that, "the differences between distinct races are often greater than those distinguishing species of animals one from the other." The expensive book sold 3,500 copies in four months and went through ten editions. Emanating from Harvard, Agassiz's pronouncements added a cosmopolitan accent to the most profound prejudice. America served as a laboratory where scientists recorded and legitimized physical, intellectual, and moral hierarchies among humans for an international audience.[25]

Amateur scientists flourished in an era when the distinction between professional and amateur had not hardened. Henry David Thoreau walked four hours every day and kept a detailed journal of the life of nature all around him. He sent specimens to Louis Agassiz and became a member of the Boston Society of Natural History. He read about vast expanses of time and distant parts of the world, pieces of which appeared in his long volume with a deceptive title: *A Week on the Concord and Merrimack Rivers*, published in 1849, an act of devotion to his deceased brother. The book, without advertising, won positive reviews but sold only about a hundred copies. Thoreau owed the printer $290, more than he earned in a year, a debt he would labor under for the next four years. In the meantime, Thoreau began a journal of measurement and reflection on nature that would grow to two million words.[26]

The landscape of the eastern United States found other interpreters and advocates in these years. George Perkins Marsh, a fellow New Englander, could hardly have differed more from Thoreau. Marsh excelled in every field of endeavor, ranging from law and public service to manufacturing and foreign diplomacy. Fluent in twenty languages, Marsh helped found the Smithsonian Institution and comparative literary study in the United States.[27]

After delivering Harvard's Phi Beta Kappa address of 1847, Marsh returned home to Rutland County in his native Vermont to judge oxen, swine, and maple sugar at an agricultural fair. There, he gave a speech that planted the seeds for one of the most important books in the history of American conservation, *Man and Nature*. Marsh celebrated the United States, as was expected at an agricultural fair, for converting "unproductive wastes into fertile fields, and filled with light and life, the dark and silent recesses of our aboriginal forests and mountains." Marsh jokingly extrapolated from recent progress to picture a day when every farmer would have a personal locomotive that required no rails, so that "every producer shall be whirled to market by the steam of his own teakettle."

But Marsh shadowed his remarks with a darker vision. He warned that the climate "has been gradually changed and ameliorated or deteriorated by human action." The "draining of swamps and the clearing of forests perceptibly effect the evaporation from the earth, and of course the mean quantity of moisture suspended in the air," Marsh observed. Fires in homes and in fields had modified "the power of the surface to reflect, absorb and radiate the rays of the sun, and consequently influence the distribution of light and heat, and the force and direction of the winds." Those changes had already begun to "create and diffuse increased warmth."

The farmers of Vermont could do something to slow that climate change, Marsh urged: allow parts of their cleared lands to return to forests. Vermont had far too many open fields for its population of people and animals. The transformations of "the physical geography of Vermont, within a single generation, are too striking to have escaped the attention of any observing person," Marsh warned. If the forests were not allowed to recover, flooding would worsen and meadows would become "broad wastes of shingle and gravel and pebbles, deserts in summer, and seas in autumn and spring." Marsh's insights would eventually gain a hearing in the conservation movement he helped lead.

A work of nature writing won an unexpectedly large readership in 1850: *Rural Hours*, published anonymously by a "lady"—Susan Fenimore Cooper, the oldest daughter of James Fenimore Cooper. The Cooper family had lived in England and Europe during Susan's adolescence, so she viewed the landscape of her ancestral community in Upstate New York upon her return through the experience of the Old World. Cooper saw God's design in nature, each flower and bird part of a larger plan, but she also read the works of naturalists such as Alexander von Humboldt, in which nature constantly changed and connected. Cooper, in her late thirties, appreciated the inspiration and wisdom of both perspectives. She immersed herself in the natural world as unobtrusively as possible, grateful for what each season offered. As she walked through the forests her grandfather and father had turned into farmsteads and a town, Cooper weighed the blessings and costs of their cultivation.

Cooper wrote lyrically about flowers, a popular topic of poetry and drawing in these decades, but brought a scientific appreciation of their "innate grace." She found in each variety of wildflower "a unity, a fitness, in the individual character of each plant to be traced most closely, not only in form, or leaf, and stem, but also in the position it chooses, and all the various accessories of its brief existence." Cooper recognized the natural cycles of death in the forests. "Old trees, dead and dying, are left standing for years, until at length they are shivered and broken by the winds, or they crumble slowly away to a shapeless stump." Such trees "have no value" to people, but they had immense value for nature. New trees took root in the debris of fallen trees, one "bare and mouldering, stained by green mildew, one a crumbling mass of fragments," to create new life from old.

People disturbed this cycle with mournful result. Cooper described farm life with respect and affection, but, like George Perkins Marsh, she regretted the waste she saw around her. She understood why "a man whose chief object in life is to make money should turn his timber into bank-notes with all possible speed," but some forbearance would make farms more beautiful and add to "their market value at the same time! Thinning woods and not blasting them; clearing only such ground as is marked for immediate tillage; preserving the wood on the hill-tops and rough side-hills; encouraging a coppice on this or that knoll; permitting bushes and young trees to grow at will along the brooks and water-courses," all would cost little and benefit much. *Rural Hours* appeared in seven editions over the next five years. In England, Charles Darwin read and admired Cooper.[28]

Shattered Voyages

By 1849, the promise of a distinctive American literature, glittering since the founding of the nation, had faded. No American approached the skill, fame, or success of the best-selling books of the preceding five years, all of them by English authors: Charlotte Brontë's *Jane Eyre*, Emily Brontë's *Wuthering Heights*, William Makepeace Thackeray's *Vanity Fair*, Charles Dickens's *Dombey and Son*, and Thomas Macaulay's *History of England*. American authors dreamed of bold works that would convey the energy and ambition of the nation surging around them, that would surpass the domestic novels of Britain.

The most brilliant writer in the United States, Edgar Allan Poe, found the years following the success of "The Raven" even harder than those before. In 1847, Poe's wife, Virginia, died of tuberculosis at the age of twenty-five. Newspapers appealed for donations for Poe, himself ill, impoverished, and devastated by the loss. Poe gratefully accepted the charity and withdrew from the frantic business of editing and reviewing to compose what he thought would be his greatest work: *Eureka: An Essay on the Material and Spiritual Universe.*[29]

Many writers put forward theories about the universe. A best-selling book, published under a pseudonym, proposed that the universe had evolved through natural laws, without the need for divine intervention. A famous British astronomer introduced the "nebular hypothesis," in which the very Sun had emerged from a swirl of gases. *Cosmos*, a massive multivolume work by the German adventurer and naturalist Alexander von Humboldt, arrived in translation in the United States in 1845. Humboldt demonstrated, with remarkable reach and detail, the interconnectedness of the universe, from its smallest to its largest elements. Edgar Allan Poe dedicated his new book to Humboldt.[30]

Poe had been fascinated with astronomy and science since his boyhood. Now, he would fuse his knowledge of scientific developments with his poetic imagination to interpret the universe itself. He scheduled a lecture in New York in February 1848 to unveil his ideas, borrowing fifteen dollars to rent a hall. He hoped for three or four hundred listeners whose ticket purchases would generate more income than he could ever make writing. A hard winter storm kept away much of the audience, but sixty people made their way to the hall.

"I have seen no portrait of POE that does justice to his pale, delicate, intellectual face and magnificent eyes," one in attendance wrote. "His lecture was a rhapsody of the most intense brilliancy. He appeared inspired, and his inspiration affected the scant audience almost painfully." Poe posited the creation of a "primordial Particle" that burst to fill "the Universe of Stars," seeding clouds that condensed to create suns and planets. Throughout the universe he envisioned, an electric force generated all "phaenomena of vitality, consciousness and Thought," resisting the gravity that would, at some distant time, "with a million-fold electric velocity," collapse all matter once again. Poe portrayed an unimaginably intricate universe unified by its oppositions, invisibly resonating.

The lecture was "the most elaborate and profound" of performances, "greeted with warm applause by the audience, who had listened with enchained attention throughout." Poe expected *Eureka* to "revolutionize the world of Physical & Metaphysical Science. I say this calmly—but I say it." The book's one hundred pages struggled to contain the vision Poe imagined, however, wavering in tone and style, confusing in assertion and speculation. Two reviews called the book "startling." Few people purchased it.

Even as he searched for the mysteries of the heavens, Poe composed two starkly contrasting works. In "Hop-Frog," a fantasy of revenge and reversal, a tormented and disabled dwarf jester persuades a king and his ministers to be covered with tar and flax to disguise themselves as eight "chained ourang-outangs" to frighten guests at a masquerade. At their entrance, Hop-Frog snatches the giddy and arrogant costumed men in their chains, hoists them to the ceiling in an iron chandelier, and burns them into "a fetid, blackened, hideous, and indistinguishable mass."

Near the same time, Poe composed a haunting and delicate poem of two childlike lovers separated by the death of young Annabel Lee:

> And neither the angels in Heaven above
> Nor the demons down under the sea
> Can ever dissever my soul from the soul
> Of the beautiful Annabel Lee

Poe's vision of men as vicious brutes, of women as pure and dying, of life as a battle between demons and angels, took haunting form.

Desperately hoping to build a new life, Poe returned to Richmond, the city of his rearing, abandonment, and first professional success. He sought out a woman he had courted early in his life, now a prosperous young widow with three children. While in Richmond, Poe lectured to "quite a full, and very fashionable audience" on "the poetic principle." A Richmond newspaper declared itself "never more delighted in our lives" than with the performance and character of a man it was now proud to call one of its own. Poe, following Percy Bysshe Shelley, compared poetry to "the desire of the moth for the star." That longing, that immeasurable and impossible distance, had defined his life's work.

Poe, dreaming anew of his own magazine, headed to New York in the fall of 1849. He somehow became lost in Baltimore along the way. Strangers discovered Poe muttering to himself, seeing "spectral and imaginary objects on the walls." Despite the efforts of a young and admiring doctor, Poe died of what was diagnosed as brain inflammation and exposure. He was quickly buried in Baltimore, before word of his death reached those who loved him. As the news spread over the wires and through columns of print, obituaries praised Poe's genius and puzzled over his mysterious death. A literary enemy printed rumors and lies about him, distortions that became an enduring caricature.

Another author confronted scandal and tragedy in these months. Margaret Fuller planned to return home from Europe in 1850 after four years of covering the bloody struggles of revolution for the *New-York Tribune*. Fuller saw in the Italian revolution a democratic promise squandered by a United States grown "stupid with the lust of gain, soiled by crime in its willing perpetuation of slavery, shamed by an unjust war." Fuller fell in love with a young Italian revolutionary and bore a son. She was crushed when the revolution failed, "the best betrayed and exiled." She, her husband, and child fled for the United States.[31]

Approaching the American coast in a storm, their ship hit

rocks off the coast of Long Island, three hundred yards from shore. As the ship slowly broke apart, crew and passengers gradually abandoned the wreck, some making their way to safety and others dying in the effort. Fuller watched, helpless, as her husband and her child drowned; she remained on board, dressed in her white nightgown, as waves washed over the wreckage and swept her from the deck. Henry David Thoreau, at the urging of Emerson, rushed to the Long Island coast to see if he could recover the manuscript of Fuller's book on Italy, but he found only empty chests. Her body was never reclaimed, though that of her child, Angelo, was. Friends buried his body in Mount Auburn Cemetery in Cambridge, under a marker for Fuller and her husband, declaring her a "genius belonging to the world."[32]

The first National Woman's Rights Convention, meeting a few months after Fuller's loss, stood in silence for the memory of a woman who would have been an intellectual leader of the movement. Emerson and colleagues gathered what they could find of Fuller's writings, which they edited to remove controversial statements and personal experiences, including the affair that led to her marriage. It became a best-selling book, appearing in thirteen editions.[33]

The loss of Margaret Fuller and Edgar Allan Poe within a few months of each other, both only forty years old, deprived the United States of two of its boldest and most versatile writers. Both had struggled against hard obstacles; both saw things other Americans chose not to see. The country would be diminished by their silence.

Chapter Eight

CONFRONTATIONS

1850–1855

The Scarlet Letter, the White Whale, and the Wide World

In 1842, Nathaniel Hawthorne and his new wife, Sophia, moved to Concord, Massachusetts, where they rented a dilapidated "manse" from Ralph Waldo Emerson and began a family. In a small room for three years, Hawthorne labored to make a living with his pen. The couple, marrying in their thirties, gloried in married life and their new daughter. Hawthorne, amused by the parade of strange seekers who came to visit Emerson, did not imbibe the spirit of transcendence in Concord. Hawthorne came to know and like Henry David Thoreau, though he could not quite comprehend the young man's purpose.

Hawthorne wrote stories that worried over aspects of human nature—guilt, sin, and mystery—to which Emerson and Thoreau gave little attention. He published *Mosses from an Old Manse* in 1846, combining stories of haunted New England, such as "Young Goodman Brown" and "Roger Malvin's Burial," with works such as "Rappaccini's Daughter" and "The Artist of the Beautiful" that dramatized the dangers and rewards of artistic creativity. The book met with a warm critical response but tepid sales.

Struggling to support his family, in 1846 Hawthorne, a loyal Democrat, gratefully accepted a political appointment to the custom house in his old hometown of Salem. After the Whigs ascended to the presidency two years later, however, Hawthorne was removed from his position. Fellow Democrats came to his defense, but Whig newspapers charged Hawthorne with political favoritism and kickbacks. Friends rallied to raise money for Hawthorne, compensating him for, they said, in "a very imperfect measure, the debt we owe you for what you have done for American Literature." Hawthorne accepted five hundred dollars, but admitted that he was "ashamed of it, and I ought to be. The fault of a failure is attributable—in a great degree, at least—to the man who fails." Sophia Hawthorne painted mythological scenes on lampshades to sell in Boston.

Hearing of Hawthorne's distress, a young publisher from Boston took the train to Salem, offering to publish two thousand copies of whatever the author had written. Hawthorne at first demurred, saying he had nothing adequate for publication. As the publisher left, however, Hawthorne pursued him to hand over the nearly completed manuscript of a long story. "It is either very good or very bad—I don't know which," Hawthorne sighed. The publisher read the pages on the train and returned the next day to implore Hawthorne to expand the tale to book length.

Hawthorne was uncertain whether the tale's theme—adultery— was a suitable or salable subject. He had suffered failure and shame, and did not want to invite even more, but decided to take the risk: "If 'The Scarlet Letter' is to be the title," Hawthorne wondered, "would it not be well to print it on the title-page in red ink?" Hawthorne expanded the text for the book with a biting account of his time in the Salem Custom House and the Whigs within. He linked the disparate texts, and the present with the past, through the fictive discovery of a fragment of cloth that inspired the tale that followed, a tale of a young woman forced to wear the letter "A" sewn at her breast.[1]

The Scarlet Letter was a horror story, with hypocrisy its monster. Nature was not a refuge, but a dangerous forest filled with inscrutable Indians and impenetrable shadows. Religion was not a balm, but a haven for liars, its preachers and congregants haunted by notions of sin they imposed upon themselves and one another. The child born of adultery bore no resemblance to the idealized lithographs of innocence that filled the ladies' magazine for which Hawthorne had written; instead, she was an unruly imp, bearing a knowledge older than her years, acknowledging "no Heavenly Father." The heroine was a woman justified in her adultery by the lack of strong sexual passion with a husband who abandoned her because he disappointed her. She proclaimed her illicit relationship legitimate because she and her lover made it "a consecration of its own. We felt it so! We said so to each other!"

Remarkably, *The Scarlet Letter*, violating so many tenets of American culture, won adoring reviews and strong sales. Hawthorne managed to seduce his readers into sympathy with a woman who had boldly and unapologetically committed bastardy. He persuaded his audience that a minister of the Gospel could be weak and evil, his faith a corruption of his soul and of those to whom he preached. Hawthorne made the venerated Puritans into vain scolds passing self-righteous and ignorant judgment. He celebrated a woman who, like himself, was exiled to the margins of a community. Like Hester Prynne, Hawthorne transformed shame into a symbol of insight into the hypocritical world around him.[2]

Though *The Scarlet Letter* did not make Hawthorne wealthy, it did provide enough income to rent a small red house in the Berkshires of western Massachusetts to escape Salem and its intrigues. It was there, in a house he did not much like, that Hawthorne met a young admirer: Herman Melville. Hawthorne, fourteen years older and in the flush of unaccustomed success with *The Scarlet Letter*, inspired Melville with his example. Flattered by the attention, Hawthorne invited the young man to stay with his family for several days. Sophia Hawthorne liked the visitor she called "Mr. Typee," seeing "Fayaway in his face." Melville soon moved his family to the Berkshires as well, borrowing money from his father-in-law to buy a farmhouse he could not afford.[3]

Melville, like Hawthorne, wrestled with the challenges of writing as a career. After the success of *Typee* and *Omoo*, Melville had published *Mardi*, a mélange of narrative and philosophizing that perplexed reviewers and readers. The recently married young man returned to the sailing stories that had made his name, quickly producing *Redburn* and *White-Jacket* in 1849 and 1850, "two *jobs* which I have done for money—being forced to it as other men are to sawing wood." After *Redburn* won a positive review, Melville noted with self-contempt in his journal that "I, the author, know [it] to be trash, & wrote it to buy some tobacco with." He determined that his next book would not compromise.[4]

Reading Hawthorne's *Mosses from an Old Manse*, Melville found inspiration in the dark allegories that shadowed the pieties of America's religious and secular faith. "What I feel most moved to write, that is banned,—it will not pay," the young author confided to Hawthorne. "Yet, altogether, write the *other* way I cannot." Hawthorne's example in his stories and *The Scarlet Letter* suggested that perhaps Melville could write books that would support his young family and yet confront moral and metaphysical depths.

Melville had begun a new book, this one about whaling, beginning with a jaunty account of a young man confronting life on a ship manned by representatives of the world's cultures. It would be called *Moby-Dick*, inspired by the true story of a ship destroyed by a white whale decades before and informed by the detailed narratives of Charles Wilkes's Exploring Expedition and the egotism of its leader. After long conversations with Hawthorne in the Berkshires, Melville began to look for deeper possibilities in the book taking shape in his mind. A story that had begun with Ishmael, a wanderer, became the story of Ahab, a cursed Israelite king who worshipped a pagan god.[5]

Melville plunged into Milton and Virgil, Shakespeare and Goethe, the Bible and Eastern religions, Alexander von Humboldt and obscure whaling volumes, weaving majestic and mundane works into his own tale. He portrayed the ship as a small world, occupied by Christians and heathens, saintly cannibals and doomed men of high character. The book became ever longer, ever darker, with no sign of redemption on any horizon.

The narrative, like a ship on the open sea, surged from one style to another. One chapter listed copious facts about whales, another explained each step in the liquefaction of blubber in flaming tryworks, another told a horrifying story of a young Black boy abandoned to the sea and insanity. Ahab delivered a ranting speech and sought to entrance his men with a gold coin hammered to the mast, not unlike the speeches in Congress that filled the papers each day in 1850. Ahab chased whales just as the United States chased territory, never satiated, killing or enslaving those in the way, dressing itself in the language of righteousness and revenge for an imaginary wrong, destroying itself with irrational hunger.[6]

As he finished the book, Melville offered a feigned warning to a sophisticated female friend: "Don't you buy it—don't you read it, when it does come out, because it is by no means the sort of book for you. It is not a piece of fine feminine Spitalsfields silk—but is of the horrible texture of a fabric that should be woven of ships' cables & hausers. A Polar wind blows through it, & birds of prey hover over it." Melville virtually dared his readers to follow him into the arcana of whale etymology, into a story that offered no glimpse of satisfying resolution, into a narrative whose voice shifted without warning. Later generations would appreciate the complexities of such a novel, but it held little appeal in 1851. Melville made only $556.37 in royalties for *Moby-Dick*, the least he had earned from any of his writing. He launched into yet another novel in anger and frustration. Upon the appearance of *Pierre* the following year, reviewers questioned the author's sanity.[7]

Nathaniel Hawthorne, for his part, visited with Melville only a few times in the winter of 1850–1851 despite the younger author's repeated invitations. Hawthorne disliked the cold and his small rental house but pushed himself to complete *The House of the Seven Gables* to build on the success of *The Scarlet Letter*. This new work also worried over the inheritances of the New England past. Its theme: "No great mistake, whether acted or endured, in our moral sphere, is ever really set right." The novel did not attract as many readers as its predecessor, and Hawthorne, once again, borrowed money. After auctioning the family's belongings, he moved his wife and children to another rented house, this one near the shore. There, he wrote *The Blithedale Romance*, a skeptical portrayal of his brief time, more than a decade before, at the utopian experiment Brook Farm. The lead female character, Zenobia, was, and was understood to be, based on Margaret Fuller. The novel proved to be no more engaged and engaging than Hawthorne himself had been at Brook Farm. It did not do well.[8]

Hawthorne complained to his publisher about his inability to compete with the "damned mob of scribbling women" who sold far more books than he did. Most prominent among those female authors was Susan Warner, whose life resembled a novel by Charles Dickens, full of stark reversals and improbable twists. She had grown up in Manhattan, her mother deceased. Susan's father lost his considerable wealth in the Panic of 1837, just as the eighteen-year-old girl came of age. The only property he retained was Constitution Island, in the Hudson River near West Point, where he had planned to erect a summer residence. Susan and her younger sister Anna moved there from their New York mansion with their aunt, ripped away from lessons in French, Italian, and piano, from fashion and social engagements, from prospects of marriage. "From dainty silks and laces," they recalled, "we came down to calicoes, fashioned by our own fingers." They chopped firewood and churned butter.[9]

The sisters searched for a way to make money. Anna created a card game for children, based on *Robinson Crusoe*, painting each card by hand. Susan decided to try writing a novel; her sister suggested she title it *The Wide, Wide World*. Her father took the completed manuscript to New York editors, but they rejected it; one simply wrote "Fudge!" on the front. George Putnam, ready to reject it as well, took the manuscript home, where his mother happened to read it. She told him he must publish it "for your fellow men." Putnam obliged half-heartedly, printing 750 copies as a Christmas book for 1850.

The Wide, Wide World told the story of a young girl growing into womanhood. Through separation, cruelty, and disdain, Ellen Montgomery succeeded by embracing a Christian faith she slowly came to understand and appreciate. The defining drama was that of Christian conversion, echoing those of readers who filled their diaries with dialogues between themselves and God, with struggles to sustain faith in the face of trials.[10]

Though much of *The Wide, Wide World* unfolded in Britain after Ellen was forced to move to Edinburgh, American reviewers proudly claimed the book as the nation's own. "Lo and behold, an American literature!" Caroline Kirkland wrote in the *North American Review*. The book reflected the true character of the United States: "humane, religious, natural, national." The "spontaneous popularity" of the novel, a "story of real life," marked "an index of national character." The reception of the book in Britain confirmed American pride in its authorship.[11]

Despite the success of *The Wide, Wide World*, Susan Warner would not see much of that world. In need of money, she had sold the rights to her book—and the many that followed—rather than collecting the enormous royalties that accrued over the decades. Her sister Anna remained prolific as well, famous for writing the beloved song for young Christians, "Jesus Loves Me." The sisters would remain together on Constitution Island the rest of their lives.

The Lamplighter, written by Maria Susanna Cummins, a first-time author in her twenties, also sold hundreds of thousands of books on both sides of the Atlantic in a matter of months in the early 1850s. Cummins's novel, like Warner's, provided vicarious experiences of being female in the middle of the nineteenth century. The stories of a young woman making her way in a hard world offered examples and warnings to those absorbed in their pages. Though called sentimental, the popular novels by women were in fact practical and strategic. They succeeded because they provided what their readers craved.[12]

The first novel written by an Indigenous American filled a different kind of popular craving—one for a fascinating outlaw. *The Life and Adventures of Joaquín Murieta: The Celebrated California Bandit* was published in 1854 in San Francisco by Yellow Bird, the Cherokee name for John Rollin Ridge. Ridge descended from Major Ridge, a Cherokee leader and kinsman of Elias Boudinot, who was assassinated for his role in negotiating the sale of land to the United States. Young Ridge, the son of a white mother, had his own violent conflicts with enemies and so moved to California in 1850. There, he wrote for newspapers obsessed with the exploits of a Mexican—or several Mexicans—named Joaquín who audaciously raided and stole from white settlers. Bounty hunters took a reward for a man they claimed to be the real Joaquín and displayed his head as proof.

Ridge invented a backstory for the bandit, showing that Joaquín had been wronged in many ways and had shown forbearance until he could tolerate no more. The Mexican's robberies and assaults were revenge for himself and for his people. Ridge made no money from the book, which proliferated for decades under different names and in other languages, but the figure of the vengeful western outlaw became forever fixed in the American imagination.[13]

Women's Voices against Slavery

Congress debated month after month in 1849 and 1850 the tangle of issues surrounding California and other territories taken from Mexico. To the surprise of many, the most volatile conflict triggered by the Compromise of 1850 turned around the Fugitive Slave Law, which had grown ever weaker over the preceding half century as state laws in the North granted due process to refugees from slavery and those accused of being refugees. The strengthened law denied to accused Black people a jury trial and habeas corpus, imposed the authority of special commissioners over local officials, paid fees to officials that rewarded conviction, and threatened fine and imprisonment for those who refused to aid in capturing fugitives. Refugees from slavery who had been living peacefully in the North for years could be seized and taken into bondage.[14]

Even white people in the North who had remained numb to the wrongs of slavery were infuriated by this injustice in their own communities. In its wake, mass meetings of indignation arose, one Washington paper reported, in "every city, and nearly every village of the North" in "negro churches, at cross-roads, in barns and market houses." As slaveholders ventured into the North to claim people they identified as their property, Black people and white allies fought back. They mobbed courthouses and jails, freeing those who had been abducted.

Despite resistance, between three hundred and five hundred

Black people were dragged into the South and into slavery through the Fugitive Slave Law. Ten to twenty thousand Black Americans moved to Canada, Mexico, and the Caribbean between 1850 and 1860 to escape the danger. Women, Black and white, stepped forward to lead a rejuvenated movement against slavery.[15]

Sojourner Truth, born in slavery in New York before the turn of the century, had decades earlier seen her six-year-old son Peter taken from her and sold among various New York owners and then into Alabama. She managed, with help from white allies, to sue successfully for his return, only to find that he had been viciously beaten and scarred. Securing her freedom and changing her name, in the 1830s and 1840s Truth found succor and power in the Methodist Church, a flamboyant prophet, the Millerite movement, and a cooperative community. There, in the Northampton Association of Education and Industry, she met William Lloyd Garrison and Frederick Douglass. Inspired by Douglass's example, Truth narrated her life story of devotion to her spiritual quest.

In her fifties by this time, Truth gained recognition as a powerful speaker. In a meeting in Providence in 1850, Truth followed Garrison and others who had raged for hours against the Fugitive Slave Law. She spoke briefly, saying that she "thanked God that the law was made—that the worst had come to worst; the best must come to best." Such bold and unpretentious statements fascinated white audiences. Truth achieved greater fame at a women's rights convention in Akron, Ohio, in May 1851. "I am a woman's rights," she announced. "I have as much muscle as any man, and can do as much work as any man. I have plowed and reaped and husked and chopped and mowed, and can any man do more than that?"

Truth chided men who feared such strength. "The poor men seem to be all in confusion and dont know what to do. Why children, if you have woman's rights give it to her and you will feel better. You will have your own rights, and they wont be so much trouble." She expressed sarcastic sympathy for the white man, who "is in a tight place, the poor slave is on him, woman is coming up on him, and he is surely between a hawk and a buzzard." Audiences delighted in Truth's honesty, expressed with a humor seldom displayed by earnest advocates of reform.[16]

While Sojourner Truth spoke in words of defiance before public audiences, Harriet Tubman worked to undermine slavery from within. Tubman escaped slavery in 1849 and through the 1850s helped dozens of others escape from Maryland through the northern states and into Canada. Tubman required secrecy rather than publicity, quiet rather than speech, but spoke to trusted audiences in the North. Leading intellectuals and abolitionists in Boston donated to her purposes as they heard her stories of bravery. "I never met with any person of any color who had more confidence in the voice of God, as spoken direct to her soul," testified one admiring white supporter. Tubman supported her work through her labor as a cook, contributing all she had to her great purpose. Tubman's example of physical risk and selflessness inspired her allies. Those same traits infuriated hapless enemies who failed to capture the small woman on her repeated raids into slavery.[17]

The Fugitive Slave Law sparked another woman into bold action. Harriet Beecher Stowe, part of a well-known family of white ministers and writers, had come of age in Cincinnati, on the Ohio River and the border with slavery. Starting in 1839, writing as "Mrs. H. B. Stowe," she contributed genteel pieces to *Godey's Lady's Book* and gathered her work into a book in 1843. Even as she wrote, Stowe suffered great personal loss in the death of a child in 1849. She and her husband, a professor, moved to Maine in 1850 for a fresh start. There, Stowe, stirred by the charged debates over fugitive slaves that she read in the papers, was appalled that many of the women she met in her new home seemed to care little about the issue.

In March 1851, Stowe contacted the editor of the *New Era*, a moderate abolitionist newspaper in Washington. Stowe proposed that she write a serial novel inspired by the Fugitive Slave Law. It would offer a "series of sketches which give the lights and shadows" of slavery. The sketches would be "written either from observation, incidents which have occurred in the sphere of my personal knowledge, or in the knowledge of my friends. I shall show the *best side* of the thing, and something *faintly approaching the worst*." Stowe felt she had no choice but to try, for "I feel now that the time has come when even a woman or a child who can speak a word for freedom and humanity is bound to speak."[18]

Stowe interwove stories that came to her, she said, like visions, visions of Black people and white, old and young, male and female, in the North and in the South, all of them swept up in the moral and physical drama of American slavery. At the center suffered an enslaved man named Tom, forced to undertake a journey from his cabin in Kentucky into the distant reaches of the South and slavery. Tom, a strong and proud man, confronted every injustice with Christian faith, lifting other enslaved people with his dignified example. The story also followed, in the opposite direction, the flight of an enslaved mother, Eliza, across the perilous, frozen Ohio River into the free but embattled soil of the North. As the forty-one weekly installments appeared, subscriptions to the *New Era* nearly tripled to thirty thousand copies.

Uncle Tom's Cabin was a social novel of the sort Americans had come to admire from Britain, rich in characters and action, revealing hidden thoughts, dramatizing conflict of both intimate and communal scale. Readers found themselves imaginatively bound with people unlike themselves. Stowe wove together the power of sermons and parlor songs, of tender poems about children, death, of mothers and children, of the New Testament and reading. The combination empowered Stowe to discuss the costs of slavery, the slave trade, and the Fugitive Slave Law as no one else had.

To connect with white readers, Stowe's Black characters embodied stereotypes ranging from the blackface foolery of Topsy to the doomed mulatto of Eliza to the pliant Christian of Tom. Each character eventually experienced conversion and elevation, but her portrayals led one Black abolitionist to exclaim in frustration that Stowe "*knows nothing about us.*" Stowe did not in fact know many Black people.[19]

Stowe ended her novel in a tone of spiritual salvation but secular despair. She disdained "the dead sea of respectable churches" and the cult of business that ruled America. She had nothing good to say of northern politicians or of those who upheld the sanctity of the Union as a reason to tolerate slavery and accept the Fugitive Slave Law. Stowe warned her fellow Christians that the "*day of vengeance*" would arrive with God's judgment for the great sin they tolerated in their midst. At the end of the novel, Stowe's Black characters flee America for Africa because she could not imagine how justice might come to them in the United States.[20]

When the bound book appeared in two volumes in the spring of 1852, three power presses and a hundred bookbinders labored to meet the demand. By the end of the year, Americans had bought three hundred thousand copies, the British a million. "It is the distinction of 'Uncle Tom's Cabin' that, it is read equally in the parlour & the kitchen & the nursery of every house," Emerson noted in his journal. "What the lady read[s] in the drawing-room in a few hours, is retailed to her in her kitchen by the cook & the chambermaid, as, week by week, they master one scene & character after another." Henry James recalled *Uncle Tom's Cabin* as his "first encounter with grownup fiction," for him as for "an immense number of people, much less a book than a state of vision, of feeling and consciousness, in which they did not sit and read and appraise and pass the time, but walked and talked and laughed and cried." Henry Wadsworth Longfellow congratulated Stowe for "one of the greatest triumphs recorded in literary history, to say nothing of the higher triumph of its moral effect."[21]

Theatrical producers of *Uncle Tom's Cabin* took whatever they wanted from Stowe's novel, for no copyright protected her. Spectacle, music, and farce animated competing versions of the play in New York City, where the show ran for hundreds of days even as other troupes spread across the North. The first time many men witnessed an antislavery story was in a play made from Stowe's novel. Stowe's characters became ubiquitous in a way impossible earlier, before the machinery of merchandizing and advertising had developed. The novel triggered an outpouring of rebuttals in the South, ranging from outraged editorials to contrived stories, but the damage to slavery had been done.[22]

Exposing Slavery to the World

William Wells Brown, who had escaped slavery through Cincinnati and taught himself to read and write as an adult, modeled his career as an abolitionist on that of Frederick Douglass. Brown spoke throughout the American North in the early 1840s, published a narrative of his life in 1847, and journeyed to the Continent and Britain in 1849. Gregarious, an excellent singer, and a showman, Brown attracted large audiences in Dublin, Paris, and London.

Brown took inspiration from the popular *Panorama of the Mississippi Valley*, which attracted hundreds of thousands of spectators in American cities and then in London. Painted on long stretches of canvas slowly unfurled on rollers, "the introduction of moving panoramas of scenery in this country by the Americans, has been the most beneficial to the progress of knowledge," noted a London paper. Brown commissioned his own panorama, twenty-four panels, each ten yards wide, depicting scenes from slavery narrated by Brown as the images passed. William and Ellen Craft, famous after their escape from slavery dressed in disguise that crossed lines of both gender and race, joined Brown after fleeing the United States. The team toured Scotland and northern England, attracting audiences of up to 1,600 people. Brown incorporated scenes from *Uncle Tom's Cabin* into his panorama and illuminated slides for his traveling presentation.[23]

In 1851, these Black abolitionists found a new stage. London opened the Great Exhibition of the Works of Industry of All Nations in the spectacular new glass Crystal Palace. People journeyed from around the world to witness the vast exhibits arrayed there. William Wells Brown advertised the hypocrisy of the United States on a day when fifteen thousand people, including the royal family, attended the exhibition. Accompanied by the Crafts and the prominent English abolitionist George Thompson, whose unmarried daughter strolled arm in arm with Brown, the party spent hours promenading through the displays. White attendees from the United States glared at them, much to Brown's satisfaction. Samuel Colt, demonstrating his revolver alongside a display about American Indians presented by the painter George Catlin, temporarily fell silent as the group passed by his exhibit.[24]

Brown and the Crafts made their way to Hiram Powers's *Greek Slave*, the artistic centerpiece of the American gallery. English observers had noted the jarring contrast between the recent actions of the United States in support of slavery and the nation's sympathy for a fictional white woman sold into Turkish slavery. A biting cartoon in *Punch* magazine portrayed "The Virginian Slave," a Black woman, partially nude, wearing heavy chains inscribed with "E Pluribus Unum," standing next to a pedestal draped with the flag of the United States. She cast her eyes upward in futile hope of deliverance.

William Wells Brown carried a copy of the cartoon into the hall, positioned it on the pedestal of the *Greek Slave*, and announced that "as an American fugitive slave, I place this 'Virginia Slave' by the side of the 'Greek Slave' as its most fitting companion." A small crowd watched the performance, American slaveowners "thoroughly muzzled" by the audacious act. A white man removed the cartoon not long after and refused to explain himself, but the story gleefully appeared in the abolitionist press.[25]

Harriet Beecher Stowe arrived in Britain in 1853 and met with enormous crowds. British convention prevented her from speaking—her husband and brother read her speech, quite ineffectively, while she sat behind them—but Stowe met many influential people at dinners and visits to their homes. Stowe projected a modest persona that won adulation, her reticence part of her appeal.

Stowe, along with Susan Warner, became one of the most popular authors in the English-speaking world. Thirty years after the belittling query of who in the world reads an American book, the answer emerged: everyone. William Wells Brown, inspired by the success of Stowe's novel, wrote his own: *Clotel*, imagining the lives of Thomas Jefferson's daughters with an enslaved woman. The book, directed at British readers, was published in England but not in the United States until the 1860s. British supporters purchased the freedom of Brown, who returned to the United States in 1854 to fight for freedom closer to home.[26]

In the United States, Frederick Douglass struggled even as *Uncle Tom's Cabin* swept to popularity. His newspaper survived only through the financial support of the abolitionist Gerrit Smith, who called for the antislavery cause to take its fight into the political realm. Douglass came to agree that too much was at stake to stand aside while Congress and the president undermined Black freedom in the North and protected slavery in the South. Douglass declared that since the Constitution guaranteed that no person could "be deprived of life, liberty, or property without due process of law," slavery anywhere in the United States was illegal. Political conflict over the issue could not be avoided.[27]

William Lloyd Garrison and his allies charged Douglass with selling out to his wealthy white patron in abandoning the anti-political principles and organization that had made him the most famous Black man in the nation. They canceled their subscriptions to his paper and spread rumors about an illicit relationship with his white English assistant, Julia Griffiths. Douglass's wife defended him, but he suffered what he called "side blows, innuendo, dark suspicions, such as avarice, faithlessness, treachery, ingratitude and what not." Harriet Beecher Stowe tried to make peace between Garrison and Douglass but failed.

In July 1852, Douglass transcended the backbiting to deliver the most powerful speech of his career and one of the greatest in United States history. He addressed nearly six hundred people in Rochester's glittering new Corinthian Hall, invited by the Rochester Ladies' Anti-Slavery Society to commemorate the Fourth of July. After a reading of the Declaration of Independence, Douglass rose to speak, his hands trembling. "Fellow-citizens, pardon me," he began, "allow me to ask, why am I called upon to speak here today? What have I, or those I represent, to do with your national independence?" Surely his white listeners knew that "I am not included within the pale of this glorious anniversary! . . . This Fourth [of] July is *yours*, not *mine*. . . . Do you mean, citizens, to mock me by asking me to speak today?"

When white Americans gathered to celebrate the glorious birth of their nation, Douglass reminded them: "Above your national, tumultuous joy, I hear the mournful wail of millions! whose chains, heavy and grievous yesterday, are today, rendered more intolerable by the jubilee shouts that reach them." If Douglass could reach the American nation celebrating its freedom, if he could have all its white citizens gathered before him, "I would today pour out a fiery stream of biting ridicule, blasting reproach, withering sarcasm, and stern rebuke. For it is not light that is needed, but fire; it is not the gentle shower, but thunder. We need the storm, the whirlwind, and the earthquake." The hypocrisy of celebrating freedom in a nation recently recommitted to slavery with the Fugitive Slave Law "brands your republicanism as a sham, your humanity as a base pretense, and your Christianity a lie."

Witnessing the South

People in the North read many contradictory things about the South: that it was rich and that it was poor, paternalistic and abusive. A young journalist, Frederick Law Olmsted, was dispatched by a fledgling newspaper, the *New York Daily Times*, to report objective accounts to readers in the North.

From a prominent family in Hartford, Olmsted had experienced previous adventures as a sailor, a merchant, and a farmer on Staten Island. In 1852, with a commission from the young newspaper looking for a way to grow its readership, he embarked on a tour of the American South to report, as dispassionately as possible, what he saw there. A handsome and personable thirty-year-old, Olmsted talked to everyone who would talk with him. On two journeys over the next two years, he traveled from Virginia to Texas, sending dozens of letters to the paper. The reports reached a large audience across the North and West.

Olmsted could not hide his disdain for almost all he saw in the South. He found the region dirty and slipshod, its farms underdeveloped and its accommodations appalling. He judged slavery a burden to slaveowners, profoundly wasteful and unproductive. While the Black people of the South varied in skill and diligence, Olmsted reported, "the great mass, as they are seen at work, under overseers, in the fields, appear very dull, idiotic, and brute-like." He did not report any scenes of whipping, though he saw overseers brandishing whips, and did not believe enslaved people were deprived of food or clothing.[28]

Olmsted offered a cautious and circuitous judgment of Black character and possibilities: "I do not think, after all I have heard to favor it, that there is any good reason to consider the negro, naturally and essentially, the moral inferior of the white." Olmsted admonished his fellow white northerners to give the Black man in the North "a fair chance to prove his own case, to prove himself a man entitled to the inalienable rights of men." Slavery damaged and stunted everyone who lived in the South, Olmsted believed, but he cautioned against pressuring the white South to end slavery. The South, trapped in bondage, could not escape it. Abolition was unrealistic and dangerous. The United States would have to live with slavery.[29]

Solomon Northup had experienced what Olmsted could not see, for he had endured slavery from inside the institution. Born a free Black man in New York, Northup had been tricked into coming to Washington, DC, in 1841 to perform with his violin. There, men drugged and kidnapped Northup and sold him into a slave trade that carried him to Louisiana. Northup labored in bondage until he approached an itinerant Canadian carpenter to request help. When the white man returned to New York, he alerted authorities of Northup's illegal seizure. In January 1853, a carriage arrived unannounced on the plantation to return him to his family. Safe in New York, Northup narrated a memoir of his horrific time in slavery, *Twelve Years a Slave*. The book's searing story, published only a few months after his deliverance, sold thirty thousand copies.[30]

In *Twelve Years a Slave*, in contrast to Olmsted's accounts, plantations appeared as brutally efficient, with large yields driven by violence because if anyone "falls behind or is a moment idle, he is whipped." Northup told the story of a young enslaved woman named Patsey, whose experience revealed the vicious capriciousness of slavery. Patsey could pick twice as much cotton as anyone else. She handled horses and mules with skill, split rails with ease, and could hoe a furrow faster than any other man or woman. "Patsey was queen of the field," Northup wrote. "She had a genial and pleasant temper, and was faithful and obedient. Naturally, she was a joyous creature, a laughing, light-hearted girl, rejoicing in the mere sense of existence."

But Patsey's back "bore the scars of a thousand stripes," for "it had fallen to her lot to be the slave of a licentious master and a jealous mistress." The enslaver could not afford to sell Patsey, his best worker, but he whipped her to appease his wife. Northup found himself dragged into the cruelty, forced to whip Patsey for visiting a nearby farm to get a piece of soap. The mistress "stood on the piazza among her children, gazing on the scene with an air of heartless satisfaction." The young enslaved woman "prayed piteously for mercy, but her prayers were vain." Patsey remained behind on the plantation after Solomon Northup left. He would relive her suffering, over and over, from lecture platforms and in the pages of his book.

The contradictory images of slavery portrayed by Olmsted and Northup proliferated across the North in infinite variations: in plays and novels, sentimental songs and abolitionist meetings, statistics and speeches. The polarities of violence and permissiveness, of inefficiency and coercion, of wealth and neglect, of care-free song and dirge, changed according to the purposes to which they were put.

Frederick Douglass published a new version of his autobiography in 1855—*My Bondage and My Freedom*. In the frontispiece, Douglass, still in his thirties, dressed in fine clothes, confronted readers with a direct gaze, nearly clenched fists, and a furrowed brow. In his text, Douglass fleshed out the scenes of his *Narrative*, published ten long years before, to provide a novelistic effect of detail and dialogue. Taking a sharper political edge than in his first book and distancing himself from the white abolitionists who had guided and constrained him in his early years, Douglass chronicled a decade of relentless work on both sides of the Atlantic on behalf of the abolitionist cause. The book sold well, replacing the story of a brave but deferential young fugitive slave with that of a mature and accomplished leader.[31]

Douglass ended his book with text from a recent talk, taking stock of the progress of the antislavery movement in 1855. He was heartened by what he saw, though he did not underestimate the challenges before the effort. "At this moment, I deem it safe to say, it is properly engrossing more minds in this country than any other subject now before the American people." The movement against slavery could be seen "moving in all directions, and in all weathers, and in all places, appearing most where desired least, and pressing hardest where most resisted. No place is exempt. The quiet prayer meeting, and the stormy halls of national debate, share its presence alike."

The powers of the nation—"the church, the government, and the people at large"—had failed to stop the antislavery movement. Although politicians temporized and revealed "northern timidity" in the face of the slave power, the determination to be rid of slavery had grown nevertheless. The efforts of politicians to stop the movement had been "as idle and fruitless as pouring oil to extinguish fire." The Compromise of 1850 had been a fraud; the Fugitive Slave Law "of positive service to the anti-slavery movement," demonstrating "the arrogant and overbearing spirit of the slave states toward the free states" and "attempting to make them parties to the crime." The southern aggression had backfired, too, by fostering among "the colored people, the hunted ones, a spirit of manly resistance well calculated to surround them with a bulwark of sympathy and respect hitherto unknown."

The movement against slavery would not disappear, Douglass announced. "It has grown too large—its friends are too numerous—its facilities too abundant—its ramifications too extended—its power too omnipotent, to be snuffed out by the contingencies of infancy." The current age, Douglass felt sure, will be known by future generations "as the age of anti-slavery literature . . . when a picture of a negro on the cover was a help to the sale of a book."[32]

Sympathies for the Slave

It was remarkable, Frederick Douglass observed in 1855, and perhaps "almost absurd to say it, considering the use that has been made of them, that we have allies in the Ethiopian songs; those songs that constitute our national music, and without which we would have no national music. They are heart songs, and finest feelings of human nature are expressed in them." Douglass acknowledged that "'Lucy Neal,' 'My Old Kentucky Home,' and 'Uncle Ned,' can make the heart sad as well as merry, and can call forth a tear as well as a smile."

As recently as 1848, Douglass himself had excoriated "the filthy scum of white society, who have stolen from us a complexion denied to them by nature, in which to make money, and pander to the corrupt taste of their white fellow-citizens." But seven years later, Douglass believed the songs "waken the sympathies for the slave, in which anti-slavery principles take root, grow and flourish."[33]

Stephen Foster played an unlikely role in the creation of American music that promised to "waken sympathies for the slave." Born on the day Thomas Jefferson and John Adams died—the Fourth of July 1826—Foster had a hard childhood. His father, once prosperous and important, struggled with drink and lawsuits. The boy grew up in boardinghouses and the homes of relatives, finding comfort in the music and singing of his older sisters. At nine years old, Foster joined local boys to perform "Zip Coon," "Jump Jim Crow," and other early blackface songs in their Pennsylvania community. Foster's "performance of these was so inimitable and true to nature," recalled a local minister, that "he was greeted with uproarious applause, and called back again and again every night the company gave an entertainment, which was three times a week."[34]

Foster studied a comic songbook, *The Parlor Companion*, which printed the words and music for blackface tunes among other kinds of music. The book provided company when he was moved to yet another group of relatives in a town on the Pennsylvania and New York border. Along the way, he heard the famous Tyrolese Minstrels, who inspired both the Virginia Minstrels and the Hutchinson Family abolitionist singers.

It was good that Foster had musical talent, for he struggled in school. He enjoyed being alone to practice his music, a relative reported to his mother, "for which he possesses a strange talent." In the winter of 1846 and 1847, Stephen moved to Cincinnati and lived in a boardinghouse while he worked as a bookkeeper. Cincinnati was booming, its population doubling in the 1840s, with tens of thousands of immigrants among three thousand Black people. Foster heard more music than ever before in his life. The Ohio River carried the diversity of the nation, with European immigrants teaching opera and piano, Black people playing music and performing dances for their own entertainment, and Irish men and women singing songs from their homeland.

As Foster worked in his office, the dreamy young man of twenty watched steamboats connecting the East, West, and South of the United States. Sometime in 1847 he wrote a song he called "Oh! Susanna." He began in imagined Black dialect: "I come from Alabama / With my Banjo on my knee / I'se gwine to Lou'siana / My true lub for to see." The "Banjo on my knee" signaled that the song was a performance by a minstrel performer, a white man in blackface, and so nothing that followed should be taken literally. The geography of the song made cruel sense in that Black people were indeed "going" from Alabama to Louisiana, where sugar plantations consumed enslaved workers from older plantation districts.

The next words advertised the song's absurdity: "It rain'd all night de day I left, / De webber it was dry; / The sun so hot I froze to def / Susanna dont you cry." Such humor was reminiscent of the Davy Crockett almanacs, clever in its hyperbole and intentional in its nonsense. Minstrels in blackface often spoke and sang in this way, hiding wit and sarcastic commentary behind buffoonery.

"Oh! Susanna" made no money for Stephen Foster in 1848, but it became enormously popular when it made its way to New York City that same year, performed onstage by Christy's Minstrels. Foster's music had become well-known even in California. "I wonder if I am putting it too strongly to say that we American people never really got together until now?" one man noted in his diary in California. The main commonality was their love for "negro melodies." Though the songs were not "real 'darkey' music exactly," the diarist admitted, the "plantation songs, as written, for instance, by Stephen Foster, are the most popular of songs among us." Miners added "some gold dust for to see" as a new verse for "Oh! Susanna."

Foster moved to New York to try to make a living with his music, composing several of his most popular songs in 1850 and

1851. "Camptown Races," also known as the song with "doo-dah" as its refrain, became extremely popular. But Foster longed to set aside "Ethiopian" tunes to write parlor songs. While rousing tunes such as "Oh! Susanna" and "Camptown Races" were often sung by groups of men in public settings, parlor songs were intended to be sung by one or two women in private. Unfortunately, Foster made only $31 from his parlor songs in the early 1850s, while he still garnered $319 from his blackface songs. He searched for a way to convey touching sentiments in the popular language of minstrelsy.[35]

Uncle Tom's Cabin offered a way forward. Foster's "My Old Kentucky Home" was inspired by Tom's memories of his cabin in Kentucky after he had been sold south. Stage productions of *Uncle Tom's Cabin* promptly incorporated Foster's new song into their productions, without credit or payment. Foster's avoidance of Black dialect and any direct mention of Tom, however, allowed white people to imagine that the song was about them. Instead of a slave driver knocking at the cabin door, it was merely "hard times."[36]

Stephen Foster did not set out to soften white northern attitudes toward Black people, but it was indeed possible that, as Frederick Douglass said, Foster's music brought that softening nevertheless. He put human emotions of longing, love, and loneliness in the mouths of imaginary Black people. Foster's brother later observed that in Stephen's songs "ridicule began to merge into sympathy. Unknown to himself, he opened the way to the hearts of the people, which led to actual interest in the black man."

The first American music composed for salons and concert halls advertised its debt to Black music. Louis Moreau Gottschalk grew up in New Orleans in the 1830s and 1840s, the son of a Jewish father from London and a young French-speaking white woman from Saint-Domingue. Recognized as a prodigy early in his life, Gottschalk was sent at the age of twelve to Paris to develop his skills. There, he came to know Frédéric Chopin and other leading musicians, who admired Gottschalk's skill at the piano. As he grew to compose his own music in his late teens, Gottschalk drew upon themes he had heard in New Orleans from the elderly Black woman who cared for him and from the city's street corners, evoking drums and songs sung by Black voices. He subtitled one composition "Song of the Blacks." European audiences loved the exotic sounds "Gottschalk of Louisiana" introduced to the repertoire dominated by Beethoven and Mozart.

Gottschalk returned to the United States in 1853. To prove his love of the land he had left, Gottschalk devised crowd-pleasing pieces, including a symphony that combined Stephen Foster's "Oh! Susanna," "Old Folks at Home," and "My Old Kentucky Home." During his tour of America, Gottschalk composed a piano piece, "The Banjo," that rang with the rhythms and textures of the increasingly ubiquitous instrument. In New Orleans, a crowd of thousands welcomed Gottschalk at ten concerts, presenting him with bouquets, medals, and rings. Gottschalk traveled throughout the Caribbean and South America to universal praise. Though he died in Buenos Aires at the age of forty, Gottschalk's legacy endured, later echoing in ragtime and jazz.[37]

Some white painters and illustrators also portrayed Black people with sensitivity in the 1850s. Lilly Martin Spencer trained in Cincinnati as a young woman in the 1840s before moving to New York. She sketched scenes from literature but found that paintings of babies and young mothers appealed to a broader audience. Converted into lithographs, the paintings spread widely. While Spencer herself did not profit from their distribution to "every corner of this continent," as one observer noted, she profited from the sale of the original painting and won offers for more.

Spencer created portraits of Black children that conveyed their individuality. A painting of a young Black girl captured her laughter as she played dress-up, peering through a homemade lorgnon. While such settings and props could easily have slipped into familiar ridicule of Black people pretending to a sophistication they did not comprehend, the warm smile of the little girl invited recognition of the common fantasies of childhood. The object of the fun was adult women who continued to play dress-up. Lithographs of Spencer's painting, *The Height of Fashion*, found their way into homes around the country.[38]

Even more popular were the lithographs produced by William Sidney Mount, an artist from Long Island. Mount established himself in the 1830s and 1840s as the first and most popular American genre painter, depicting country dances, courting, horse trading, and cider making, many of them subtle political parables appreciated by a sophisticated New York City clientele who had grown up in the country themselves. Mount, like his patrons, knew formerly enslaved people on Long Island and admired those who had been kind to him as a boy.

Invited by a patron to create a scene that recalled a warm relationship between a white youngster and an older Black person, Mount painted *Eel Spearing at Setauket*. There, a small white boy (modeled by the patron's nephew) intently steadies a boat as a dignified middle-aged Black woman stands at the bow and prepares to spear an eel in the shallow clear water. The luminous effect created an accomplished painting as well as a rare portrayal of friendship crossing lines of race, gender, and age.[39]

Mount achieved greater success with a painting and lithograph from 1847, *The Power of Music*. Mount featured an older Black man, dressed in patched work clothes, having momentarily set aside his axe to listen to a young white man in a barn playing his violin for two admiring older friends. The Black man pauses outside, unseen, smiling slightly, perhaps enjoying the skills of a former student. Such a man in Mount's youth, Anthony Hannibal Clapp, was a fine violinist, much admired by Mount's family, and had perhaps taught Mount to play. Critics understood what Mount had accomplished in the painting: "His humor is of that rich and legitimate quality which cultivates the love of our kind, and awakens an interest in all that has come from our Maker's hand. It inclines us to cast away any contempt which may lurk in our minds for those in manner or circumstances not exactly to our taste."[40]

In the late 1850s, Mount was commissioned to produce paintings for two lithographs, to be marketed in Europe as well as the United States, featuring Black men playing, stereotypically, a banjo and bones. Mount recruited models from men he knew, capturing their unique identities, style, dignity, and skill. The players dressed a bit flamboyantly, as traveling musicians might, and smiled with self-confidence and pride. The young man in *The Banjo Player*—modeled on George Freeman of Long Island— played an instrument of recent style and with appropriate positioning of his hands. The older man, in clothing still stylish if a bit more worn, conveyed a sense of the dexterity required to play complex rhythms on the bones, suitable for dancing without other accompaniment. Lithographs of the paintings spread widely in the United States.[41]

A younger white artist established himself with similar themes. Eastman Johnson had studied in Düsseldorf to become a history painter. He worked with an American who lived there, Emanuel Leutze, who painted *Washington Crossing the Delaware* in 1851, a painting in high European style that some Americans loved but that others found ill-suited for democratic tastes. Johnson, well-traveled in Europe and familiar with the latest styles, saw that leading European painters often painted poor and marginal people with sympathy. Johnson proved adept in that work and decided to pursue genre painting instead of history painting. Returning to the United States in the late 1850s, Johnson found suitable American subjects in a dilapidated kitchen at Mount Vernon and in an alley behind his family's home in Washington.[42]

Johnson painted a complex scene in a work he called *Negro Life at the South*, disguising its origins in the nation's capital. (A subsequent purchaser of the painting would later change the title to *Old Kentucky Home*, named after Foster's song.) Like Mount, Johnson placed a Black musician at the center of the composition; a handsome banjo player entertains two boys, one listening intently and another dancing with his mother. A couple courts, the woman of light skin tone listening to a darker suitor; upstairs, a woman brings her baby outside to enjoy the music. Two girls notice a young white woman entering the scene, apparently admiring what she hears. The setting is old and decaying, but the scene is vibrant with human vitality and connection.[43]

Johnson's humane approach was striking. Despite the impoverished setting, one reviewer observed, the scene offered a valuable evocation of "human beings in new and vivid aspects." People purchased many lithographs and photographs of the painting. Art could allow people, at least for a moment, to glimpse the humanity of Black people at a time when their humanity was callously denied.[44]

Poetry, too, played an important role in the campaign against slavery, for poems' form and figurative language were charged with emotional meaning for nineteenth-century audiences. A young Black woman, Frances Ellen Watkins, sold twelve thousand copies of her book of poems in the late 1850s as she spoke across the North to raise money for the Underground Railroad. Her poem of 1858, "Bury Me in a Free Land," spoke with the voice of a woman begging not to be buried where slavery ruled:

I could not rest if I heard the tread / Of a coffle gang to
    shambles led,
And the mother's shriek of wild despair / Rise like a curse
    on the trembling air

I could not sleep if I saw the lash / Drinking her blood at
    each fearful gash,
And I saw her babes torn from her breast / Like trembling
    doves from their parent nest.

Listening to Watkins, one audience member wrote, "There
swept over me, in a chill wave of horror, the realization that this
noble woman . . . might have been sold on the auction-block, to
the highest bidder." Female writers and speakers such as Watkins evoked sympathies for the slave in ways that men could not,
Black people in ways white people could not, poetry in ways prose
could not.[45]

As Frederick Douglass saw, the narratives, lectures, novels,
plays, fairs, toys, editorials, petition campaigns, poems, and political efforts of the antislavery movement—even songs in dialect—
exerted a cumulative effect on white northerners. The question
looming in the 1850s was whether such sympathy for the slave
could be translated into political power and moral resolve.[46]

Chapter Nine

CULMINATIONS

1855–1860

Popular America

As the American publishing industry grew stronger and more sophisticated in the late 1850s, authors reached readers who would not have purchased American books before. The most popular books of the decade had nothing to do with the political conflict that filled the front pages of newspapers. Americans read, instead, about humbug, mythical Indians, and sarcastic and successful women.

P. T. Barnum wrote *Barnum's Own Story* to escape financial collapse. He succeeded, selling more than 160,000 copies of his autobiography in the United States in 1855. People expected exaggeration if not outright lying from Barnum, and they found it as he told of his early adventures with the Feejee Mermaid and other frauds. The respectable *New York Herald* simply noted that "it would be hard to find a more disgusting mess of trash, and the book seems to have been published to show to what vile uses printers' ink may be put." Another reviewer spoke with equal hyperbole to the contrary: Barnum's book was, quite simply, "the most readable work ever published."

Americans read in *Barnum's Own Story* of the salesmanship, enterprise, novelty, and self-promotion in which America excelled. They were alternately appalled and fascinated. Barnum revealed the deceit and humbug of his early years to prove that he had changed into a philanthropic, abstemious, high-minded man. Readers, predictably, focused on Barnum's admissions of guilt rather than on his conversion. Barnum, his feelings hurt, deposited his royalties and launched a profitable tour of England.[1]

Americans proved eager to read, too, an idealized poem about the sad but inevitable disappearance of the American Indian. Henry Wadsworth Longfellow, the nation's most popular poet, beloved both for his short poems and for his long verse narrative *Evangeline*, pored over a four-volume compilation of miscellaneous information about American Indians gathered by Henry R. Schoolcraft. Longfellow settled upon the name Hiawatha for its melodious sound. He adopted the national epic of Finland—*Kalevala*—for its drum-like meter. From a photograph, he selected the scenic falls of Minnehaha in Minnesota for a setting. Longfellow larded his pages with footnotes to prove its supposed authenticity. Though parodied for its easily mimicked rhythm and stilted language, the poem remained popular for generations. *The Song of Hiawatha* inspired painters, sculptors, and composers as well as manufacturers of chewing tobacco, soap, and other wares who looked for an authentic American aura for their product.[2]

The most popular female writer of the mid-1850s defied the portrayal of women as helpless and weak, portrayals that often had little to do with the aspirations and accomplishments of actual women. Sara Payson Willis had married happily and bore three daughters. In 1845, however, her husband and one of her children died of typhoid. At the age of thirty-four, pressured by her parents and siblings, Willis reluctantly married a man with whom she grew increasingly miserable. She divorced him. Without support from her family, Willis wrote light articles for a small weekly Boston paper to sustain herself and her children.

Willis's humorous pieces met instant success as they were reprinted by other papers around the country and in England. With Fanny Fern as her pen name, Willis toyed with the conventions of sentimentality and parodied self-absorbed husbands. In one piece, she ridiculed young wives who cried too easily, advising them to avoid tears by steering clear of "smoky chimneys, and old coats, and young babies!" In any case, "you miserable little whimperer, what have you to cry for? A-i-n-t y-o-u m-a-r-r-i-e-d? Isn't that the summum bonum—the height of feminine ambition?" Fern was sympathetic to women but did not pander. Nathaniel Hawthorne admired Fern, who "writes as if the devil was in her." In fact, he told his publisher, "If you meet her, I wish you would let her know how much I admire her."[3]

Fern wrote a barely disguised autobiography that told the story of a desperate young widow who transformed herself into a successful writer. *Ruth Hall: A Domestic Tale of the Present Time* appeared in 1854. The novel, written in a casual and innovative style, ridiculed well-known men, including the author's brother, who had refused to help the struggling writer. Fanny Fern remained one of the most popular, and prosperous, columnists in the United States for decades, a favorite of men and women alike.[4]

The painter Lilly Spencer also parodied images of genteel womanhood. Spencer's work took viewers into kitchens and nurseries, where male artists seldom ventured, to meet a laughing woman reaching out a flour-covered hand to offer a handshake or a flirtatious young woman warning, invitingly, that if the viewer kisses her he will be kissing the molasses she had tasted in her cooking. Spencer made fun of a young husband (modeled on her own) sent out for shopping, failing publicly in his efforts to keep fish, eggs, and a plucked chicken in his basket. Lithographs and hand-colored photographs of Spencer's work decorated homes across the country.[5]

Images, in fact, proliferated wherever Americans looked in the 1850s. A single photograph could produce hundreds of thousands of lithographs. Illustrated newspapers employed teams of engravers to turn photographs into publishable images overnight. Weekly magazines presented elaborate pictorial spreads from around the country and the world. Bibles and gift books assumed ever more ornate forms, inside and out.

The United States perfected daguerreotypes to their highest form, winning every prize at the Great Exhibition in London's Crystal Palace in 1851, a year when three million daguerreotypes were taken in America. The length of exposure for a daguerreotype declined from an excruciating five minutes to two or three seconds, so that even children might be included, and the price of an image fell from five dollars to twenty-five cents. But the unique beauty of a daguerreotype, shimmering with silver and copper, could not compete in cost or convenience with a glass-plate negative printed on inexpensive and lightweight paper, a format that became ever more popular. Stereoscopes, using paper images, created a novel sensation, offering an unprecedented three-dimensional effect through an inexpensive optical device suitable for parlor use.

The moving panorama, with scenes of characters and places passing on long rolls of canvas, attained great popularity in the 1850s. Americans played leading roles in developing this novel combination of entertainment and instruction, attended by millions in Britain and Europe and across the United States. Panoramas, sometimes accompanied by sound effects, depicted the path of the Mississippi River and the adventures of whaling voyages in the South Pacific. The *Seven Mile Mirror!* took viewers across two thousand miles of the Great Lakes on seven miles of canvas. A *Moving Panorama of the Drunkard*, accompanied by a chorus of singers, told a "thrilling, mirthful, sad, moral, and instructive" story of intemperance. A *Grand Panorama of American Slavery* ended each presentation with Henry "Box" Brown emerging from the crate in which he had escaped bondage.[6]

Two Black artists in Cincinnati collaborated on a panorama of America that wove Black people into the fabric of the nation's history: *Ball's Splendid Mammoth Pictorial Tour of the United States, Comprising Views of the African Slave Trade; of Northern and Southern Cities; of Cotton and Sugar Plantations; of the Mississippi, Ohio and Susquehanna Rivers, Niagara Falls, & C.* Born free in Virginia, J. P. Ball had moved to Cincinnati as a young man and established the largest daguerreotype studio in the West, employing nine photographers so that clients would not have to wait to have their portraits taken. For his panorama, Ball proudly advertised that it had been "painted by Negroes." Its fifty-three paintings reached floor to ceiling and stretched six hundred yards. It reached large audiences in Cincinnati and Boston, a celebration of Black accomplishment even as it exposed audiences to the geography of slavery.[7]

Ball employed the Black artist Robert Duncanson, born free in 1823, to paint backgrounds and tint the images of his daguerreotypes. Duncanson had begun his career as a housepainter with his family in Michigan, but taught himself to paint portraits by copying prints. He moved to Cincinnati for the greater opportunities for work despite the limitations for Black people in the border city. Duncanson developed an interest in landscape painting, inspired by the Hudson River School.[8]

In 1851, Duncanson won a valuable commission from Nicholas Longworth, a wealthy horticulturalist opposed to slavery. Longworth hired Duncanson to paint eight landscape murals—each nine feet by six and a half feet—for the entryway to his mansion, Belmont House. The murals evoked the Ohio landscape in ways both literal and imaginative.[9]

After completing his murals, Duncanson, like American artists and antislavery advocates before him, traveled to England and Europe to improve his skills and to win new patrons. Longworth supplied a letter of introduction to Hiram Powers, the Cincinnati sculptor who had won international fame with the *Greek Slave* a few years before. Duncanson met with great success in Britain, where the press praised, and aristocrats purchased, his pictures. Duncanson enjoyed the freedom he later found in Canada, where he influenced other painters. He would return to the United States when slavery no longer dominated the landscape.

Among the most popular traveling panoramas were those of the American West, composed from daguerreotypes, sketches, and paintings. Moving panoramas took visitors into Indian Nations, traversed the Overland Trail, and introduced the exotic land of California. Thrilling scenery of mountains and rock formations alternated with images of the "horrors of the desert," where, the narrator intoned, viewers witnessed "broken wagons, dying animals, and men feeding on their carcasses, groaning in the agonies of despair and death." The *Pantoscope of California* met with "triumphant success." When it arrived in Boston, excursion parties on railroads came from distant towns to see the spectacle.[10]

Artist Thomas Ayres produced sketches and paintings of the Yosemite Valley drawn soon after white Americans found the site in the 1850s. His work filled the magazines and the imaginations of people in the East, and tourism to the valley began almost immediately. In the Sierra mountains of California, two men stripped the bark from a giant sequoia to display in American cities and then in London. Doing so, they proved how magnificent and ancient the forests of the West were, and how they would be exploited.[11]

Herman Melville viewed the profusion of word and image with

bitter insight. Trying to make a living with his writing, Melville adapted to the world of popular magazines. He published taut and engaging stories in the ambitious new *Putnam's Monthly Magazine of American Literature, Science, and Art*, which was devoted to American writers and whose editor admired Melville's complex stories of miscommunication and deception. "Bartleby, the Scrivener" depicted an urban world of offices and paper, of bosses and clerks, with dark humor and an unreliable narrator. "Benito Cereno" dramatized the confusion, even inability, of white people who attempted to understand Black slavery. The collection of stories that Melville gathered from that work into *The Piazza Tales* won warm reviews for the "peculiar richness of language, descriptive vitality, and splendidly sombre imagination which are the author's characteristics." Some noted the similarity to the stories of Edgar Allan Poe. Book buyers, though, were not interested in collected magazine articles and the book failed to meet the costs of publication.[12]

Melville imagined a novel that moved with the pace of magazine sketches. He published *The Confidence-Man: His Masquerade*, on April Fool's Day in 1857. There, Melville portrayed conversations on a Mississippi River steamboat, each a scene of deceit in one form or another. The confidence man seeks to win "trust" by tailoring his appearance and his pitch to the self-deceptions of each of the many marks on board. Melville used the strange book to depict familiar characters in American life: "fellows who, whether in stocks, politics, breadstuffs, morals, metaphysics, religion—be it what it may" seek advantage by deceiving voters, customers, converts, or readers. Most reviewers declared themselves unamused and unedified. It would be Melville's last novel.[13]

Melville's wealthy father-in-law funded a trip to the Holy Land in hopes it would revive the author's spirits after the many literary experiments and disappointments of the 1850s. Nathaniel

Hawthorne, finally enjoying the political sinecure from the Democrats for which he had longed, welcomed Melville in Liverpool. There, the old friend was struck by Melville's despondency. "He can neither believe, nor be comfortable in his unbelief; and he is too honest and courageous not to try to do one or the other," Hawthorne wrote sympathetically. Melville, just turning forty in 1859, continued to write for an audience that would not appear in his lifetime, until a new century discovered Ishmael, Bartleby, and Cereno.[14]

Mines and Wells

The American economy, after dramatic developments and shocking downturns over the preceding half century, began to cohere and accelerate in the 1850s. Technologies long in the making finally matured. The railroad and the telegraph, heavily promoted for decades, became true systems in the 1850s, connecting across great distances and creating new economic regions. The sewing machine, the object of endless battles over patents and credit for invention, finally gained a foothold after 1852, when I. M. Singer & Company employed women to demonstrate its practicality in the home. McCormick's reaper, though imagined in Virginia in the 1830s, found rapid adoption on the prairies of the Midwest in the 1850s, after railroads and installment credit made it widely accessible. Levi Strauss, a young Jewish immigrant born in Bavaria, represented his family's New York–based mercantile business in San Francisco, alert to opportunities in rugged work clothing, as well as the latest styles in hats and scarves.[15]

A fundamental transition in the American economy, and in American life, arrived in the 1850s when fossil fuels came to the fore. Individuals and industries sought more efficient, hotter-burning fuels than the wood they had consumed in voracious amounts for the preceding two hundred years. The cities of the East had long used soft bituminous coal for gas light systems and for home heating. Plentiful and easy to ignite, bituminous coal was also smoky and sooty. Pittsburgh, without adequate water-power, had turned to nearby coal early in its history. "The city is darkened with smoke," Horace Mann observed in 1840; "the air is full of it, the sun is obscured by it." The nation's use of bituminous coal tripled between 1840 and 1850, and then doubled again in the 1850s.[16]

People knew that the hard anthracite coal of Pennsylvania would generate far more heat for railroads, steamboats, and factories than bituminous coal if methods could be devised to release and contain that energy. Railroad companies found ways to burn anthracite without melting grates and other equipment, enabling ever more powerful engines. More than half of the steamboats plying American waters burned the fuel. The use of anthracite grew even faster than bituminous, the three million tons delivered in 1850 growing to over eight million by 1860. The spread of canals throughout the North over the preceding quarter-century made it possible to transport the heavy mineral from remote mines to cities and factories. Sealed stoves replaced open hearths in the 1850s, when more than nine in ten homes used coal. Coal became cheaper than wood in New York and Philadelphia.[17]

Iron production soared along with the coal that powered its creation, from 150,000 tons in 1847 to more than 500,000 tons in 1860. To have produced that much iron with wood would have required more than three and a half million acres of timberland. And coal was necessary to mine coal: the steam engines that drained mines and ventilated shafts in the mines ran on the fuel.

The coal regime concentrated heavily in the Northeast, especially Pennsylvania. The South, by contrast, had no great need for coal nor access to it except for the iron furnaces of Virginia. The South's homes did not require as much heat as those in the North and the region's primary industry, cotton agriculture, had little need for steam power. The enslaved population of the South was tragically suited as the source of energy of the region. While the South built railroads at a rapid rate in the 1850s, and while southern cities and towns grew and turned to gaslight, the region did not need, nor benefit from, the boatloads of coal that increasingly powered the Northeast.[18]

Southern forests, however, became newly important as a source of energy as American whaling ships leaving New Bedford and Nantucket could not meet the demand for oil. Voyages stretched ever longer in time and distance as ships hunted whales beyond their familiar haunts. Sailors deserted more frequently, and fewer young men rushed to sign on. As the price of whale oil increased, people looked for other ways to light their homes and businesses.

Camphene, a mixture of spirits of turpentine and distilled alcohol, became the most popular source of light. Also called "burning fluid" or "spirit gas," the product cost less than half the price of whale oil and burned brighter and left less residue than the oil "obtained by perilous adventure on the stormy sea with monsters of the deep." But camphene was notoriously volatile and easily spilled as people filled or carried lamps. The "progress of the age, and the ingenuity of man, have introduced no engines of destruction so potent as camphene," one editorial warned. Articles about fires and disfigurement caused by camphene filled newspapers, feeding outrage: "When will people cease to use this infernal stuff?" one editor demanded to know.[19]

The working poor had no choice but to use the "infernal stuff." The hundreds of clothing businesses established in New York in the 1840s shifted production of finished clothing from skilled male tailors to piecework by seamstresses in their own homes.

Tens of thousands of women and children, not paid enough to live on, worked by the light of camphene lamps into the night. Laboring "in the upper story of some poor, ill-constructed, unventilated house in a filthy street," women and their daughters gathered around the lamps, producing shirts for four cents each—less than half what a man earned.

As the demand for camphene grew, so did slavery in the piney woods of the South. The sandy and swampy soil of eastern North Carolina, its pine trees attesting to its worthlessness for farming, had been bypassed as unprofitable for generations. The sudden demand for camphene, however, induced slaveholders to purchase the cheap land and send young enslaved men into remote forests to slash the pines to produce turpentine. The process required hard tasks stretched over a year. The turn to camphene demonstrated the continuing interdependence of northern development and southern slavery.

The decline of whale oil had another consequence: the development of a new lubricant and fuel, petroleum. The Senecas of Pennsylvania had long used the oil oozing from the ground to anoint their bodies. Later, entrepreneurs marketed petroleum in patent medicines. As coal producers became annoyed by the seepage of the oil into their mines, some set out to find a more profitable use for petroleum. In 1854, they sent a sample to the chemist Benjamin Silliman of Yale University to determine its qualities. He reported that "the lamp burning this fuel gave as much light as any which they had seen, that the oil was spent more economically, and the uniformity of the light was greater than in Camphene, burning for twelve hours without a sensible diminution, and without smoke."

Investors sent Edwin Drake to Oil Creek in Pennsylvania to try a novel approach: drilling a hole to recover petroleum intentionally. Drake met with ridicule and resistance. After several failed attempts, investors lost heart and wrote Drake to tell him to cease the efforts. The letter took so long to reach the remote site, however, that it arrived after Drake and his workers finally succeeded in capturing oil from a well in 1859. By the next year, the Titusville well was producing 450,000 gallons of oil, reaching 3 million gallons two years later.[20]

Song of America

Out of the tumult and jostling of the early 1850s, an American poet emerged to capture America in the making. He invented a form of startling verse capacious enough for the challenge.

In Concord, on the Fourth of July 1855, Ralph Waldo Emerson and his wife, Lydian, draped their front gate in black to mourn the political state of the nation in the era of the Kansas-Nebraska Act. Yet a package arrived that day, carrying a slim book that celebrated the new nation. Titled *Leaves of Grass*, the volume bore no author's name. The ornate cover, green with raised golden letters sprouting roots and tendrils, enclosed wide pages carrying long, unrhymed lines. Inside, an engraving from a daguerreotype portrayed an image of the author as unlikely as the book's cover and title. A bearded young man looked intently at the reader, his hat tipped to one side, his shirt unbuttoned at the collar, one hand on his hip and another in his pocket.[21]

Emerson looked into the unbidden book and then read through it again. Unsure how to describe *Leaves of Grass* when he shared it with friends, he praised it as "the best piece of American Buddhism that anyone has had strength to write, American to the bone." He called it "a remarkable mixture of the *Bhagavad Gita* and the *New York Herald*." Emerson wrote the author, Walt Whitman, a letter of praise, congratulating him on his great accomplishment.

Whitman's book met a call Emerson himself had made more than a decade before in a ringing essay, "The Poet." Emerson's call was an invitation for a new voice: "Our log-rolling, our stumps and their politics, our fisheries, our Negroes, and Indians, our boasts, and our repudiations, the wrath of rogues, and the pusillanimity of honest men, the Northern trade, the Southern planting, the Western clearing, Oregon and Texas, are yet unsung."[22]

In New York in 1848, Walt Whitman heard Emerson repeat his call for a poet worthy of American scenes. Whitman read everything he could find by Emerson during his lunch breaks as he framed houses in the early 1850s in Brooklyn. Whitman would remember that he had been "simmering, simmering" and then "Emerson brought him to a boil." Before 1855, Whitman had been many things—a journalist, an editor, a writer of a temperance novel, a conventional poet, a carpenter, a devotee of mesmerism and phrenology, a storekeeper, a devoted brother and son—but the thirty-six-year-old man had not distinguished himself in any calling. He had been a strong and outspoken Democrat, but fell away from the party and the journalistic patronage it offered. He knew Brooklyn, Long Island, and Manhattan intimately, but took only one trip, to New Orleans, where he worked for three months before being fired. Whitman loafed, as he bragged, observing the cacophonous city of New York. He loved opera and theater. He met young men on his long, winding walks, craving their friendship and embrace.[23]

Amid this watching, listening, and reading, Whitman invented a form suited for the poem that was America. Whitman, who paid to have his book published and set its type himself, recognized the great gift Emerson had bestowed with his letter of congratulation. Whitman immediately published Emerson's endorsement, without asking permission, and prepared an expanded edition of *Leaves of Grass* that would bear an excerpt of Emerson's endorsement printed in gilded letters on the spine. Emerson, tolerant of the public use of his private endorsement, shared the book with his friends. Thoreau admired the volume and carried it around Concord in defiance of anyone who might be disturbed by its boldness.

The title announced the deep democratic purposes of the poems: leaves of grass, each distinct and yet one no better than any other. Whitman put himself above no one, among everyone: "If you want me again look for me under your boot-soles." And if

> Missing me in one place search another,
> I stop some where waiting for you.

The grass, he "guesses," is a "uniform hieroglyphic," that people were like grass: "Sprouting alike in broad zones and narrow zones / Growing among black folks as among white." Whitman named the people who are essentially one and the same despite their names: "Kanuk, Tuckahoe, Congressman, Cuff, I give them the same. I receive them the same." The Canadian, the Virginia planter, the politician, the enslaved man—all are grass and alike in their individuality.

Whitman wrote poetry for everyone, of everyone. There was no formal scheme to bind the words, no arcane or foreign vocabulary, no allusions to classical works that only the educated would know. He composed lists, in no descending or ascending order. To read Whitman was to walk on the streets and docks of New York in the 1850s, to see without judging, to celebrate oneself as a way of celebrating all selves. Sex was capacious for Whitman, with love for men and women, for touch as well as devotion, for longing as well as fulfillment. He accepted it all, grateful for it all.

Whitman welcomed and did not judge religion: "I hear and

behold God in every object, yet I understand God not in the least." Whitman worshipped the everyday: "I see something of God each hour of the twenty-four, and each moment then, / In the faces of men and women I see God, and in my own face in the glass; / I find letters from God dropped in the street, and every one is signed by God's name, / And I leave them where they are, for I know that others will punctually come forever and ever."

In the second edition of his book, published in 1856 and longer than the first, Whitman connected the past, present, and future in a poem that would become known as "Crossing Brooklyn Ferry": "I am with you, you men and women of a generation, or ever so many generations hence." Looking centuries ahead, Whitman assured the reader to follow many years later: "Just as you feel when you look on the river and sky, so I felt." Whitman acknowledged that he, like others, and perhaps the reader, was "wayward, vain, greedy, shallow, sly, cowardly, malignant; the wolf, the snake, the hog, not wanting in me." Americans were not perfect, for humans were not perfect. And yet they were divine for all their shortcomings.

The heartiest welcome to *Leaves of Grass* came from Fanny Fern, another self-made author. The "world needed" a poet such as Whitman, she announced, "enamored of *women* not *ladies, men* not *gentlemen*." The world required "a man who dared speak out his strong, honest thoughts, in the face of pusillanimous, toady-ing, republican aristocracy; dictionary-men, hypocrites, cliques and creeds; it needed a large-hearted, untainted, self-reliant, fear-less son of the Stars and Stripes."

Fern admired Whitman's resistance to a publisher who, she slyly remarked, would have forced the poet's lines "to be arranged, re-arranged and disarranged to his circumscribed liking, till they hung limp, tame, spiritless, and scentless." She was "not unaware that the charge of coarseness and sensuality, has been affixed" to Whitman's writing, but Fern defied the critics who would "shroud the eyes of the nursing babe lest it should see its mother's breast." Fern quoted *Leaves of Grass* at length and offered an invitation to Mr. Whitman: "Please accept the cordial grasp of a woman's hand."[24]

Most reviewers would not extend their hand. A critic in *Frank Leslie's Illustrated Newspaper* announced that "we have upon our table (and shall put into the fire)" a copy of *Leaves of Grass*. "We shall not aid in extending the sale of this intensely vulgar, nay, absolutely beastly book, by telling our readers where it may be purchased." The review castigated Emerson for his endorsement of such a book and archly encouraged a grand jury to investigate Whitman to see if his poetry constituted a crime. Whitman longed to be loved by the America he celebrated. But he was not. Whitman disappeared from view, spending his nights in a bohemian tavern, spending his days writing hymns to America that America ignored.[25]

Life in the Woods and the World

Henry David Thoreau set the manuscript on Walden aside for more than two years before he returned to its revision and expansion. The book grew more layered and allusive, filled with moral examples from the Greeks and Buddhists as well as from apparently mundane forms of nature, creating a narrative at once scientific and lyrical, practical and mystical.

Thoreau rejected the American credo of striving, conformity, materialism, and possession, lives of "quiet desperation" he discovered in others. Amid "this restless, nervous, bustling, trivial Nineteenth Century," Thoreau urged readers to simplify their lives, to find that in quiet and acceptance "the laws of the universe will appear less complex, and solitude will not be solitude, nor poverty poverty, nor weakness weakness." Thoreau reassured his readers that "if a man does not keep pace with his companions, perhaps it is because he hears a different drummer."

Thoreau explored his world through many dimensions. He carefully measured the great depths of Walden Pond and then played a flute in a boat on its surface as he fished at midnight. "A lake is the landscape's most beautiful and expressive feature," he wrote. "It is earth's eye; looking into which the beholder measures the depth of his own nature." "Sky water" reflected perfectly: "It is a mirror which no stone can crack, whose quicksilver will never wear off, whose gilding Nature continually repairs." Ponds "are too pure to have a market value; they contain no muck. How much more beautiful than our lives, how much more transparent than our characters, are they!"[26]

Thoreau tried out different parts of *Walden* on local audiences. They appreciated his sense of humor as well as the mocking and sometimes self-mocking tone of his adventures, at once earthy and visionary. He lived at Walden for two years, two months, and two days, but turned his narrative into the story of a single year, the seasons turning, the water thawing and freezing, crops ripening, birds migrating. His purpose was to see anew, to notice parts of life that seemed beneath notice. Nature for Thoreau was not a symbol, not a reflection of human need or spirituality, but the world itself. People stumbled through and disturbed that world without comprehending it and thus not comprehending themselves. *Walden* was an experiment to see what would happen if, instead of pushing through nature or pushing nature around, we paused before nature long enough to see it live and breathe, to see it change and die on its own terms.

Thoreau did grow a crop, and did till some of the poor soil at the pond. In that new field, Thoreau planted beans, an intentionally lowly crop, native to the region and grown by its Natives, and not much in demand despite its use in baked beans. Thoreau could not hope to make much money from beans, as his farming neighbors told him. Though the twelve bushels he produced ranked him fourth in the county in total production, Thoreau's yield was meager. The average Massachusetts farmer produced twenty bushels of beans from an acre; Thoreau, eight. In contrast to the heroic model of agriculture promoted by farming magazines and newspapers, Thoreau did not seek to tailor the soil to human use. He took from the hard land what it would naturally provide. After a year's experiment, he resolved not to raise beans for market again, but to see if virtues of "sincerity, truth, simplicity" might not grow instead, and with less "manurance."[27]

Walden, even with its iconoclasm, found warm reviews when it appeared in 1854. "Get the book," wrote one Boston paper. "You will like it. It is original and refreshing; and from the brain of a live man." In England, the famous novelist George Eliot praised Thoreau's "deep poetic sensibility" and the "sturdy sense mingled with his unworldliness"; another British reviewer called it "a brave book, one in a million, an honour to America, a gift to men," a book "worth reading and re-reading." Despite such words of endorsement and encouragement, the book failed to find an audience in America or abroad in the few years remaining in Thoreau's life. People did not know what to do with such a book. Thoreau demanded that people reconsider their lives in every dimension, a reconsideration few sought.[28]

Nature preoccupied other thoughtful Americans as well in the 1850s. Asher Durand, head of the influential National Academy of Design in New York, encouraged young painters to approach nature on its own terms. The best picture did not call attention to itself, Durand counseled, but "at once takes possession of you—draws you into it—you traverse it—breathe its atmosphere—feel its sunshine, and you repose in its shade without thinking of its design or execution, effect or color." Durand took delight in the precision required to represent nature honestly, of painting rocks and trees in shifting light. He painted in the open air, the first major American painter to do so.

A young poet living in Amherst, Massachusetts, evolved her own language of nature. Emily Dickinson wrote for herself, in poems she stitched together and then put away, written in words skeptical and wry, on a "slant," as she put it. Dickinson crafted hymns to nature that echoed the form but not the substance of what she had heard in church. In one of the first pieces she saved, Dickinson evoked a trinity from her meadow, the Holy Ghost as a light wind:

In the name of the Bee–
And of the Butterfly–
And of the Breeze–Amen!

For Dickinson, like Susan Fenimore Cooper, Henry David Thoreau, and Asher Durand, visions of America hovered in a natural world to be approached with humility, gratitude, and reverence.[29]

The reverence for nature asserted itself even in the midst of the nation's largest city. A bold endeavor in New York cultivated nature to elevate and instruct a crowded and anxious people. Plans for a central park had circulated for years even as the rocky land in the middle of the island of Manhattan harbored stinking industries, the shanties of otherwise homeless people, wandering livestock, and outposts of Black families seeking refuge.

Andrew Jackson Downing, the leading landscape architect in the nation, pressed the city to act in 1848. Downing, a handsome young man of charm and connection, had recently received a commission to remake the swampy area in Washington, DC, between the United States Capitol and the White House into a beautiful garden. He proposed to relieve the straight lines of Washington's streets with winding paths and groups of trees. Downing put forward a similar vision for New York, but his plans perished in 1852 when the steamboat carrying him from his home on the Hudson River, in a race with another boat, exploded and burned. Downing saved his wife and others but drowned as he tried to rescue another woman. His loss at the age of thirty-six, many feared, would stop the progress on New York's central park.[30]

Wealthy landowners mobilized to promote the city, raise their land values, reduce disease, and instill habits of decorum in the teeming population. They persuaded city leaders to set aside more than eight hundred acres of the most valuable land in the United States for the park. Its shape was awkward and unnatural—a large rectangle in the middle of Manhattan island—and filled with rock, but the project stirred many in the city. Labor leaders, eager for work for their men, joined in the call for the park, as did temperance reformers and public health advocates.

Frederick Law Olmsted, looking for new opportunities after finishing the second important but unprofitable volume of his southern travels, took a position to supervise preliminary work at the park while the city solicited proposals for the park's design. In the meantime, Olmsted established a winning partnership with Charles Vaux, who had worked with Andrew Jackson Downing, to propose a park that would orchestrate its elements into a tranquil and instructive tapestry, "a specimen of God's handiwork."[31]

Olmsted and Vaux oversaw an enterprise of enormous ambition and cost. Over a thousand workers with picks and wheelbarrows moved more than 2.5 million cubic yards of stone and earth, altering every part of the landscape to make the result appear natural. In the winter of 1858, while other parts of the place—named, with economy of language and imagination, Central Park—remained under construction, ice skating ponds opened and attracted a hundred thousand people each day from all backgrounds. In the summer of 1859, the Ramble opened, its maze of paths, outcroppings, and shrubs mimicking the pleasures of wilderness. Two million visitors came to the park that year, testifying to the American hunger for nature even if sculpted by man. Work on the park would continue for years to come.

The Throne of the Despot

The slave South's wealth, power, and global standing grew through the 1850s, and so did its arrogance and assertion. The South's politicians forged alliances with self-interested counterparts in the North and West to protect the interests of slavery, using the machinery and rhetoric of party politics to unify white men around the belief that the perpetual enslavement of Black people secured white freedom and prosperity. By the 1850s this formula had become an article of faith for millions of white Americans. Even as the price of enslaved people mounted and the percentage of white families who could claim ownership of a Black person declined to only a quarter of the white population in the South, white southerners increasingly identified themselves as a slaveholding people. No one who disagreed dared speak out in the South.

Americans expressed disgust with politics and politicians through the second half of the 1850s. The Whigs dissolved in hapless disarray. The Free Soil Party and the Know-Nothings failed to sustain early success. The Democrats bickered and splintered, the party's weak presidents occupying the White House but dividing the party. A new Republican Party struggled to combine nativists, aggressive evangelicals, practical businessmen, and abolitionist voters in opposition to the power and expansion of the slave South. Violence in Kansas and in Congress testified to the broken politics.[32]

Frederick Douglass's path across this treacherous terrain traced its fault lines and dangers. Celebrated and despised as the embodiment of Black accomplishment and determination,

Douglass moved cautiously. He had declared, unlike the Garrisonian wing of abolitionism, that politics offered the best way toward ending slavery, but the shifting ground of the late 1850s offered no clear path. With his book *My Bondage and My Freedom* selling thousands of copies in 1855 and large crowds coming to hear him wherever he spoke, Douglass had to determine the best way forward.

Douglass, unlike most Americans, welcomed the political chaos. "The disintegration of the once powerful political Parties is a cheering and significant sign of the times," he declared. "The throne of the despot is trembling to its deep foundations. There is a good time coming." He sought to exacerbate what he called the "irrepressible conflict" between the North and the South.[33]

Douglass distrusted the new Republican Party, for its leaders talked about the rights and opportunities of white people and ignored the aspirations of Black Americans. Republicans expected slavery to die of its own sickness and weakness once it was contained, perhaps in a hundred years. "Instead of walking straight up to the giant wrong and demanding its utter overthrow," Douglass warned, the Republicans "are talking of limiting it, circumscribing it, surrounding it with free States, and leaving it to die of inward decay."[34]

Douglass, on the other hand, recognized that Republican attacks on the "Slave Power" aided the abolition cause by weakening the South's hold on national dominance. He was willing to support Republicans "not merely for what they are but for what we have good reason to believe they will become." Douglass supported the Republican candidate for president in 1856, John C. Frémont, a political neophyte. Although Frémont lost his bid for the presidency, he won a third of the national vote and the electoral votes of every northern state except Pennsylvania, Illinois, and Indiana. If the Republicans could win one more key northern state in the next election, they would take the presidency. It was a remarkable debut for the new party.

The *Dred Scott* decision by the United States Supreme Court in 1857 demonstrated the arrogance of the Slave Power's control of the federal government. Chief Justice Roger B. Taney declared that Black people had no rights that white people were bound to honor and that the Missouri Compromise, blocking the spread of slavery in territories, was unconstitutional. Douglass and the Republicans warned that the court would issue another decision declaring that slavery was legal even in states that had abolished the institution. The United States, Republicans claimed, would become all-enslaved if it did not become all free.

In the wake of *Dred Scott*, Douglass began to consider violent resistance. He welcomed John Brown into his home for three weeks in early 1858. Brown had become famous for killing men he portrayed as advocates of slavery in Kansas and for his passionate speeches before abolitionist audiences in New England. At Douglass's home, Brown crafted an elaborate constitution for a new free state he planned to establish in western Virginia, after he freed enslaved people to join him. Brown had yet to raise the money he needed for any action, so he and Douglass went their separate ways. Douglass set off across the Midwest, speaking to audiences angry at the South and the Slave Power but uncertain of the way forward. John Brown followed another path.

In 1857, visiting Concord on a speaking tour, John Brown was introduced to Emerson, who, in turn, invited Brown to stay at his house. The invitation signaled Emerson's slow but profound transformation toward antislavery. Emerson had struggled over slavery for two decades. Early on, he had denounced organized reform of any sort. In his famous 1841 essay "Self-Reliance," Emerson counseled that rather than indulge an "incredible tenderness for black folk a thousand miles off" it would be better to "go love thy infant; love thy woodchopper: be good natured and modest." One event after another, however, changed Emerson's mind. In 1844 and 1845, he spoke, alongside Douglass, against the admission of the slave state of Texas and embraced abolition. The Fugitive Slave Law crisis of the early 1850s, especially the apostasy of Massachusetts senator Daniel Webster and the capture of fugitive enslaved man Anthony Burns in Boston in 1854, pushed Emerson into greater advocacy for Black people. These events carried the moral stench of slavery into Massachusetts itself.

Emerson used his literary and lecturing fame, ever mounting in the United States and Great Britain, to lend credibility and visibility to the abolitionist cause. In 1855, Emerson spoke against slavery before large crowds in Boston, New York, Philadelphia, and elsewhere. Abolitionists expressed amazement and gratitude that the voice of Transcendentalism now touched the ground: "No more feeling in the skies, after the absolute, but sharp observations on human life and manners," one exclaimed. "Never was such a change, apparently, as from the Emerson of '45 to the Emerson of '55."

Emerson's fame led critics to denounce the Sage of Concord: "Denunciation and blasphemy by the wholesale," complained a Boston newspaper, "is no longer a strange thing" in the events where Emerson spoke, nor was "treason." After the attack on Massachusetts senator Charles Sumner in the United States Capitol in May 1856, Emerson declared he did "not see how a barbarous community and a civilized community can constitute one state. I think we must get rid of slavery, or we must get rid of freedom." He urged listeners "to give largely, lavishly" to provide rifles to free-state settlers in Kansas. Emerson knew that such comments expended the social capital he had built over the preceding two decades among the educated and powerful, for "Judges, Bank

Presidents, Railroad men, men of fashion, lawyers universally all take the side of slavery."[35]

Thoreau, having only local fame and notoriety, used boldness rather than standing to aid the antislavery cause. He spent a night in jail in 1845 to oppose the war with Mexico and, ten years later, gave a blistering speech, "Slavery in Massachusetts," after Webster's support for the Fugitive Slave Act and Burns's arrest. On the Fourth of July in 1854, speaking alongside William Lloyd Garrison and Sojourner Truth beneath an American flag turned upside-down in a sign of national distress, Thoreau charged that northerners "fail now and always to face the facts." Massachusetts was deeply and directly implicated in slavery. Northern politicians offered only "half measures and make-shifts." While they vacillated, "the debt accumulates." Only abolition would free the nation. Thoreau's speech circulated widely under the headline "Words That Burn." Thoreau was impressed when he met John Brown in Concord in early 1857. Brown returned to Concord in 1859 and met wealthy abolitionists who offered support for his vague plans for a blow against the Slave Power.[36]

Beyond abolitionist circles, conflicting visions of the American future crystallized in the late 1850s. The Democrats proclaimed the virtues of passive government, white dominance, religious tolerance, the welcoming of immigrants, and the preservation of the Union. They would build national prosperity by enabling slaveholders to profit from their human property and share that prosperity with northern and western merchants, farmers, and workers. National unity would grow from constitutionally protected rights in property, including enslaved people. The Democrats would promote slavery's growth with the return of fugitive slaves, the construction of southern railroads to the Pacific, and taking Cuba or parts of Central America if the opportunity arose.

The Democrats envisioned no future for Black people beyond continued servitude and constricted rights in the rest of the nation. The Democrats spoke a language of ridicule, contempt, and hostility toward Black Americans and their white advocates.

The Republicans' vision of national prosperity portrayed a different American future. It would unleash the most productive parts of the new economy by connecting and strengthening the East, Midwest, and West. They saw the South, and the Democrats who protected the South, as retrograde in morality, economic life, and social progress. Over time, the Republicans argued, slavery, if constrained within its current borders, would die of its own corruption and inefficiencies. They asserted the superiority of free labor and the rights of the northern white majority of the United States, increasing in numbers and progress every day. The Republicans would oppose slavery's expansion but would not promote immediate abolition. They were sympathetic to Black people in slavery and sometimes in the North, though most Republicans did not advocate social equality. The Democrats played upon Republican inconsistencies and divisions over race with gleeful energy, calling the party the Black Republicans.[37]

Americans had acknowledged the possibility of disunion for as long as there had been a union. In the late 1850s, however, northerners and southerners articulated visions of two distinct and irreconcilable societies within the United States. In March 1858, South Carolina senator James Henry Hammond proclaimed the virtues of the South: "Look at her. Eight hundred fifty thousand square miles. As large as Great Britain, France, Austria, Prussia and Spain. Is not that territory enough to make an empire that shall rule the world?" he boasted. Though the North was proud of its wealth, "the South have sustained you in great measure. You are our factors. You fetch and carry for us." Southern capital allowed the North "to keep your machinery together and in motion." What would happen if the South were "to discharge you; suppose we were to take our business out of your hands;—we should consign you to anarchy and poverty."[38]

The South's power did not lie only in its size and wealth, but in its martial character as well. "At any time, the South can raise, equip, and maintain in the field, a larger army than any Power of the earth can send against her, and an army of soldiers—men brought up on horseback, with guns in their hands," Hammond bragged. Such an army would not be necessary, however, for why "would any sane nation make war on cotton? Without firing a gun, without drawing a sword, should they make war on us we could bring the whole world to our feet." Should the South withhold cotton from the market for three years, "England would topple headlong and carry the whole civilized world with her, save the South. No, you dare not make war on cotton. No power on earth dares to make war upon it. Cotton is king."

Hammond declared that "the greatest strength of the South arises from the harmony of her political and social institutions. This harmony gives her a frame of society, the best in the world, and an extent of political freedom, combined with entire security, such as no other people ever enjoyed upon the face of the earth." Hammond announced that "in all social systems there must be a class to do the menial duties, to perform the drudgery of life. That is, a class requiring but a low order of intellect and but little skill. Its requisites are vigor, docility, fidelity. Such a class you must have, or you would not have that other class which leads progress, civilization, and refinement." That laboring class "constitutes the very mud-sill"—the buried foundation of a house—"of society and of political government." In the South, "we call them slaves." In the North, the mud-sill was the white laboring class; the North dared not call it such, but "you have it; it is there; it is everywhere; it is eternal." Hammond, with cotton wealth pouring from slave labor into his new plantation house in South Carolina, filled with books, paintings, and statues from Europe, declared himself unafraid.

Republicans agreed with Hammond and other southerners that the North and South had created incompatible social orders. Abraham Lincoln, a state legislator from Illinois, received the nomination of the Republicans to run against powerful Senator Stephen Douglas for a seat in the US Senate. In June 1858, Lincoln delivered an address declaring that "this government cannot endure, permanently half *slave* and half *free*." Lincoln argued that the United States faced two paths forward: "Either the *opponents* of slavery, will arrest the further spread of it, and place it where the public mind shall rest in the belief that it is in the course of ultimate extinction; or its *advocates* will push it forward, till it shall become alike lawful in *all* the States, *old* as well as *new*— *North* as well as *South*." Lincoln's speech focused on issues of history, precedent, and the Constitution, charging Douglas and the Democrats with violating American ideals when they sought to allow slavery the right to expand.[39]

The speech powered Lincoln's national visibility, as did the seven debates that followed across the state of Illinois in the fall of 1858. The debates, many attended by more than ten thousand people, were enabled by railroads, recorded by stenographers, disseminated by telegraph, and published across the vast network of newspapers that reached into every American community. The debates marked a new kind of media saturation, and each debate focused on the fight over slavery. Lincoln won the popular vote, but Douglas was elected by the gerrymandered Illinois senate. Lincoln, meanwhile, became a leading contender for the Republican nomination for president in 1860.

William H. Seward, senator from New York and a longtime opponent of slavery, stood as a better-known potential candidate for the Republicans. In October 1858, Seward delivered a campaign speech in Rochester that elaborated on the differences between the North and the South. Seward accepted James Henry Hammond's portrayal of the United States as defined by two distinct societies. "Our country is a theatre, which exhibits, in full operation, two radically different political systems," Seward argued, "the one resting on the basis of servile or slave labor, the other on voluntary labor of freemen." He stated that the sins of slavery were obvious to all: "The slave system is one of constant danger, distrust, suspicion, and watchfulness." That it displays "the lowest degree of which human nature is capable, to guard against mutiny and insurrection." Doing so, the slave system "wastes energies which otherwise might be employed in national development and aggrandizement." The American political theater, fortunately, pitted a worthy opponent against slavery: "the free-labor system." Its virtues contrasted with the sins of slavery, for free labor "secures universal contentment, and brings into the highest possible activity all the physical, moral, and social energies of the whole state."

The conflicting systems had lived parallel lives for the last two generations, each growing stronger. Now, "a new and extended network of railroads and other avenues, and an internal commerce which daily becomes more intimate" meant that "these antagonistic systems are continually coming into closer contact, and collision results." The future could only bring "an irrepressible conflict between opposing and enduring forces."

Seward drew out the moral: "the United States must and will, sooner or later, become either entirely a slaveholding nation, or entirely a free-labor nation." That meant that "either the cotton and rice fields of South Carolina and the sugar plantations of Louisiana will ultimately be tilled by free labor" or "the rye fields and wheat fields of Massachusetts and New York must again be

surrendered by their farmers to slave culture." The inevitable conflict between slavery and free labor "renders all such pretended
compromises, when made, vain and ephemeral." No compromise
would save the United States. The nation of disconnected frontiers and itinerant prophets had coalesced into a nation of copper
wires and iron rails, turning upon itself.[40]

The conflict between the North and the South focused on
the future of agriculture rather than on fights between agrarian
and industrial visions. The North remained anchored in farming, an interest that grew as the Midwest became settled and the
farms of the East abandoned wheat for urban markets in dairy,
fruits, and vegetables. Agricultural journals and fairs flourished
as farm machinery and fertilizers proliferated. Rural areas developed prosperous small towns, and in turn connected to larger
towns and cities. Population density increased across the North,
from the longest-settled areas in the East to the newly settled
communities in the West. Young men could expect to move up
from farm laborer to landowner or even a lawyer, not unlike
Abraham Lincoln.[41]

The slave South participated in its own form of agricultural
improvement. James Henry Hammond, like other slaveholders,
worked to modernize their plantations, adding phosphorus-rich
marl to soils depleted by cotton. Journals such as the *Southern Cul-
tivator* and *DeBow's Review* spread news of improved techniques
of tilling, of diversification into wine, silk, and fruit. To more effi-
ciently manage their enslaved labor force, planters installed clocks
and bells to regulate time. White doctors described strategies to
treat enslaved women bearing children, and white ministers reassured slaveholders that they served God's purposes by holding
others in bondage. Railroad building surged across the South in
the late 1850s, as did slave-based industry in cities such as Richmond. Cotton prices and the prices for enslaved people attained

all-time highs. Leaders of the slave South argued that they were on the cusp of unprecedented wealth and autonomy, and they had reason to believe so.[42]

A young North Carolinian, Hinton Rowan Helper, passionately disagreed. He argued in 1857 that the South would undergo a crisis when nonslaveholders recognized that Black slavery damaged white people as well. Building an elaborate, if flawed, statistical argument, Helper attempted to prove that slavery retarded every aspect of progress in the South, from literacy and wealth to democracy and self-respect. He dismissed the most common argument in defense of slavery, that it reflected God's will, for "to say that one man was created to domineer over another is to call in question the justice, mercy, and goodness of God."[43]

Helper expressed sympathy for enslaved people, who "toiled unceasingly from the gray of dawn till the dusk of eve." Their "cruel task-masters" inflicted "heartless separations from the tenderness of the kindred, with epithets, with scoldings, with execrations, and with the lash—and, not unfrequently, with the fatal bludgeon or the more deadly weapon." The cruelty stole from the enslaved, for "from the labor of their hands, and from the fruit of their loins, the human mongers of the South have become wealthy, insolent, corrupt, and tyrannical."

Since no New York firm wanted to alienate the southern market, Helper struggled to get his book published and paid to have it produced. Horace Greeley of the *New-York Tribune* released a strong review, however, and word of the book spread quickly. William Lloyd Garrison's *Liberator* declared *The Impending Crisis of the South* as "in some respects more valuable than any other works that has yet appeared on the subject of slavery." Because Helper's book confirmed the northerners' vision of a weak and corrupt South, the Republican Party commissioned a brief edition to distribute across the North.

Suffering and Salvation

The celebratory vision of the North contrasted with the reality of a financial crisis that saw demand for American grains plummet after the end of a war in the Crimea in 1856. The winter of 1857–1858 brought severe unemployment. In New York City, up to a hundred thousand people were without jobs. Strikes broke out in New England textile plants, Pennsylvania coal and iron mines, and shoe manufacturers across the North. Railroad construction, which had grown feverishly through the early 1850s, suddenly halted. Westward migration in the North slowed, and so did immigration from Ireland and Germany. The sudden rise of unions and outbreaks of strikes alarmed middle-class people and employers, who heard protests of inequity and inequality they had long ignored or denied.[44]

The economic development of the 1850s, it turned out, had left many workers behind. All women suffered brutally low wages, as did Black people of both genders. The richest 10 percent of Americans had owned half of all wealth at the time of Revolution; by the 1850s, they owned nearly three quarters. Labor markets were isolated, leaving pockets of vulnerability when local industries slowed or stopped.[45]

A song by Stephen Foster, "Hard Times Come No More," evoked urban suffering:

> While we seek mirth and beauty, and music light and gay,
> There are frail forms fainting at the door;
> Though their voices are silent, their pleading looks will say
> Oh! Hard Times, come again no more.

A painter in Pittsburgh, David Gilmour Blythe, painted gangs of boys on their own, their hard, barely human, expressions conveying neglect and threat.[46]

Many Americans blamed the Panic of 1857 on the moral state of the nation, grown slack and self-indulgent after so many years of prosperity. How else to explain the suffering that so quickly afflicted families in the most advanced parts of the American economy? In 1857, a religious revival surged along the networks of Protestant churches, organizations, and publications that blanketed the United States, beginning in Boston and New York and spreading to cities across the North.[47]

The revival of 1857 became known as the "businessman's revival," for it attracted a disproportionate number of male worshippers from the commercial districts of major cities. Men dressed in office attire were novel attendees of religious services, where women still predominated. With prayer meetings carefully arranged for the lunch hour, attendees agreed not to pray or speak too long, not to introduce issues of politics or other secular concerns, and to treat each other with civility. A new organization, the Young Men's Christian Association, or YMCA, worked to carry the message to college campuses and other places revivals might not otherwise reach. Workingmen attended their own meetings, organized by trade, with shoemakers and shipbuilders, firefighters and carpenters recruiting friends.

For the first time, the secular press paid attention to the revivals in their cities. Horace Greeley's *New-York Tribune* and its competitors spread news of the revival. Sending out daily reports of the latest converts, telling stories of Jessie Frémont dropping a golden ring in the collection plate, or of a prominent boxer confessing his sins in public, the newspapers made news out of religion. Church leaders in one city after another urged their congregations to keep up, to prove that Christianity flourished in their midst no less than among their rivals.

Through the winter of 1857 and into the spring of 1858, Christians took heart from the revivals. Preachers avoided politics in their sermons and prayers, hoping that a spirit of fellow feeling might calm the political vituperation that tore at the United States. Hundreds of thousands of people joined churches and renewed their commitment to Christian charity, praying that individual regeneration might lead to national repentance.

The revival, however, did not fulfill those hopes. White Christians in the South read of the northern revivals with skepticism. The South had outstripped the North in rates of church membership through the 1850s and did not feel itself in need of revival. As white Christians saw it, the South had not bred the problems that the northern revival sought to redress—unemployment, homelessness, labor unrest, abolitionism, and women's rights. The South largely avoided the dislocations of the panic, as prices for cotton held. Prices for enslaved people mounted to an all-time peak in 1860.[48]

Across the nation, signs of social dissolution rose in the 1850s. The United States registered the highest rates of homicide in the world, as men shot one another, as men carrying ropes proclaimed themselves vigilantes. Violence racked cities, where gangs claimed territories and terrorized their rivals. Men killed one another with broadswords in Kansas. Migrants on the overland trails equipped themselves with firearms to fight the Natives whose lands they crossed. Immigrants fought with one another and against those who did not welcome them in the United States. United States soldiers fought against the Lakotas, Cheyennes, Apaches, Arapahos, and Navajos throughout the West. Mormon militia, in alliance with and disguised as Paiute Indians, killed more than a hundred emigrants in the Mountain Meadows Massacre. At women's rights conventions, men shouted down the speakers and hissed when they called for equality. The 1858 meeting in New York dissolved in the face of rowdyism "amid great confusion."[49]

The new nation lacked the resilience to weather the long-building crisis that threatened to engulf everyone and everything. No one could find the language to imagine a Union that was not divided. Americans had exhausted their goodwill, patience, trust, and empathy over the preceding decades. They had consumed themselves with vituperation, not only politically but on many fronts, so that the only honest language seemed the language of resentment and distrust, of cynicism and suspicion. Fantasies of violence, suffered and inflicted, filled imaginations. The network of partisan newspapers, telegraph lines, and political patronage spun over the preceding decades amplified bitter rhetoric into every American community. Despite efforts to rebuild the ruins of Mount Vernon and market *Washington Crossing the Delaware*, a sense of shared patriotism proved impossible to sustain.[50]

Epilogue

THE SWORD
AND THE NOOSE

1859–1861

John Brown advanced his plans in secret in the summer of 1859. His goal was to take the federal armory at Harpers Ferry, West Virginia, and from there attract enslaved people who would rise in a mass revolt. Brown met Frederick Douglass at a remote quarry in Chambersburg, Pennsylvania, near the Maryland border, to share his plans and plead for his participation. Douglass told Brown the plan would not work and would, in fact, make things worse for enslaved people. But Brown proceeded, nevertheless. The raid failed and Brown lost sons and other allies. A Virginia court ruled that Brown would be hanged on December 2. Brown used the intervening weeks to preach his gospel of rebellion and to warn of his vision of a land purged with blood.

Brown's attack on Harpers Ferry, as he intended, inflamed both sides of the Mason-Dixon Line. Frederick Douglass, warned that he had been linked to Brown and would be arrested, fled for Canada and then for Great Britain, where he spoke to enormous and admiring audiences in late 1859 and early 1860. In Concord, Ralph Waldo Emerson admired Brown's bravery but thought he "lost his head" in his plans for the aborted attack. Emerson raised money for Brown's defense, referring to him as "that new saint" who would "make the gallows like the cross." Emerson and his wife welcomed Brown's children into their home so they could go to school. Frances Watkins, a Black poet and speaker, wrote Brown in prison: "Virginia has no bolts or bars through which I dread to send you my sympathy. . . . I thank you, that you have been brave enough to reach out your hands to the crushed and blighted of my race. You have rocked the bloody Bastille; and I hope that from your sad fate great good things may arise to the cause of freedom." Watkins reached out to Brown's wife, "the noble wife of the hero of the nineteenth century," assuring her that a "republic that produces such a wife and mother may hope for better days."[1]

Henry David Thoreau announced that he would give a speech about John Brown even though friends and families counseled against it. In a jammed hall in Concord, filled with people hostile to Brown and to the speaker, Thoreau asked a question he had asked since his jailing for opposition to the war with Mexico: "Is it not possible that an individual may be right and a government wrong? Are laws to be enforced simply because they were made?" Thoreau gave over much of his speech to quotations from Brown himself, emphasizing love instead of vengeance. "I pity the poor in bondage that have none to help them; that is why I am here; not to gratify any personal animosity, revenge, or vindictive spirit," Thoreau read. "It is my sympathy with the oppressed and the wronged, that are as good as you, and as precious in the sight of God."[2]

Organizers of an event in Boston invited Thoreau, by telegraph, to give his speech again a few days later. He spoke before 2,500 people, to great applause, and then again in Worcester. Spread by papers across the country, "A Plea for Captain John Brown" gave Thoreau the widest audience of anything he had written. He hoped to publish the speech as a pamphlet to raise money for the Brown family, but no publisher would consider such a controversial step. Back in Concord, Thoreau drove a "Mr. X" in a wagon to the train station at night to escape to Canada. The passenger, as Thoreau suspected, had participated in Brown's raid.[3]

Lydia Maria Child had no reason to expect a response when she wrote Virginia governor John Wise to ask if she might visit John Brown before his execution. Child and her husband had fallen deeper into debt after their failed attempt to grow sugar beets to replace cane sugar produced by slave labor. She no longer edited a newspaper and had broken ties with some of her former allies in the abolitionist movement. Child wrote Wise nevertheless, asking him to pass along an enclosed letter to Brown. She did not hide her loyalties. "I have been for years an uncompromising abolitionist," she told the governor. She wished to dress Brown's wounds and "speak soothingly" to the captive. Wise responded theatrically, as he was inclined to do. "Why," he asked, "should you not be so allowed, Madam?" He would personally protect her, even though she sought to succor "one who whetted knives of butchery for our mothers, sisters, daughters and babes." Satisfied with his gallant response, Wise sent the correspondence to the newspapers. Brown also replied to Child, graciously declining her offer to visit but suggesting that she might help his family instead.

To Child's astonishment, her exchange with Governor Wise appeared in the *New-York Tribune*. Suddenly finding herself with a national audience, she replied. Child reminded Wise of the white South's brutality against anyone "who happened to have black, brown, or yellow complexion." The South had denied any recourse other than violence, since southern politicians had gagged petitions, rammed through the Fugitive Slave Law, applauded the beating of Charles Sumner in the US Senate chamber, and violated democracy in Kansas. "The people of the North had a very strong attachment to the Union," but "you have weakened it beyond all power of restoration." If the South wished to secede, as it so often threatened, it might be for the best.

A white woman in the South, the wife of United States senator James Mason, responded to Child as a fellow Christian. "You would soothe with sisterly and motherly care the hoary-headed murderer of Harper's Ferry!" Margaretta Mason of Virginia exclaimed. "A man whose aim and intention was to incite the horrors of a servile war—to condemn women of your own race . . . to see their husbands and fathers murdered, their children butchered, the ground strewed with the brains of their babes." The hypocrisy of abolitionists infuriated Mason. "Would you stand by the bedside of an old negro, dying of a hopeless disease, to alleviate his sufferings as far as human aid could?" Mason asked, certain of the answer. "Did you ever sit up until the 'wee hours' to complete a dress for a motherless child, that she might appear on Christmas day in a new one?" The slaveowning women of the South "do these and more for our servants, and why? Because we endeavor to do our duty in that state of life it has pleased God to place us."

Child replied in kind. "It would be extremely difficult to find any woman in our villages who does not sew for the poor, and watch with the sick, whenever occasion requires." As for Christmas dresses: "We pay our domestics generous wages, with which they can purchase as many Christmas gowns as they please," rather than making them "receive their clothing as a charity, after being deprived of just payment for their labor." In her most biting rebuff to the slaveowning mother, Child pointed out in the North "after we have helped the mothers, we do not sell the babies." The *Tribune* printed the entire exchange, as did the *Liberator*. The American Anti-Slavery Society published the letters in pamphlet form. At five cents each, they sold three hundred thousand copies.[4]

Child had another important role to play in these years, one less public but more enduring. A Black woman had long attempted to tell her story but could not make her voice heard. Harriet Jacobs had lived in a garret for seven years to flee the sexual assaults of her enslaver and to save her children, fathered by another white man, from sale. After escaping from North Carolina in 1842, she moved to Brooklyn. Harassed even there by the man who claimed to own her, Jacobs moved to Boston and then to Rochester, where she worked in the abolitionist bookstore above Frederick Douglass's *North Star*. Allies purchased her freedom.

In the early 1850s, Jacobs met Quaker activists who urged her to write her story. Presented as a novel, the narrative told of sexual exploitation in a way no other work dared. Recognizing that bearing children out of wedlock removed her from the sympathy of some, Jacobs reminded readers that "the condition of a slave confuses all principles of morality, and, in fact, renders the practice of them impossible." As a result, "I have placed myself before you, to be judged as a woman whether I deserve your pity or contempt."

Jacobs and her allies approached Harriet Beecher Stowe to collaborate soon after the appearance of *Uncle Tom's Cabin*. The now-famous author declined, instead planning to use Jacobs's story in her own writing. Jacobs decided to tell her story in her own voice, "a history of my life entirely by itself." Publishers in Britain as well as the United States showed no interest, though one said they would consider producing a book if Lydia Maria Child offered a preface. In the summer of 1860, the fifty-year-old Jacobs met the sixty-year-old Child at the American Anti-Slavery Society in Boston. They worked together over the coming months to polish the book for publication.

Child's introduction vouched for the author's character and truthfulness. It also warned readers that "I am well aware that many will accuse me of indecorum for presenting these pages to the public, for the experiences of this intelligent and much-injured woman belong to a class which some call delicate subjects, and some indelicate." Sex, especially interracial sex, was not considered suitable for a respectable book, even about slavery, "but the public ought to be made acquainted with its monstrous features." Child took responsibility for presenting a story with the "veil withdrawn." She did so "for my sisters in bondage, who are suffering wrongs so foul, that our ears are too delicate to listen to them."

As Child and Jacobs finished revisions, the publisher went bankrupt. Somehow, Jacobs gathered enough money to cover the book's expenses on her own. When the book appeared—*Incidents in the Life of a Slave Girl: Written by Herself*—no author was listed, only Child as the editor. The story was told through a pseudonym, Linda Brent. The book finally appeared in early 1861, when the agony of slavery became the focus of the world's attention. In the late twentieth century, Harriet Jacobs and her story would be recognized as among the most eloquent portrayals of the lives of Black women in American slavery.[5]

As Jacobs struggled to publish her book, the nation tore itself apart. Frederick Douglass, though disappointed in the Republican platform of 1860 because "it is opposed to the political power of slavery, rather than to slavery itself," recognized that Republican victory could "humble the slave power and defeat all plans for giving slavery any further guarantee of permanence." Douglass had come to admire the Republican nominee, Abraham Lincoln of Illinois. Though "untried," Lincoln showed "great firmness of will." When President-elect Lincoln, threatened by assassins, entered Washington under the cover of night in March 1861, Douglass noted the irony: "Mr. Lincoln entered the Capital as the poor, hunted fugitive slave reaches the North, in disguise, seeking concealment, evading pursuers, by the underground railroad."[6]

Lincoln's inaugural address, eagerly awaited by the nation, appalled Douglass in its promise to protect slavery where it existed and to return fugitive slaves. Douglass lamented the "weakness, timidity, and conciliation" in Lincoln's speech. Despite Lincoln's words of reassurance, South Carolina and other southern states moved to secede upon Lincoln's election. Emerson perceived the situation clearly: "The furious slaveholder does not see that the one thing he is doing, by night & by day, is, to destroy slavery." In secession, the white South abandoned the protections the nation and the new president offered slavery. "They who help & they who hinder are all equally diligent in hastening its downfall," Emerson grimly noted.[7]

Later generations would blame abolitionists such as Douglass and Stowe, Emerson and Thoreau, for causing the Civil War, for forcing the South to secede. The story was untrue, for Lincoln was elected by a northern majority who, like Lincoln himself, had no intention of abolishing slavery or going to war.

Though the vision of American freedom that abolitionists had sustained for more than thirty years did not cause the war, however, it did cause emancipation. Over the next few years, through powerful Republican allies in Congress, through petition campaigns by women and personal meetings with Lincoln, through the bravery of Black soldiers on the battlefield and the dedication of Black men and women in the field hospitals, the stubborn advocates for freedom seized the opening of war to fulfill the most profound transformation in the nation's history. In their victory, the abolitionists and their allies proved the power of a vision sustained in the face of disheartening history.

Acknowledgments

This book began to take shape in an undergraduate seminar at the University of Richmond where we read classics of American literature in historical context. I'm grateful for the students' patience, humor, and goodwill in that sometimes-bracing experience. They helped me see familiar works through young eyes, helped me glimpse what might still matter in long-ago words.

As I researched and wrote this book, the pandemic that began in 2020 saw obligations disappear or become virtual. I requested book after book from the university's library and interlibrary loan. Staff members wrapped them in paper and plastic, leaving them on a table at the building's entrance. I retrieved them in a mask, carrying them home in bags and backpacks, excited and daunted as I unwrapped them. I did not have a chance to thank those who did such favors for me, including work-study students under the guidance of the professionals in the library, so I thank them now: Kevin Butterfield, Emily Bradford, Anna Creech, Marcia Whitehead, Cassandra Taylor-Anderson, Sam Schuth, and Travis Smith. I'm also grateful for those who built and sustain the Internet Archive, JSTOR, Project Muse, Wikimedia, the Library of Congress, and digital archives that share the past online.

I delivered a series of remote lectures at universities around the country for Phi Beta Kappa during the pandemic, trying out ideas and approaches for this book. I missed the personal connection and dinners we would have enjoyed otherwise, of course, but I appreciated the stimulating online conversations all the more. As the virus diminished, I taught a seminar for the Gilder Lehrman Institute of American History at Gettysburg College in the summer of 2022, where teachers from around the country helped me to see new dimensions of the era. I'm grateful for their friendly honesty as well as for the support of James Basker and Daniel Percoco of Gilder Lehrman. My friend and ally at New American History, Annie Evans, helped me understand how this book might speak to teachers and students of many ages.

Throughout much of the writing of this book I depended on my great friend Brian Balogh. Brian claims to know nothing about this era—though that's a misrepresentation of the facts—but his perspective as a twentieth-century historian helped me think about why these stories might matter today. Our friend Peter Onuf, who knows everything about this era, read an early version as well; his approval of my approach gave me confidence to proceed. William G. Thomas III and I have been allies for a long time and so he could level with me, and he did. I'm grateful, too, for the early readings of Rachael Ayers, Hannah Ayers, Lance Warren, and Tony Field, all of whom steered me in useful directions. Nathaniel Ayers has, once again, brought patience and skill to bear on this book's images. Avery Meredith, budding photographer, graced me with the jacket photo.

The book would not have been possible without the support and advice of Steve Forman, my longtime editor and friend. Steve has made *American Visions* better in every way. An author could not be luckier than to have Steve. Mike van Mantgem did a wonderful job with the copyediting.

And, as in all my books, the acknowledgments culminate with Abby Ayers. She was trapped in a house with this book from start to finish, forced to hear about it at lunch and dinner and during walks in between. If that wasn't enough, she agreed to embark on a great adventure, visiting places I write about in this book in a camper Abby christened "Bertha." We covered a lot of territory, recording the journey in an online journal, seeing this history refracted in our own time. That adventure is part of the journey Abby and I have been on together for half a century. I have treasured every mile.

Notes

PREFACE

1 Excellent books portray the political and economic history of this period.
See Alan Taylor, *American Republics: A Continental History of the United States, 1783–1850* (New York: W. W. Norton, 2021); Steven Hahn, *A Nation without Borders: The United States and Its World in an Age of Civil Wars, 1830–1910* (New York: Viking, 2016); Daniel Walker Howe, *What Hath God Wrought: The Transformation of America, 1815–1848* (New York: Oxford University Press, 2007); and Sean Wilentz, *The Rise of American Democracy: Jefferson to Lincoln* (New York: W. W. Norton, 2005).

   David S. Reynolds, *Waking Giant: America in the Age of Jackson* (New York: Harper, 2009) gives culture a prominent role in his story, as he does in a series of books from his pioneering *Beneath the American Renaissance: The Subversive Imagination in the Age of Emerson and Melville* (Cambridge, MA: Harvard University Press, 1988) to *Abe: Abraham Lincoln in His Times* (New York: Penguin Press, 2020). A recent exploration is Alexander Nemerov, *The Forest: A Fable of America in the 1830s* (Princeton: Princeton University Press, 2023).

CHAPTER ONE: REVELATIONS—1800–1829

1 Anne F. Hyde, *Empires, Nations, and Families: A History of the North American West, 1800–1860* (Lincoln: University of Nebraska Press, 2012); Hyde, *Born of Lakes and Plains: Mixed-Descent Peoples and the Making of the American West* (New York: W. W. Norton, 2022); Pekka Hämäläinen, *Indigenous Continent: The Epic Contest for North America* (New York: Liveright, 2022); Samantha Seeley, *Race, Removal, and the Right to Remain: Migration and the Making of the United States* (Chapel Hill: University of North Carolina Press, 2021); Michael John Witgen, *Seeing Red: Indigenous Land, American Expansion, and the Political Economy of Plunder in North America* (Chapel Hill: University of North Carolina Press, 2022).

2 Adam Jortner, *The Gods of Prophetstown: The Battle of Tippecanoe and the Holy War for the American Frontier* (New York: Oxford University Press, 2012), 97–202, quotes on 102, 174–75, and 176; Peter Cozzens, *Tecumseh and the Prophet: The Shawnee Brothers Who Defied a Nation* (New York:

Alfred A. Knopf, 2020); Conevery Bolton Valencius, *The Lost History of the New Madrid Earthquakes* (Chicago: University of Chicago Press, 2013), 57–77, 94–97, and 102–22; R. David Edmunds, *The Shawnee Prophet* (Lincoln: University of Nebraska Press, 1985); Kathleen DuVal, *The Native Ground: Indians and Colonists in the Heart of the Continent* (Philadelphia: University of Pennsylvania Press, 2007), 207–8.

3　Hämäläinen, *Indigenous Continent*, 367–75.

4　John Dunn Hunter, *Memoirs of a Captivity among the Indians of North America* (London: Longman, Hurst, 1823), 45–46.

5　Quoted in Valencius, *New Madrid Earthquakes*, 106–7.

6　James W. Parins, *Literacy and Intellectual Life in the Cherokee Nation, 1820–1906* (Norman: University of Oklahoma Press, 2013); Margaret Bender, *Signs of Cherokee Culture: Sequoyah's Syllabary in Eastern Cherokee Life* (Chapel Hill: University of North Carolina Press, 2002); April R. Summitt, *Sequoyah and the Invention of the Cherokee Alphabet* (Santa Barbara: ABC-CLIO, 2012); William G. McLoughlin, *Cherokee Renascence in the New Republic* (Princeton, NJ: Princeton University Press, 1987).

7　Catherine Allgor, *A Perfect Union: Dolley Madison and the Creation of the American Nation* (New York: Henry Holt, 2006).

8　Kariann Akemi Yokota argues that "Americans' (particularly Anglo-American elites') sense of nationhood remained inchoate throughout the early national period," because "the problem of how to form a nation with clear, well-established internal ties of ethnicity, geography, and consanguinity presented numerous imponderables for these newly minted Americans." For the founders, "the revolutionary victory was the first, rather than the last step in gaining freedom from the mother country." Yokota, *Unbecoming British: How Revolutionary America Became a Postcolonial Nation* (New York: Oxford University Press, 2011), 9–11.

9　Allgor, *Perfect Union*, 159–61.

10　Allgor, *Perfect Union*, 6–7.

11　Allgor, *Perfect Union*, 188.

12　Allgor, *Perfect Union*, quote on 212.

13　Gregg D. Kimball, *American City, Southern Place: A Cultural History of Antebellum Richmond* (Athens: University of Georgia Press, 2000); Michael L. Nicholls, *Whispers of Rebellion: Narrating Gabriel's Rebellion* (Charlottesville: University of Virginia Press, 2012).

14　Meredith Henne Baker, *The Richmond Theater Fire: Early America's First Great Disaster* (Baton Rouge: Louisiana State University Press, 2012), quotes on 8–9, 17–19.

15　Alan Taylor, *The Internal Enemy: Slavery and War in Virginia, 1772–1832* (New York: W. W. Norton, 2013), 114, 135.

16　Quoted in Baker, *Richmond Theater Fire*, 178–79; Christopher Grasso, *Skepticism and American Faith: From the Revolution to the Civil War* (New York: Oxford University Press, 2018), 202, 213.

17　Alan Taylor, *The Civil War of 1812: American Citizens, British Subjects,*

Irish Rebels, and Indian Allies (New York: Alfred A. Knopf, 2010), 244–45; Troy Bickham, *The Weight of Vengeance: The United States, the British Empire, and the War of 1812* (New York: Oxford University Press, 2012); François Furstenberg, "The Significance of the Trans-Appalachian Frontier in Atlantic History," *American Historical Review* 113 (June 2008): 647–77; Pietro S. Nivola and Peter J. Kastor, *What So Proudly We Hailed: Essays on the Contemporary Meaning of the War of 1812* (Washington, DC: Brookings Institution Press, 2012).

18 Taylor, *Internal Enemy*, 271–72.

19 Allgor, *Perfect Union*, Prologue, 313–18.

20 Quoted in Taylor, *Internal Enemy*, 305.

21 Mark Clague, *O Say Can You Hear? A Cultural Biography of* The Star-Spangled Banner (New York: W. W. Norton, 2022), 20–30; Billy Coleman, *Harnessing Harmony: Music, Power, and Politics in the United States, 1788–1865* (Chapel Hill: University of North Carolina Press, 2020), 23–44; Marc Ferris, *Star-Spangled Banner: The Unlikely Story of America's National Anthem* (Baltimore: Johns Hopkins University Press, 2014); Marc Leepson, *What So Proudly We Hailed: Francis Scott Key, A Life* (New York: St. Martin's Press, 2014); Laura Lohman, *Hail Columbia! American Music and Politics in the Early Nation* (New York: Oxford University Press, 2020).

22 Nicole Eustace, *1812: War and the Passions of Patriotism* (Philadelphia: University of Pennsylvania Press, 2012); Nicole Eustace, ed., *Warring for America: Cultural Contests in the Era of 1812* (Chapel Hill: University of North Carolina Press, 2017).

23 George William Van Cleve, *A Slaveholders' Union: Slavery, Politics, and the Constitution in the Early Republic* (Chicago: University of Chicago Press, 2010), 228–29.

24 Paul J. Polgar, *Standard-Bearers of Equality: America's First Abolition Movement* (Chapel Hill: University of North Carolina Press, 2019), quote on 3; Manisha Sinha, *The Slave's Cause: A History of Abolition* (New Haven, CT: Yale University Press, 2016); Patrick Rael, *Eighty-Eight Years: The Long Death of Slavery in the United States, 1777–1865* (Athens: University of Georgia Press, 2015); William G. Thomas III, *A Question of Freedom: The Families Who Challenged Slavery from the Nation's Founding to the Civil War* (New Haven, CT: Yale University Press, 2020); Kerri K. Greenidge, *The Grimkes: The Legacy of Slavery in an American Family* (New York: Liveright, 2022), 38–43.

25 Lamont D. Thomas, *Rise to Be a People: A Biography of Paul Cuffe* (Urbana: University of Illinois Press, 1986), quote on 108; James Campbell, *Middle Passages: African American Journeys to Africa, 1787–2005* (New York: Penguin Press, 2006), 34–50; Marie Tyler-McGraw, *An African Republic: Black and White Virginians in the Making of Liberia* (Chapel Hill: University of North Carolina Press, 2007); David Brion Davis, *The Problem of Slavery in the Age of Emancipation* (New York: Alfred A. Knopf, 2014), 167–92.

26 Speech at the American Colonization Society, December 21, 1816; James C. Klotter, *Henry Clay: The Man Who Would Be President* (New York: Oxford University Press, 2018); Eric Burin, *Slavery and the Peculiar Solution: A History of the American Colonization Society* (Gainesville: University Press of Florida, 2005); Bjorn F. Stillion Southard, *Peculiar Rhetoric: Slavery, Freedom, and the African Colonization Movement* (Jackson: University Press of Mississippi, 2019).

27 Thomas, *Rise to Be a People*, quotes on 114 and 115.

28 Charles F. Irons, *The Origins of Proslavery Christianity: White and Black Evangelicals in Colonial and Antebellum Virginia* (Chapel Hill: University of North Carolina Press, 2008), quote on 120.

29 Kurt Leichtle and Bruce Carveth, *Crusade against Slavery: Edward Coles, Pioneer of Freedom* (Carbondale: Southern Illinois University Press, 2011), with quotes on 47–49, 65, and 70; Suzanne Cooper Guasco, *Confronting Slavery: Edward Coles and the Rise of Antislavery Politics in Nineteenth-Century America* (DeKalb: Northern Illinois University Press, 2013); M. Scott Heerman, *The Alchemy of Slavery : Human Bondage and Emancipation in the Illinois Country, 1730–1865* (Philadelphia: University of Pennsylvania Press, 2018).

30 Melvin Patrick Ely, *Israel on the Appomattox: A Southern Experiment in Black Freedom from the 1790s through the Civil War* (New York: Alfred A. Knopf, 2004); Thomas, *A Question of Freedom*; Warren Eugene Milteer Jr., *Beyond Slavery's Shadow: Free People of Color in the South* (Chapel Hill: University of North Carolina Press, 2021); Michael P. Johnson and James L. Roark, *Black Masters: A Free Family of Color in the Old South* (New York: W. W. Norton, 1984); Watson Jennison, *Cultivating Race: The Expansion of Slavery in Georgia, 1750–1860* (Lexington: University of Kentucky Press, 2012).

31 Jeffrey L. Pasley and John Craig Hammond, eds., *A Fire Bell in the Past: The Missouri Crisis at 200,* Volume I, *Western Slavery, National Impasse,* and Volume II, *The "Missouri Question" and Its Answers* (Columbia: University of Missouri Press, 2021); Alan Taylor, *American Republics: A Continental History of the United States, 1783–1850* (New York: W. W. Norton, 2020), 180–83.

32 Andrew H. Browning, *The Panic of 1819: The First Great Depression* (Columbia: University of Missouri Press, 2019); Diane Mutti Burke, *On Slavery's Border: Missouri's Small Slaveholding Households, 1815–1865* (Athens: University of Georgia Press, 2010); Robert Pierce Forbes, *The Missouri Compromise and Its Aftermath: Slavery and the Meaning of America* (Chapel Hill: University of North Carolina Press, 2007).

33 Jeremy Schipper, *Denmark Vesey's Bible: The Thwarted Revolt That Put Slavery and Scripture on Trial* (Princeton, NJ: Princeton University Press, 2022); Mark A. Noll, *America's Book: The Rise and Decline of a Bible Civilization* (New York: Oxford University Press, 2022), 226–30; Douglas R. Egerton, *He Shall Go Out Free: The Lives of Denmark Vesey*, revised and updated edition (Lanham, MD: Rowman & Littlefield, 2004); Michael

P. Johnson, "Denmark Vesey's Church," *Journal of Southern History* 86, no. 4 (November 2020): 805–48; Maurie D. McInnis, *The Politics of Taste in Antebellum Charleston* (Chapel Hill: University of North Carolina Press, 2005); Ethan J. Kytle and and Blain Roberts, *Denmark Vesey's Garden: Slavery and Memory in the Cradle of the Confederacy* (New York: The New Press, 2018); James O'Neil Spady, ed., *Fugitive Movements: Commemorating the Denmark Vesey Affair and Black Radical Antislavery in the Atlantic World* (Columbia: University of South Carolina Press, 2022).

34 Quoted in Egerton, *He Shall Go Out Free*, 130.

35 Lloyd S. Kramer, *Lafayette in Two Worlds: Public Cultures and Personal Identities in an Age of Revolution* (Chapel Hill: University of North Carolina Press, 1996).

36 Lafayette quoted on 194 and 219 in Kramer, *Lafayette*.

37 Celia Morris Eckhardt, *Fanny Wright: Rebel in America* (Cambridge, MA: Harvard University Press, 1984), quotes on 105, 110.

38 Quoted in Eckhardt, *Fanny Wright*, 88.

39 Quoted in Eckhardt, *Fanny Wright*, 96.

40 Elizabeth Ann Bartlett, *Liberty, Equality, Sorority: The Origins and Interpretation of American Feminist Thought: Frances Wright, Sarah Grimke, and Margaret Fuller* (Brooklyn, NY: Carlson, 1994), quoted on 28.

41 Quoted in Eckhardt, *Fanny Wright*, 222–23.

42 Charles Grandison Finney, *Memoirs of Rev. Charles G. Finney* (New York: Fleming H. Revell, 1876); Charles E. Hambrick-Stowe, *Charles G. Finney and the Spirit of American Evangelicalism* (Grand Rapids, MI: William B. Eerdmans, 1996); Marianne Perciaccante, *Calling Down Fire: Charles Grandison Finney and Revivalism in Jefferson County, New York, 1800–1840* (Albany: State University of New York Press, 2003).

43 The account that follows is drawn from Finney's *Memoirs*, Chapters I–V.

44 David Paul Nord, "Benevolent Books: Printing, Religion, and Reform," in Robert A. Gross and Mary Kelley, *A History of the Book in America*, Volume 2, *An Extensive Republic: Print, Culture, and Society in the New Nation, 1790–1840* (Chapel Hill: University of North Carolina Press, 2010), 221–46.

45 *A Brief History of the American Tract Society, Instituted at Boston, 1814: and Its Relations to the American Tract Society at New York, Instituted 1825* (Boston: Press of T. R. Marvin, 1857), at https://archive.lib.msu.edu /AFS/dmc/ssb/public/all/briefhistory/brie.html; Nord, "Benevolent Books," 233.

46 Richard R. John, *Spreading the News: The American Postal System from Franklin to Morse* (Cambridge, MA: Harvard University Press, 1995), quote on 184–85; Robert H. Abzug, *Cosmos Crumbling: American Reform and the Religious Imagination* (New York: Oxford University Press, 1994), 114–15.

47 John, *Spreading the News*, quote on 85.

48 Richard Lyman Bushman, *Joseph Smith: Rough Stone Rolling* (New York: Alfred A. Knopf, 2005), 3–56; Paul C. Gutjahr, *The Book of Mormon: A Biography* (Princeton, NJ: Princeton University Press, 2012), 3–37.

49 Quoted in Bushman, *Joseph Smith*, 37.

50 Quoted in Bushman, *Joseph Smith*, 39. The following account unfolds over 40–56 in Bushman.

51 William Kerrigan, *Johnny Appleseed and the American Orchard* (Baltimore: Johns Hopkins University Press, 2012), quoted on 37–38, 145–46; Devin P. Zuber, *A Language of Things: Emanuel Swedenborg and the American Environmental Imagination* (Charlottesville: University of Virginia Press, 2019).

52 Kerrigan, *Johnny Appleseed*, quote on 137.

53 Kerrigan, *Johnny Appleseed*, quote on 145.

CHAPTER TWO: RECKONINGS—1820–1832

1 Sydney Smith, *Edinburgh Review* (January 1820).

2 Jane P. Tompkins, *Sensational Designs: The Cultural Work of American Fiction 1790–1860* (New York: Oxford University Press, 1985); Cathy N. Davidson, *Revolution and the Word: The Rise of the Novel in America* (New York: Oxford University Press, 1986); Steven Watts, *The Romance of Real Life: Charles Brockden Brown and the Origins of American Culture* (Baltimore: Johns Hopkins University Press, 1994); Jeffrey Andrew Weinstock, *Charles Brockden Brown* (Cardiff: University of Wales Press, 2011); Robert S. Levine, *Dislocating Race and Nation: Episodes in Nineteenth-Century American Literary Nationalism* (Chapel Hill: University of North Carolina Press, 2008). See the excellent online archive at https://brockdenbrown.cah.ucf.edu/volumes.php.

3 Quoted in Levine, *Dislocating*, 37–38.

4 Catherine Allgor, *A Perfect Union: Dolley Madison and the Creation of the American Nation* (New York: Henry Holt, 2006), 222; Andrew Burstein, *The Original Knickerbocker: The Life of Washington Irving* (New York: Basic Books, 2008); Brian Jay Jones, *Washington Irving: An American Original* (New York: Arcade Publishing, 2008); Jeffrey Rubin-Dorsky, *Adrift in the Old World: The Psychological Pilgrimage of Washington Irving* (Chicago: University of Chicago Press, 1988), 65–122; Andrew Burstein and Nancy Isenberg, eds., *Rip Van Winkle's Republic: Washington Irving in History and Memory* (Baton Rouge: Louisiana State University Press, 2022).

5 Quoted in Burstein, *Original Knickerbocker*, 149–50.

6 Wayne Franklin, *James Fenimore Cooper: The Early Years* (New Haven, CT: Yale University Press, 2007), quote on 248.

7 Franklin, *Cooper*, quoted on 271; Alan Taylor, *William Cooper's Town: Power and Persuasion on the Frontier of the Early American Republic* (New York: Random House, 1995).

8 Philip F. Gura, *Truth's Ragged Edge: The Rise of the American Novel* (New York: Farrar, Straus & Giroux, 2013), 40–46; Edward Watts and David J. Carlson, eds., *John Neal and Nineteenth-Century American Literature and Culture* (Lewisburg, PA: Bucknell University Press, 2012); Neal's fascinating life is related in a particularly detailed Wikipedia entry, a democratic form he would appreciate. The "son of a bitch" information is from there.

9   Quoted in Watts and Carlson, eds., *John Neal*, xxv, xxiv.

10 Gura, *Truth's Ragged Edge*, 49–64; Mary Kelly, ed., *Hope Leslie, or, Early Times in Massachusetts* (New Brunswick, NJ: Rutgers University Press, 1987).

11 Gregory Nobles, *John James Audubon: The Nature of the American Woodsman* (Philadelphia: University of Pennsylvania Press, 2017); Jennifer L. Roberts, *Transporting Visions: The Movement of Images in Early America* (Berkeley: University of California Press, 2014), 69–115.

12 Christopher Irmscher and Richard J. King, *Audubon at Sea: The Coastal and Transatlantic Adventures of John James Audubon* (Chicago: University of Chicago Press, 2022).

13 Alan Wallach, "Thomas Cole: Landscape and the Course of American Empire," in William H. Truettner and Alan Wallach, eds., *Thomas Cole: Landscape into History* (New Haven, CT: Yale University Press with the National Museum of American Art, 1994), 23–84, quote on 25.

14 Roberta Gray Katz, "Thomas Cole: Reading the Paintings from *The Last of the Mohicans*," presented at the 18th Cooper Seminar, State University of New York College at Oneonta, July 2011, placed online in July 2013 at http://jfcoopersociety.org/articles/suny/2011suny-Katz.html; James F. Beard Jr., "Cooper and His Artistic Contemporaries," *New York History* 35, no. 4 (1954): 480–95.

15 Francesca Orestano, "John Neal, the Rise of the Critick, and the Rise of American Art," in Watts and Carlson, eds., *John Neal*, 123–44, quote on 134.

16 Sean Wilentz, *The Rise of American Democracy: Jefferson to Lincoln* (New York: W. W. Norton, 2005), 168–78; Claudio Saunt, *A New Order of Things: Property, Power, and the Transformation of the Creek Indians, 1733–1816* (Cambridge: Cambridge University Press, 1999), 233–36; Matthew J. Clavin, *Aiming for Pensacola: Fugitive Slaves on the Atlantic and Southern Frontiers* (Cambridge, MA: Harvard University Press, 2015), 40–47; Nathaniel Millett, *The Maroons of Prospect Bluff and Their Quest for Freedom in the Atlantic World* (Gainesville: University Press of Florida, 2013).

17 David S. Heidler and Jeanne T. Heidler, *The Rise of Andrew Jackson: Myth, Manipulation, and the Making of Modern Politics* (New York: Basic Books, 2018); Wilentz, *Rise of American Democracy*; William J. Cooper, *The Lost Founding Father: John Quincy Adams and the Transformation of American Politics* (New York: Liveright, 2017).

18 Rachel Stephens, *Selling Andrew Jackson: Ralph E. W. Earl and the Politics of Portraiture* (Columbia: University of South Carolina Press, 2018), 120–21. On the Bank War, see Stephen W. Campbell, *The Bank War and the Partisan Press: Newspapers, Financial Institutions, and the Post Office in Jacksonian America* (Lawrence: University Press of Kansas, 2019); Stephen Mihm, "The Fog of War: Jackson, Biddle, and the Destruction of the Bank of the United States," in Sean Patrick Adams, ed., *A Companion to the Era of Andrew Jackson* (Chichester, UK: Wiley-Blackwell, 2013), 348–75.

19 Stephens, *Selling Andrew Jackson*, 134–35; Norma Basch, "Marriage, Morals, and Politics in the Election of 1828," *Journal of American History* 80 (1993): 890–918.

20 Donald B. Cole, *Vindicating Andrew Jackson: The 1828 Election and the Rise of the Two-Party System* (Lawrence: University Press of Kansas, 2009), 181; Mark R. Cheathem, *Andrew Jackson, Southerner* (Baton Rouge: Louisiana State University Press, 2014), 116–17; Heidler and Heidler, *Rise of Andrew Jackson*; Alex Zakaras, *The Roots of American Individualism: Political Myth in the Age of Jackson* (Princeton, NJ: Princeton University Press, 2022).

21 See Kirsten E. Wood, "'One Woman So Dangerous to Public Morals': Gender and Power in the Eaton Affair," *Journal of the Early Republic* 17 (Summer 1997): 237–75; John F. Marszalek, *The Petticoat Affair: Manners, Mutiny, and Sex in Andrew Jackson's White House* (New York: Free Press, 1997); Patricia Brady, *A Being So Gentle: The Frontier Love Story of Rachel and Andrew Jackson* (New York: Palgrave Macmillan, 2011); Andrew Burstein, *The Passions of Andrew Jackson* (New York: Alfred A. Knopf, 2003); Margaret Eaton, *The Autobiography of Peggy Eaton* (New York: Charles Scribner's Sons, 1932).

22 Kenneth H. Wheeler, *Modern Cronies: Southern Industrialism from Gold Rush to Convict Labor* (Athens: University of Georgia Press, 2021).

23 Claudio Saunt, *Unworthy Republic: The Dispossession of Native Americans and the Road to Indian Territory* (New York: W. W. Norton, 2020), 69–76, 82–83; Michael John Witgen, *Seeing Red: Indigenous Land, American Expansion, and the Political Economy of Plunder in North America* (Chapel Hill: University of North Carolina Press, 2022); Watson Jennison, *Cultivating Race: The Expansion of Slavery in Georgia, 1750–1860* (Lexington: University Press of Kentucky, 2012).

24 Mary Hershberger, "Mobilizing Women, Anticipating Abolition: The Struggle against Indian Removal in the 1830s," *Journal of American History* 86 (June 1999): 15–40; Susan Zaeske, *Signatures of Citizenship: Petitioning, Antislavery, and Women's Political Identity* (Chapel Hill: University of North Carolina Press, 2003); Alisse Portnoy, *Their Right to Speak: Women's Activism in the Indian and Slave Debates* (Cambridge, MA: Harvard University Press, 2005); Tiya Miles, "'Circular Reasoning': Recentering Cherokee Women in the Antiremoval Campaigns," *American Quarterly* 61 (June 2009): 221–43; and Natalie Joy, "The Indian's Cause: Abolitionists and Native American Rights," *Journal of the Civil War Era* 8 (June 2018): 215–42.

25 Saunt, *Unworthy Republic*, quotes on 69–70; Amy Dunham Strand, *Language, Gender, and Citizenship in American Literature, 1789–1919* (New York: Routledge, 2009).

26 Peter P. Hinks, ed., *David Walker's Appeal to the Coloured Citizens of the World* (University Park: Pennsylvania State University Press, 2000); Paul J. Polgar, *Standard-Bearers of Equality: America's First Abolition Movement* (Chapel Hill: University of North Carolina Press, 2019), 309–15.

27 Levine, *Dislocating Race and Nation*, 88–110.

28 Marcy J. Dinius, "'Look!! Look!!! at This!!!!': The Radical Typography of David Walker's 'Appeal,'" *PMLA* 126 (January 2011): 55–72; Lori Leavell, "'Not intended exclusively for the slave states': Antebellum Recirculation of David Walker's 'Appeal,'" *Callaloo* 38 (Summer 2015): 679–95.

29 Barry O'Connell, ed., *On Our Own Ground: The Complete Writings of William Apess, a Pequot* (Amherst: University of Massachusetts Press, 1992), 155–61.

30 Robert H. Gudmestad, *Steamboats and the Rise of the Cotton Kingdom* (Baton Rouge: Louisiana State University Press, 2011), 1–7; Walter Johnson, *River of Dark Dreams: Slavery and Empire in the Cotton Kingdom* (Cambridge, MA: Harvard University Press, 2013).

31 Gudmestad, *Steamboats*, 15–18; "*Enterprise* (1814)," Wikipedia, at https://en.wikipedia.org/wiki/Enterprise (1814); Louisiana State Exhibit Museum, "The Battle of New Orleans," at http://laexhibitmuseum.org/historic-objects/battle-of-new-orleans/.

32 Peter L. Bernstein, *Wedding of the Waters: The Erie Canal and the Making of a Great Nation* (New York: W. W. Norton, 2005), 204–11, quote on 336–37; Carol Sheriff, *The Artificial River: The Erie Canal and the Paradox of Progress, 1817–1862* (New York: Hill and Wang, 1996).

33 John Lauritz Larson, *Internal Improvement: National Public Works and the Promise of Popular Government in the Early United States* (Chapel Hill: University of North Carolina Press, 2001), quote on 75–76.

34 Van Buren quoted in Bernstein, *Wedding of the Waters*, 196–97.

35 Craig Miner, *A Most Magnificent Machine: America Adopts the Railroad, 1825–1862* (Lawrence: University Press of Kansas, 2010), 1; Kathleen Waters Sander, *John W. Garrett and the Baltimore and Ohio Railroad* (Baltimore: Johns Hopkins University Press, 2017), quote on 36; David Schley, *Steam City: Railroads, Urban Space, and Corporate Capitalism in Nineteenth-Century Baltimore* (Chicago: University of Chicago Press, 2020), quote on 26–27.

36 Schley, *Steam City*, with quotes on 1, 26–27, 29.

37 Miner, *Most Magnificent Machine*, 33–52, quote on 47; Aaron W. Marrs, *Railroads in the Old South: Pursuing Progress in a Slave Society* (Baltimore: Johns Hopkins University Press, 2009) and William G. Thomas, *The Iron Way: Railroads, the Civil War, and the Making of Modern America* (New Haven, CT: Yale University Press, 2011), emphasize the compatibility of the railroad with the slave South.

CHAPTER THREE: REBELLIONS—1827–1836

1 Martha S. Jones, *Vanguard: How Black Women Broke Barriers, Won the Vote, and Insisted on Equality for All* (New York: Basic Books, 2021), 23–28, quote on 28.

2 Kristin Waters, *Maria W. Stewart and the Roots of Black Political Thought* (Jackson: University Press of Mississippi, 2021); Valerie C. Cooper,

Word, Like Fire: Maria Stewart, the Bible, and the Rights of African Americans (Charlottesville: University of Virginia Press, 2012), 81–84; Marilyn Richardson, ed., *Maria W. Stewart: America's First Black Woman Political Writer: Essays and Speeches* (Bloomington: Indiana University Press, 1987). For a rich portrayal of Black Boston in these years, see Steven Kantrowitz, *More than Freedom: Fighting for Black Citizenship in a White Republic, 1829–1889* (New York: Penguin, 2012).

3   Charles F. Irons, *The Origins of Proslavery Christianity: White and Black Evangelicals in Colonial and Antebellum Virginia* (Chapel Hill: University of North Carolina Press, 2008).

4   The following narrative is based on Scot French, *The Rebellious Slave: Nat Turner in American Memory* (New York: Houghton Mifflin, 2004), quotes on 1, 2, 3, 54.

5   French, *Rebellious Slave*, 46–56.

6   Christopher Tomlins, *In the Matter of Nat Turner: A Speculative History* (Princeton, NJ: Princeton University Press, 2020).

7   David J. Allmendinger Jr., *Nat Turner and the Rising in Southampton County* (Baltimore: Johns Hopkins University Press, 2014); Patrick H. Breen, *The Land Shall Be Deluged in Blood: A New History of the Nat Turner Revolt* (New York: Oxford University Press, 2015); Vanessa M. Holden, *Surviving Southampton: African American Women and Resistance in Nat Turner's Community* (Urbana: University of Illinois Press, 2021).

8   Eva Sheppard Wolf, *Race and Liberty in the New Nation: Emancipation in Virginia from the Revolution to Nat Turner's Rebellion* (Baton Rouge: Louisiana State University Press. 2006), 242–45.

9   Thomas Roderick Dew, *Review of the Debate in the Virginia Legislature of 1831 and 1832* (Richmond: T. W. White, 1832).

10 Alison Goodyear Freehling, *Drift toward Dissolution: The Virginia Slavery Debate of 1831–1832* (Baton Rouge: Louisiana State University Press, 1982); William W. Freehling, *The Road to Disunion: Secessionists at Bay, 1776–1854* (New York: Oxford University Press, 1990); Robert Pierce Forbes, *The Missouri Compromise and Its Aftermath: Slavery and the Meaning of America* (Chapel Hill: University of North Carolina Press, 2007); Tomlins, *In the Matter of Nat Turner*; Michael O'Brien, *Conjectures of Order: Intellectual Life and the American South, 1810–1860* (Chapel Hill: University of North Carolina Press, 2001), and Alfred J. Brophy, *University, Court, and Slave: Proslavery Academic Thought and Southern Jurisprudence, 1831–1861* (New York: Oxford University Press, 2016).

11 Quoted in French, *Rebellious Slave*, 31–32.

12 Waters, *Maria W. Stewart*, quote on 224–25. The next two paragraphs quote Stewart in Waters, on 229–30 and 243.

13 Leo Damrosch, *Tocqueville's Discovery of America* (New York: Farrar, Straus & Giroux, 2010); Sheldon S. Wolin, *Tocqueville between Two Worlds* (Princeton, NJ: Princeton University Press, 2009); James T. Schleifer, *The Chicago Companion to Tocqueville's Democracy in America*

(Chicago: University of Chicago Press, 2012); Arthur Kaledin, *Tocqueville and His America: A Darker Horizon* (New Haven, CT: Yale University Press, 2011); Olivier Zunz, ed., and Arthur Goldhammer, trans., *Alexis de Tocqueville and Gustave de Beaumont in America: Their Friendship and Their Travels* (Charlottesville: University of Virginia Press, 2010); Zunz, *The Man Who Understood Democracy: The Life of Alexis de Tocqueville* (Princeton, NJ: Princeton University Press, 2022).

14 Alexis de Tocqueville, *Democracy in America*, translated by Arthur Goldhammer (New York: Library of America, 2004), 611. The following quotes are from ("freest") 625, ("hurls") 326, ("individualism") 585, ("some religious") 595, and ("deposit") 600.

15 Damrosch, *Tocqueville's Discovery*, quote on 187.

16 For a helpful overview, see Frank Towers, "The Rise of the Whig Party," in Sean Patrick Adams, ed., *A Companion to the Era of Andrew Jackson* (Chichester, UK: Wiley-Blackwell, 2013), 328–47. The fullest account is Michael F. Holt, *The Rise and Fall of the American Whig Party: Jacksonian Politics and the Onset of the Civil War* (New York: Oxford University Press, 1999).

17 Tocqueville, *Democracy*, quotes on 367, 395–96, and 419.

18 Rogers M. Smith, *Civic Ideals: Conflicting Visions of Citizenship in U.S. History* (New Haven, CT: Yale University Press, 1997) and Alex Zakaras, *The Roots of American Individualism: Political Myth in the Age of Jackson* (Princeton, NJ: Princeton University Press, 2022).

19 Patrick J. Jung, *The Black Hawk War of 1832* (Norman: University of Oklahoma Press, 2007), 172.

20 As with *The Confessions of Nat Turner,* authorship could not be easily established for a book whose significance grew from its claims of authenticity. Roger L. Nichols, ed., *Black Hawk's Autobiography* (Ames: Iowa State University, 1999), Introduction; quotes on 22, 41–42.

21 *History of the Indian tribes of North America, with biographical sketches and anecdotes of the principal chiefs: Embellished with one hundred and twenty portraits, from the Indian Gallery in the Department of War, at Washington,* by Thomas L. McKenney and James Hall (Philadelphia: Edward C. Biddle, 1836–1844), quote on 3; Peter J. Kastor, *William Clark's World: Describing America in an Age of Unknowns* (New Haven, CT: Yale University Press, 2011), 228–33; James David Horan, *The McKenney-Hall Portrait Gallery of American Indians* (New York: Crown Publishers, 1972), 61.

22 Brian W. Dippie et al., *George Catlin and His Indian Gallery* (Washington, DC, New York, and London: Smithsonian American Art Museum in association with W. W. Norton, 2002), quote on 41.

23 Philip F. Gura, *The Life of William Apess, Pequot* (Chapel Hill: University of North Carolina Press, 2015), 13; Benita Eisler, *The Red Man's Bones: George Catlin, Artist and Showman* (New York: W. W. Norton, 2013); Stephanie Pratt and Joan Carpenter Troccoli, *George Catlin: American Indian Portraits* (London: National Portrait Gallery, 2013).

24 Brian Jay Jones, *Washington Irving: An American Original* (New York: Arcade, 2008), 294–95.

25 James P. Ronda, "'We Have a Country': Race, Geography, and the Invention of Indian Territory," *Journal of the Early Republic* 19 (Winter 1999): 739–55; Claudio Saunt, *Unworthy Republic: The Dispossession of Native Americans and the Road to Indian Territory* (New York: W. W. Norton, 2020).

26 Jones, *Washington Irving*, quotes on 302, 305–6; Mark K. Burns, "'Ineffectual Chase': Indians, Prairies, Buffalo, and the Quest for the Authentic West in Washington Irving's 'A Tour on the Prairies,'" *Western American Literature* 42 (Spring 2007): 54–79.

27 John Francis McDermott, ed., *Washington Irving, A Tour on the Prairies* (Norman: University of Oklahoma Press, 1956), xxix.

28 Jones, *Washington Irving*, 318; Angela Calcaterra, *Literary Indians: Aesthetics and Encounter in American Literature to 1920* (Chapel Hill: University of North Carolina Press, 2018), Chapter 4.

29 Saunt, *Unworthy Republic*, 273–79; Gregory Smithers, *Native Southerners: Indigenous History from Origins to Removal* (Norman: University of Oklahoma Press, 2019); Barbara Krauthamer, *Black Slaves, Indian Masters: Slavery, Emancipation, and Citizenship in the Native American South* (Chapel Hill: University of North Carolina Press, 2013).

30 Jane Dinwoodie, "Evading Indian Removal in the American South," *Journal of American History* 108 (June 2021): 17–41; Edward L. Ayers, *Southern Journey: The Migrations of the American South, 1790–2020* (Baton Rouge: Louisiana State University Press, 2020), Part 1.

31 Saunt, *Unworthy Republic*, 282–308, quote on 295; C. S. Monaco, *The Second Seminole War and the Limits of American Aggression* (Baltimore: Johns Hopkins University Press, 2018).

32 Saunt, *Unworthy Republic*, 307–8; Apess, quoted on 256.

33 Gregg Cantrell, *Stephen F. Austin: Empresario of Texas* (Austin: Texas State Historical Association, 2016); James L. Haley, *Sam Houston* (Norman: University of Oklahoma Press, 2002), quotes on 109, 118. See Andrew J. Torget, *Seeds of Empire: Cotton, Slavery, and the Transformation of the Texas Borderlands, 1800–1850* (Chapel Hill: University of North Carolina Press, 2015) and Alice L. Baumgartner, *South to Freedom: Runaway Slaves to Mexico and the Road to the Civil War* (New York: Basic Books, 2020).

34 Carolyn L. Karcher, *The First Woman in the Republic: A Cultural Biography of Lydia Maria Child* (Durham, NC: Duke University Press, 1998) and Lydia Moland, *Lydia Maria Child: A Radical American Life* (Chicago: University of Chicago Press, 2022).

35 Moland, *Child*, quotes on 93 and 107.

36 Lydia Maria Child, *An Appeal in Favor of that Class of Americans Called Africans* (Coleridge, NY: John Taylor, 1836), quotes on 1, 195, 198, 289.

37 Gerda Lerner, *The Grimke Sisters from South Carolina: Pioneers for Women's Rights and Abolition* (Chapel Hill: University of North Carolina Press, 2004; 1967); Mark Perry, *Lift Up Thy Voice: The Sarah and Angelina Grimké Family's Journey from Slaveholders to Civil Rights Leaders* (New York: Viking, 2001).

38 Kerri K. Greenidge, *The Grimkes: The Legacy of Slavery in an American Family* (New York: Liveright, 2022).

39 Quoted in Greenridge, *Grimkés*, 65.

40 Richard John, *Spreading the News: The American Postal System from Franklin to Morse* (Cambridge, MA: Harvard University Press, 1995), 260–80.

41 Leonard L. Richards, *Gentlemen of Property and Standing: Anti-Abolition Mobs in Jacksonian America* (New York: Oxford University Press, 1970).

42 Quoted in Lerner, *Grimké Sisters*, 123–24; Greenidge, *Grimkes*, 65–67.

43 Angelina Emily Grimké, *An Appeal to the Christian Women of the South* (New York: American Anti-Slavery Society, 1836), quotes on 3–4, 17, 22, 25–27, 30–31.

44 Kristina R. Gaddy, *Well of Souls: Uncovering the Banjo's Hidden History* (New York: W. W. Norton, 2022).

45 Brian Roberts, *Blackface Nation: Race, Reform, and Identity in American Popular Music, 1812–1925* (Chicago: University of Chicago Press, 2017); Eric Lott, *Love & Theft: Blackface Minstrelsy and the American Working Class* (New York: Oxford University Press, 1995); Robert Hornback, *Racism and Early Blackface Comic Traditions: From the Old World to the New* (Cham, Switzerland: Palgrave Macmillan, 2018).

CHAPTER FOUR: REFLECTIONS—1836–1848

1 Robert D. Richardson, *Emerson: The Mind on Fire* (Berkeley: University of California Press, 1996), with quotes from 51, 146–48.

2 Robert A. Gross, *The Transcendentalists and Their World* (New York: Farrar, Straus & Giroux, 2021).

3 Barbara Packer, "The Transcendentalists," in Sacvan Bercovitch, ed., *The Cambridge History of American Literature*, Volume 2, *1820–1865* (Cambridge: Cambridge University Press, 1995), 329–604, with quote from 392–93; Gross, *Transcendentalists*, 433–38; Joel Myerson, Sandra Harbert Petrulionis, and Laura Dassow Walls, eds., *The Oxford Handbook of Transcendentalism* (New York: Oxford University Press, 2010).

4 Richardson, *Emerson*, quote on 260.

5 Ralph Waldo Emerson, *Essays and Lectures*, Joel Porte, ed. (New York: Library of America, 1983), 53–71.

6 Laura Dassow Walls, *Henry David Thoreau: A Life* (Chicago: University of Chicago Press, 2017), 78–81, quote on 81.

7 Emerson, "The Divinity School Address," in *Essays and Lectures*, 77; Gross, *Transcendentalists*, 676–77.

8 Richardson, *Emerson*; David Dowling, *Emerson's Protégés: Mentoring and Marketing Transcendentalism's Future* (New Haven, CT: Yale University Press, 2014).

9 Megan Marshall, *Margaret Fuller: A New American Life* (New York: Houghton Mifflin Harcourt, 2013), 135, 132–33; John Matteson, *The Lives of Margaret Fuller: A Biography* (New York: W. W. Norton, 2012).

10 Marshall, *Margaret Fuller*, 133.

11 Marshall, *Margaret Fuller*, 149–54, quote on 147; Matteson, *Lives*, 175–76.

12 Robert Arbour, "Mr. Emerson's Playful Lyceum: Polyvocal Promotion on the Lecture Circuit," in Tom F. Wright, ed., *The Cosmopolitan Lyceum: Lecture Culture and the Globe in Nineteenth-Century America* (Amherst: University of Massachusetts Press, 2013), 93–112, quotes on 103–4, 105; Donald M. Scott, "The Popular Lecture and the Creation of a Public in Mid-Nineteenth-Century America," *Journal of American History* 66 (March 1980): 791–809; Mary Kupiec Cayton, "The Making of an American Prophet: Emerson, His Audiences, and the Rise of the Culture Industry in Nineteenth-Century America," *American Historical Review* 92 (June 1987): 597–620, with quote on 609; Wesley T. Mott, "'The Age of the First Person Singular': Emerson and Individualism," in Joel Myerson, ed., *A Historical Guide to Ralph Waldo Emerson* (New York: Oxford University Press, 2000), 61–100.

13 Quoted in Richardson, *Emerson*, 369 and 373.

14 Matteson, *Lives*, 219–48; Marshall, *Margaret Fuller*, 202–17; S. M. Fuller, *Summer on the Lakes, in 1843* (Boston: Little, Brown, 2012), at Project Gutenberg at https://www.gutenberg.org/files/11526/11526-h /11526-h.htm; Jeffrey Steele, ed., *The Essential Margaret Fuller* (New Brunswick, NJ: Rutgers University Press, 1992), xiii; Aaron Sachs, *Arcadian America: The Death and Life of an Environmental Tradition* (New Haven, CT: Yale University Press, 2013), 77–81.

15 Jonathan Messerli, *Horace Mann: A Biography* (New York: Alfred A. Knopf, 1972), 249, 492–93.

16 Carl F. Kaestle, *Pillars of the Republic: Common Schools and American Society, 1780–1860* (New York: Hill and Wang, 1983), 75–135; Johann N. Neem, *Democracy's Schools: The Rise of Public Education in America* (Baltimore: Johns Hopkins University Press, 2017).

17 Bob Pepperman Taylor, *Horace Mann's Troubling Legacy: The Education of Democratic Citizens* (Lawrence: University Press of Kansas, 2010).

18 Caroline Matilda Kirkland, *A New Home - Who'll Follow? Or, Glimpses of Western Life* (New York: C. F. Francis, 1839), chap. XLV.

19 John Loughery, *Dagger John: Archbishop John Hughes and the Making of Irish America* (Ithaca, NY: Cornell University Press, 2018), 122–38, quote on 124.

20 Andie Tucker, "Newspapers and Periodicals," in Robert A. Gross and Mary Kelley, eds., *A History of the Book in America*, Volume 2, *An Extensive Republic: Print, Culture, and Society in the New Nation, 1790–1840* (Chapel Hill: University of North Carolina Press, 2010), 389–408; Matthew Goodman, *The Sun and the Moon: The Remarkable True Account of Hoaxers, Showmen, Dueling Journalists, and Lunar Man-Bats in Nineteenth-Century New York* (New York: Basic Books, 2008).

21 Meredith McGill, *American Literature and the Culture of Reprinting, 1834–1853* (Philadelphia: University of Pennsylvania Press, 2003); Jack Larkin, "'Printing is something every village has in it': Rural

Printing and Publishing," in Gross and Kelley, *History of the Book in America*, 145–60.

22 Georgia B. Barnhill, "Transformations in Pictorial Printing," in Gross and Kelley, *History of the Book in America*, 422–40.

23 Patricia Okker, *Our Sister Editors: Sarah J. Hale and the Tradition of Nineteenth-Century American Women Editors* (Athens: University of Georgia Press, 1995), 33; Isabelle Lehuu, *Carnival on the Page: Popular Print Media in Antebellum America* (Chapel Hill: University of North Carolina Press, 2000), 3–11.

24 Jane Tompkins, *Sensational Designs: The Cultural Work of American Fiction, 1790–1860* (New York: Oxford University Press, 1985), 3–39, with quote on 13; David Leverenz, "Men Writing in the Early Republic," in Gross and Kelley, *History of the Book in America*, 350–63, quote from the Boston paper on 352. Full accounts of Hawthorne's life and work appear in James R. Mellow, *Nathaniel Hawthorne in His Times* (Boston: Houghton Mifflin, 1980) and Brenda Wineapple, *Hawthorne: A Life* (New York: Alfred A. Knopf, 2003).

25 John Tresch, *The Reason for the Darkness of the Night: Edgar Allan Poe and the Forging of American Science* (New York: Farrar, Straus & Giroux, 2021), 7–108.

26 McGill, *American Literature*, 149–76, with quote on 164; J. Gerald Kennedy and Jerome McGann, *Poe and the Remapping of Antebellum Print Culture* (Baton Rouge: Louisiana State University Press, 2012).

27 Kenneth Silverman, *Edgar A. Poe: Mournful and Never-Ending Remembrance* (New York: HarperCollins, 1991), quote on 137.

28 McGill, *American Literature*, 149–76; Kennedy and McGann, *Poe and Remapping*; Silverman, *Edgar A. Poe*, 140–49.

29 Colin Woodard, *Union: The Struggle to Forge the Story of United States Nationhood* (New York: Viking, 2020), 75–88; Michael Davitt Bell, "Conditions of Literary Vocation," in Bercovitch, ed., *The Cambridge History of American Literature*, 61.

30 Lara Langer Cohen, *The Fabrication of American Literature: Fraudulence and Antebellum Print Culture* (Philadelphia: University of Pennsylvania Press, 2012); Lloyd Pratt, *Archives of American Time: Literature and Modernity in the Nineteenth Century* (Philadelphia: University of Pennsylvania Press, 2010).

31 Alan Wallach, "Thomas Cole: Landscape and the Course of American Empire," in William H. Truettner and Alan Wallach, eds., *Thomas Cole: Landscape into History* (New Haven, CT: Yale University Press, 1994), 23–111, quote on 51.

32 Quoted in Wallach, "Thomas Cole," 67, 73, 82–84, 95.

33 Elizabeth Mankin Kornhauser, "Manifesto for an American Sublime: Thomas Cole's *The Oxbow*," in Elizabeth Mankin Kornhauser and Tim Barringer, *Thomas Cole's Journey: Atlantic Crossings* (New York: Metropolitan Museum of Art, 2018), 62–95, quote on 76; Karl Kusserow, "The Trouble with Empire," in Karl Kusserow and Alan C. Braddock,

eds., *Nature's Nation: American Art and Environment* (New Haven, CT: Yale University Press, 2018), 103–39, quote on 106.

34 Van Gosse, *The First Reconstruction: Black Politics in America from the Revolution to the Civil War* (Chapel Hill: University of North Carolina Press, 2021); Kate Masur, *Until Justice Be Done: America's First Civil Rights Movement, from the Revolution to Reconstruction* (New York: W. W. Norton, 2021); Eric Foner, *Gateway to Freedom: The Hidden History of the Underground Railroad* (New York: W. W. Norton, 2015); Timothy D. Walker, ed., *Sailing to Freedom: Maritime Dimensions of the Underground Railroad* (Amherst: University of Massachusetts Press, 2021).

35 Paul Simon, *Freedom's Champion: Elijah Lovejoy* (Carbondale: Southern Illinois University Press, 1994); Walter P. Johnson, *The Broken Heart of America: St. Louis and the Violent History of the United States* (New York: Basic Books, 2020), 73–83.

36 Elizabeth Ann Bartlett, ed., *Sarah Grimké: Letters on the Equality of the Sexes and Other Essays* (New Haven, CT: Yale University Press, 1988), quotes on 1–3, 102.

37 Lydia Moland, *Lydia Maria Child: A Radical American Life* (Chicago: University of Chicago Press, 2022), quotes on 163–64.

38 Gerda Lerner, *The Grimké Sisters of South Carolina: Pioneers for Women's Rights and Abolition* (Chapel Hill: University of North Carolina Press, 2004), 173–77; Robert H. Abzug, *Passionate Liberator: Theodore Dwight Weld and the Dilemma of Reform* (New York: Oxford University Press, 1980); Kerri K. Greenidge, *The Grimkes: The Legacy of Slavery in an American Family* (New York: Liveright, 2022).

39 Daniel Carpenter and Colin D. Moore, "When Canvassers Became Activists: Antislavery Petitioning and the Political Mobilization of American Women," *American Political Science Review* 108 (2014): 479–98; Lerner, *Grimké Sisters*, quote on 190–92. On petitioning, see Nancy Hewitt, *Women's Activism and Social Change: Rochester, New York, 1822–1872* (New York: Oxford University Press, 1984); Julie Roy Jeffrey, *The Great Silent Army of Abolitionism: Ordinary Women in the Antislavery Movement* (Chapel Hill: University of North Carolina Press, 1998); Jean Fagan Yellin and John C. Van Horne, eds., *The Abolitionist Sisterhood: Women's Political Culture in Antebellum America* (Ithaca, NY: Cornell University Press, 1994); and Susan Zaeske, *Signatures of Citizenship* (Chapel Hill: University of North Carolina Press, 2003).

40 William J. Cooper, *The Lost Founding Father: John Quincy Adams and the Transformation of American Politics* (New York: Liveright, 2017), 326–55, quotes on 341, 59, 360.

41 Theodore Dwight Weld, *American Slavery As It Is: Testimony of a Thousand Witnesses* (Chapel Hill: University of North Carolina Library, DocSouth edition, 2011), 16–20.

42 Manisha Sinha, *The Slave's Cause: A History of Abolition* (New Haven, CT: Yale University Press, 2016), 256–65; Corey M. Brooks, *Liberty Power: Antislavery Third Parties and the Transformation of American Politics*

(Chicago: University of Chicago Press, 2016); Carol Faulkner, *Lucretia Mott's Heresy: Abolition and Women's Rights in Nineteenth-Century America* (Philadelphia: University of Pennsylvania Press, 2011). The classic account of Quakers and abolitionism is David Brion Davis, *The Problem of Slavery in the Age of Revolution, 1770-1823* (Ithaca: Cornell University Press, 1975).

43 Henry Mayer, *All on Fire: William Lloyd Garrison and the Abolition of Slavery* (New York: St. Martin's, 1998), quote on 283, and W. Caleb McDaniel, *The Problem of Democracy in the Age of Slavery: Garrisonian Abolitionists and Transatlantic Reform* (Baton Rouge: Louisiana State University Press, 2013).

44 David W. Blight, *Frederick Douglass: Prophet of Freedom* (New York: Simon & Schuster, 2018), with quotes from 99–100 and 103.

45 Jonathan Daniel Wells, *The Kidnapping Club: Wall Street, Slavery, and Resistance on the Eve of the Civil War* (New York: Bold Type Books, 2020).

46 Gosse, *First Reconstruction*, quote on 29–30; see the rich resources at the Colored Conventions Project at https://coloredconventions.org.

47 Gary S. Selby, "Mocking the Sacred: Frederick Douglass's 'Slaveholder's Sermon' and the Antebellum Debate over Religion and Slavery," *Quarterly Journal of Speech* 88 (August 2002): 326–41, with quotes from 330–31, 333, and 337–38.

48 For a detailed accounting of these years, see Gregory P. Lampe, *Frederick Douglass: Freedom's Voice, 1818–1845* (East Lansing: Michigan State University Press, 1998), quote from viii.

49 Blight, *Frederick Douglass*, 131–33.

50 Phillip Troutman, "Grapevine in the Slave Market: African American Geopolitical Literacy and the 1841 *Creole* Revolt," in Walter Johnson, ed., *The Chattel Principle: Internal Slave Trades in the Americas* (New Haven, CT: Yale University Press, 2005), 203–33; Gerald Horne, *Negro Comrades of the Crown: African Americans and the British Empire Fight the U.S. before Emancipation* (New York: New York University Press, 2012); Walter Johnson, "White Lies: Human Property and Domestic Slavery Aboard the Slave Ship *Creole*," *Atlantic Studies* 5 (August 2005): 237–63.

51 William G. Thomas III, *A Question of Freedom: The Families Who Challenged Slavery from the Nation's Founding to the Civil War* (New Haven, CT: Yale University Press, 2020), 309–14, with quote from 310.

CHAPTER FIVE: EXPLORATIONS—1832–1848

1 Scott A. Sandage, *Born Losers: A History of Failure in America* (Cambridge, MA: Harvard University Press, 2005), quote on 88–89.

2 Stanley L. Engerman and Kenneth L. Sokoloff, "Technology and Industrialization, 1790–1914," in Stanley L. Engerman and Robert E. Gallman, eds., *The Cambridge Economic History of the United States*, Volume 2, *The Long Nineteenth Century* (New York: Cambridge University Press, 2000), 372–79; John Lauritz Larson, *The Market*

Revolution in America: Liberty, Ambition, and the Eclipse of the Common Good (New York: Cambridge University Press, 2010), 82.

Recent works on the evolution of the American economy in this era have disassembled long-familiar generalizations such as "revolutions" of transportation and markets. See Jonathan Levy, *The Ages of American Capitalism: A History of the United States* (New York: Random House, 2021); Kenneth Lipartito, "Reassembling the Economic: New Departures in Historical Materialism," *American Historical Review* 121 (February 2016): 101–39; Michael Zakim and Gary J. Kornblith, eds., *Capitalism Takes Command: The Social Transformation of Nineteenth-Century America* (Chicago: University of Chicago Press, 2012); Steven Hahn, *A Nation without Borders: The United States and Its World in an Age of Civil Wars, 1830–1910* (New York: Viking, 2016); Eli Cook, *The Pricing of Progress: Economic Indicators and the Capitalization of American Life* (Cambridge, MA: Harvard University Press, 2017); Christy Ford Chapin, "United States Financial History," in the *Oxford Research Encyclopedia*, published online March 25, 2021, at https://doi.org/10.1093/acrefore/9780199329175.013.894.

3 Joshua D. Rothman, "The Contours of Cotton Capitalism: Speculation, Slavery, and Economic Panic in Mississippi, 1832–1841," in Sven Beckert and Seth Rockman, eds., *Slavery's Capitalism: A New History of American Economic Development* (Philadelphia: University of Pennsylvania Press, 2016), 122–46; Joshua D. Rothman, *Flush Times and Fever Dreams: A Story of Capitalism and Slavery in the Age of Jackson* (Athens: University of Georgia Press, 2012), 3–4.

On the domestic slave trade, see Michael Tadman, *Speculators and Slaves: Masters, Traders, and Slaves in the Old South* (Madison: University of Wisconsin Press, 1996); Walter Johnson, *Soul by Soul: Inside the Antebellum Slave Market* (Cambridge, MA: Harvard University Press, 1999); Ira Berlin, *Generations of Captivity: A History of African-American Slaves* (Cambridge, MA: Harvard University Press, 2003); Calvin Schermerhorn, *Money over Mastery, Family over Freedom: Slavery in the Antebellum Upper South* (Baltimore: Johns Hopkins University Press, 2011); Maurie D. McInnis, *Slaves Waiting for Sale: Abolitionist Art and the American Slave Trade* (Chicago: University of Chicago Press, 2013); Walter Johnson, *River of Dark Dreams: Slavery and Empire in the Cotton Kingdom* (Cambridge, MA: Harvard University Press, 2013); Calvin Schermerhorn, *The Business of Slavery and the Rise of American Capitalism, 1815–1860* (New Haven, CT: Yale University Press, 2015) and Calvin Schermerhorn, *Unrequited Toil: A History of United States Slavery* (Cambridge: Cambridge University Press, 2018); Caitlin Rosenthal, *Accounting for Slavery: Masters and Management* (Cambridge, MA: Harvard University Press, 2018); Joshua D. Rothman, *The Ledger and the Chain: How Domestic Slave Traders Shaped America* (New York: Basic Books, 2021).

4 Gregory D. Smithers, *Native Southerners: Indigenous History from Origins to Removal* (Norman: University of Oklahoma Press, 2019), 168–70;

Alaina E. Roberts, *I've Been Here All the While: Black Freedom on Native Land* (Philadelphia: University of Pennsylvania Press, 2021), 12–28; Pekka Hämäläinen, *Indigenous Continent: The Epic Contest for North America* (New York: Liveright, 2022).

5 Joshua A. Lynn, *Preserving the White Man's Republic: Jacksonian Democracy, Race, and the Transformation of American Conservatism* (Charlottesville: University of Virginia Press, 2019); Daniel Peart and Adam I. P. Smith, eds., *Practicing Democracy: Popular Politics in the United States from the Constitution to the Civil War* (Charlottesville: University of Virginia Press, 2015), especially Introduction, 5–15, and Reeve Huston, "Rethinking the Origins of Partisan Development in the United States, 1795–1840," 64–65; Donald J. Ratcliffe, "The Nullification Crisis, Southern Discontents, and the American Political Process," *American Nineteenth-Century History* 1 (Summer 2000): 1–30; J. M. Opal, *Avenging the People: Andrew Jackson, the Rule of Law, and the American Nation* (New York: Oxford University Press, 2017).

6 Stephen W. Campbell, *The Bank War and the Partisan Press: Newspapers, Financial Institutions, and the Post Office in Jacksonian America* (Lawrence: University Press of Kansas, 2019); Stephen Mihm, "The Fog of War: Jackson, Biddle, and the Destruction of the Bank of the US," in Sean Patrick Adams, ed., *A Companion to the Era of Andrew Jackson* (Chichester, UK: Wiley-Blackwell, 2013), 348–75; Sharon Ann Murphy, *Other People's Money: How Banking Worked in the Early American Republic* (Baltimore: Johns Hopkins University Press, 2017), 83–84; Robert H. Wiebe, *The Opening of American Society: From the Adoption of the Constitution to the Eve of Disunion* (New York: Alfred A. Knopf, 1984), 151–52.

7 Michael A. Lofaro, ed., *Davy Crockett: The Man, the Legend, the Legacy, 1786–1986* (Knoxville: University of Tennessee Press, 1985), 104.

8 David Crockett, *Autobiography of David Crockett* (New York: Charles Scribner's Sons, 1923), 132–36.

9 Olivier Zunz, ed., and Arthur Goldhammer, trans., *Alexis de Tocqueville and Gustave de Beaumont in America: Their Friendship and Their Travels* (Charlottesville: University of Virginia Press, 2010), 351.

10 James Atkins Shackford, *David Crockett: The Man and the Legend* (Lincoln: University of Nebraska Press, 1996), 212; James E. Crisp, *Sleuthing the Alamo: Davy Crockett's Last Stand and Other Mysteries of the Texas Revolution* (New York: Oxford University Press, 2005); James E. Crisp and Dan Kilgore, *How Did Davy Die? And Why Do We Care So Much?* (College Station: Texas A&M University Press, 2010).

11 Alice L. Baumgartner, *South to Freedom: Runaway Slaves to Mexico and the Road to the Civil War* (New York: Basic Books, 2020), 116–19; Alan Taylor, *American Republics: A Continental History of the United States, 1783–1850* (New York: W. W. Norton, 2021), 322–23; Andrew J. Torget, *Seeds of Empire: Cotton, Slavery, and the Transformation of the Texas Borderlands, 1800–1850* (Chapel Hill: University of North Carolina

Press, 2015), 260; Gerald Horne, *The Counter Revolution of 1836: Texas Slavery & Jim Crow and the Roots of American Fascism* (New York: International Publishers, 2022).

12 Carroll Smith-Rosenberg, "Davey Crockett as Trickster: Pornography, Liminality and Symbolic Inversion in Victorian America," *Journal of Contemporary History* 17 (1982): 325–50; Lara Langer Cohen, *The Fabrication of American Literature: Fraudulence and Antebellum Print Culture* (Philadelphia: University of Pennsylvania Press, 2012).

13 Donald B. Cole, *Martin Van Buren and the American Political System* (Princeton, NJ: Princeton University Press, 2014), 257–81; Joshua A. Lynn, *Preserving the White Man's Republic: Jacksonian Democracy, Race, and the Transformation of American Conservatism* (Charlottesville: University of Virginia Press, 2019).

14 Frank Towers, "The Rise of the Whig Party," and Robert J. Cook, "Fanfare for the Common Man? Political Participation in Jacksonian America," in Adams, ed., *A Companion to the Era of Andrew Jackson*, 328–47 and 532–48, respectively; Alasdair Roberts, *America's First Great Depression: Economic Crisis and Political Disorder after the Panic of 1837* (Ithaca, NY: Cornell University Press, 2012), quotes on 43 and 104.

15 Levy, *Ages of American Capitalism*, 122–23; Jessica Lepler, *The Many Panics of 1837: People, Politics, and the Creation of a Transnational Financial Crisis* (Cambridge: Cambridge University Press, 2013), 214, 221, with quotes from 142–46; Lance E. Davis and Robert J. Cull, "International Capital Movements, Domestic Capital Markets, and American Economic Growth, 1820–1914," in Stanley L. Engerman and Robert E. Gallman, eds., *Cambridge Economic History of the United States* (New York: Cambridge University Press, 1996), 733–812, detail on 737–38.

16 Michael F. Holt, "The Election of 1840, Voter Mobilization, and the Emergence of the Second American Party System: A Reappraisal of Jacksonian Voting Behavior," in Holt, *Political Parties and American Political Development from the Age of Jackson to the Age of Lincoln* (Baton Rouge: Louisiana State University Press, 1992); Michael F. Holt, *The Rise and Fall of the American Whig Party: Jacksonian Politics and the Onset of the Civil War* (New York: Oxford University Press, 1999); Peart and Smith, eds., *Practicing Democracy*, 1–15, and Huston, "Rethinking the Origins of Partisan Development," 64–65.

17 Glenn C. Altschuler and Stuart M. Blumin, *Rude Republic: Americans and Their Politics in the Nineteenth Century* (Princeton, NJ: Princeton University Press, 2000), quote on 18; Elizabeth R. Varon, *We Mean to Be Counted: White Women and Politics in Antebellum Virginia* (Chapel Hill: University of North Carolina Press, 1998).

18 Allan Metcalf, *OK: The Improbable Story of America's Greatest Word* (New York: Oxford University Press, 2011).

19 Richard J. Ellis, *Old Tip vs. the Sly Fox: The 1840 Election and the Making of a Partisan Nation* (Lawrence: University Press of Kansas, 2020), 276–77.

20 Briton Cooper Busch, *Whaling Will Never Do for Me: The American Whaleman in the Nineteenth Century* (Lexington: University Press of Kentucky, 2015), 3–5; Eric Jay Dolin, *Leviathan: The History of Whaling in America* (New York: W. W. Norton, 2007); Lance E. Davis, Robert E. Gallman, and Karin Gleiter, *In Pursuit of Leviathan: Technology, Institutions, Productivity, and Profits in American Whaling, 1816–1906* (Chicago: University of Chicago Press, 1997); David W. Blight, *Frederick Douglass: Prophet of Freedom* (New York: Simon & Schuster, 2018), 89–91; Andrew Delbanco, *Melville: His World and Work* (New York: Alfred A. Knopf, 2005), 37–41.

21 Jeremy Zallen, *American Lucifers: The Dark History of Artificial Light, 1750–1865* (Chapel Hill: University of North Carolina Press, 2019), 49–52, with quote on 49.

22 Delbanco, *Melville*, quotes on 68 and 70.

23 Sumner La Croix, *Hawai'i: Eight Hundred Years of Political and Economic Change* (Chicago: University of Chicago Press, 2019).

24 Edward P. Crapol, *John Tyler, the Accidental President* (Chapel Hill: University of North Carolina Press, 2012), 130–73, with quotes on 147–48, 154–55, and 164.

25 Quote from Crapol, *John Tyler*, 144.

26 Nathaniel Philbrick, *Sea of Glory: America's Voyage of Discovery, The U.S. Exploring Expedition, 1838–1842* (New York: Viking, 2003), and Crapol, *John Tyler*, 144–47.

27 Richard Kurin, *The Smithsonian's History of America in 101 Objects* (New York: Penguin Press, 2013).

28 Delbanco, *Melville*, 37–45, 66–86; Stephen Railton, *Authorship and Audience: Literary Performance in the American Renaissance* (Princeton, NJ: Princeton University Press, 1991), 152–57.

29 Aaron Sachs, *Up from the Depths: Herman Melville, Lewis Mumford, and Rediscovery in Dark Times* (Princeton, NJ: Princeton University Press, 2022).

30 Anne Farrar Hyde, *An American Vision: Far Western Landscape and National Culture, 1820–1920* (New York: New York University Press, 1990), 1–11.

31 Steve Inskeep, *Imperfect Union: How Jessie and John Frémont Mapped the West, Invented Celebrity, and Helped Cause the Civil War* (New York: Penguin Press, 2020); John C. Frémont, *Frémont's First Impressions: The Original Report of His Exploring Expeditions of 1842–1844*, Anne F. Hyde, ed. (Lincoln, NE: Bison Books, 2012), with a valuable introduction.

32 Thomas Richards Jr., *Breakaway Americas: The Unmanifest Future of the Jacksonian United States* (Baltimore: Johns Hopkins University Press, 2020), 183–87.

33 Hyde, *American Vision*, 3–5, 13–14.

34 Will Bagley, *So Rugged and Mountainous: Blazing the Trails to Oregon and California* (Norman: University of Oklahoma Press, 2010), 206–8.

35 John Mack Faragher, *Women and Men on the Overland Trail* (New

Haven, CT: Yale University Press, 1979), 14–36; Bagley, *So Rugged and Mountainous*, 215–16, 230; Annette Kolodny, *The Land before Her: Fantasy and Experience of the American Frontiers, 1630–1860* (Chapel Hill: University of North Carolina Press, 1984).

36 John D. Unruh Jr., *The Plains Across: The Overland Emigrants and the Trans-Mississippi West, 1840–1860* (Urbana: University of Illinois Press, 1979); William G. Robbins, *Oregon: This Storied Land*, 2nd ed. (Seattle: University of Washington Press, 2020), 45–46.

37 Richard L. Bushman, *Joseph Smith: Rough Stone Rolling* (New York: Alfred A. Knopf, 2005), chapters 19–22.

38 Bushman, *Joseph Smith*, 410, 416, 423.

39 Benjamin E. Park, *Kingdom of Nauvoo: The Rise and Fall of a Religious Empire on the American Frontier* (New York: Liveright, 2020), 62–67; Laurel Thatcher Ulrich, *A House Full of Females: Plural Marriage and Women's Rights in Early Mormonism, 1835–1870* (New York: Alfred A. Knopf, 2017).

40 Alex Beam, *American Crucifixion: The Murder of Joseph Smith and the Fate of the Mormon Church* (New York: PublicAffairs, 2014).

41 Mark A. Noll, *America's Book: The Rise and Decline of a Bible Civilization* (New York: Oxford University Press, 2022), 252–53; Ronald L. Numbers and Jonathan M. Butler, *The Disappointed: Millerism and Millenarianism in the Nineteenth Century* (Knoxville: University of Tennessee Press, 1993); Ronald L. Numbers, *Prophetess of Health: Ellen G. White and the Origins of Seventh-Day Adventist Health Reform* (Knoxville: University of Tennessee Press, 1992). Quote of White at https://en.wikipedia.org/wiki/Ellen_G._White.

42 Quoted in Menahem Blondheim, *News over the Wires: The Telegraph and the Flow of Public Information in America, 1844–1897* (Cambridge, MA: Harvard University Press, 1994), 33.

43 Kenneth Silverman, *Lightning Man: The Accursed Life of Samuel F. B. Morse* (New York: Alfred A. Knopf, 2003), quotes on 236–37, 238–39, 240–41, and 242.

44 Benjamin Sidney Michael Schwantes, *The Train and the Telegraph: A Revisionist History* (Baltimore: Johns Hopkins University Press, 2019); Edmund Russell, "Capitalism Matters: How Financial and Technological Innovations Shaped U.S. Telegraphs, 1845–1860," *Technology and Culture* 63 (January 2022): 31–60.

45 Timothy J. Henderson, *A Glorious Defeat: Mexico and Its War with the United States* (New York: Hill and Wang, 2008), xviii–31; Brian DeLay, *War of a Thousand Deserts: Indian Raids and the U.S.-Mexican War* (New Haven, CT: Yale University Press, 2010); Pekka Hämäläinen, *Indigenous Continent: The Epic Contest for North America* (New York: Liveright, 2022), 422–30.

46 Emerson quoted in Robert Johannsen, introduction to Sam W. Haynes and Christopher Morris, eds., *Manifest Destiny and Empire: American Antebellum Expansionism* (College Station: Texas A&M University

Press, 1997), 12–13; Richard Slotkin, *The Fatal Environment: The Myth of the Frontier in the Age of Industrialization, 1800–1890* (New York: Atheneum, 1985), 175; Andrés Reséndez, *Changing National Identities at the Frontier: Texas and New Mexico, 1800–1850* (Cambridge: Cambridge University Press, 2004), 197–236.

47 John L O'Sullivan, "Annexation," *United States Magazine and Democratic Review*, Volume 17 (New York: 1845), 5–6, 9–10, in https://www .americanyawp.com/reader/manifest-destiny/john-osullivan-declares -americas-manifest-destiny-1845/.

48 Reginald Horsman, *Race and Manifest Destiny: The Origins of American Racial Anglo-Saxonism* (Cambridge, MA: Harvard University Press, 1981), with quotes from 240, 273, 260, 261, and 269–71; Perry Miller, *The Raven and the Whale: Poe, Melville, and the New York Literary Scene* (New York: Harcourt, Brace, 1956; Baltimore: Johns Hopkins University Press, 1997); Edward L. Widmer, *Young America: The Flowering of Democracy in New York City* (New York: Oxford University Press, 1999), 16–17; Yonatan Eyal, *The Young America Movement and the Transformation of the Democratic Party, 1828–1861* (Cambridge: Cambridge University Press, 2007).

49 Catlin quoted in Thomas R. Hietala, "'This Splendid Juggernaut': Westward a Nation and Its People," in Haynes and Morris, eds., *Manifest Destiny*, 48–67, with quotes on 49–50.

50 Thomas Hietala, *Manifest Design: Anxious Aggrandizement in Late Jacksonian America* (Ithaca, NY: Cornell University Press, 1985), viii; Matthew Karp, *This Vast Southern Empire: Slaveholders at the Helm of American Foreign Policy* (Cambridge, MA: Harvard University Press, 2016), 6–7, 12; Edward E. Baptist, *Creating an Old South: Middle Florida's Plantation Frontier before the Civil War* (Chapel Hill: University of North Carolina Press, 2002); Paul Frymer, *Building an American Empire: The Era of Territorial and Political Expansion* (Princeton, NJ: Princeton University Press, 2017), 136–37.

51 Robert W. Johannsen, *To the Halls of the Montezumas: The Mexican War in the American Imagination* (New York: Oxford University Press, 1985), 14–19, 20, 176, 86, 190–91.

52 Bryan F. LeBeau, *Currier & Ives: America Imagined* (Washington, DC: Smithsonian Institution Press, 2001), 64–66; Johannsen, *To the Halls*, 12; Walton Rawls, *The Great Book of Currier and Ives' America* (New York: Abbeville Press, 1979), 294–95.

53 Amy Kaplan, *The Anarchy of Empire in the Making of U.S. Culture* (Cambridge, MA: Harvard University Press, 2002), 35.

54 Amy Greenberg, *A Wicked War: Polk, Clay, Lincoln, and the 1846 U.S. Invasion of Mexico* (New York: Alfred A. Knopf, 2012), 201, 223.

55 Hietala, *Manifest Design*, 2–3; Kaplan, *Anarchy of Empire*, 26; Henderson, *Glorious Defeat*, 177, 179; Polk quoted in Karp, *This Vast Southern Empire*, 123.

56 Justin Wolff, *Richard Caton Woodville: American Painter, Artful Dodger* (Princeton, NJ: Princeton University Press, 2002), with quote on 102.

57 Laura Dassow Walls, *Henry David Thoreau: A Life* (Chicago: University of Chicago Press, 2017), 208–13.

58 Lindsay Schakenbach Regele, "Industrial Manifest Destiny: American Firearms Manufacturing and Antebellum Expansion," *Business History Review* 92 (Spring 2018): 57–83, with quotes from 77 and 80; Herbert G. Houze and Elizabeth Mankin Kornhauser, ed., *Samuel Colt: Arms, Art, and Invention* (New Haven, CT: Yale University Press, 2007); Pamela Haag, *The Gunning of America: Business and the Making of American Gun Culture* (New York: Basic Books, 2016).

CHAPTER SIX: BOUNDARIES—1840–1845

1 Helen Lefkowitz Horowitz, *Rereading Sex: Battles over Sexual Knowledge and Suppression in Nineteenth-Century America* (New York: Alfred A. Knopf, 2002), 543–74; Janet Farrell Brodie, *Contraception and Abortion in Nineteenth-Century America* (Ithaca, NY: Cornell University Press, 1994); Andrea Tone, *Devices and Desires: A History of Contraceptives in America* (New York: Hill and Wang, 2001).

2 See Horowitz, *Rereading Sex*, 75–85, 159–60, 202–5, with quotes on 75–76, 85, and 114.

3 April Haynes, "The Trials of Frederick Hollick: Obscenity, Sex Education, and Medical Democracy in the Antebellum United States," *Journal of the History of Sexuality* 12 (October 2003); April R. Haynes, *Riotous Flesh: Women, Physiology, and the Solitary Vice in Nineteenth-Century America* (Chicago: University of Chicago Press, 2015), 107–31.

4 Stephen Nissenbaum, *Sex, Diet, and Debility in Jacksonian America: Sylvester Graham and Health Reform* (Westport, CT: Greenwood Press, 1980), quote on xi.

5 Simone M. Caron, *Who Chooses? American Reproductive History since 1830* (Gainesville: University Press of Florida, 2008), 15–24; Andrea Tone, ed., *Controlling Reproduction: An American History* (Lanham, MD: Rowman & Littlefield, 1996), 62–63; Brodie, *Contraception and Abortion*; James Mohr, *Abortion in America: The Origins and Evolution of National Policy, 1800–1900* (Oxford: Oxford University Press, 1978).

6 Horowitz, *Rereading Sex*, 198–209; Dana Medoro, *Certain Concealments: Poe, Hawthorne, and Early Nineteenth-Century Abortion* (Amherst: University of Massachusetts Press, 2022), 1–18; Jennifer Wright, *Madame Restell: The Life, Death, and Resurrection of Old New York's Most Fabulous, Fearless, and Infamous Abortionist* (New York: Hachette Books, 2023).

7 Nissenbaum, *Sex, Diet, and Debility*, 15; Horowitz, *Rereading Sex*, 96–97.

8 Haynes, *Riotous Flesh*, 1–25, 56–80.

9 Nissenbaum, *Sex, Diet, and Debility*, 147; Stephen Tomlinson, *Head Masters: Phrenology, Secular Education, and Nineteenth-Century Social Thought* (Tuscaloosa: University of Alabama Press, 2005); James Poskett, *Materials of the Mind: Phrenology, Race, and the Global History of Science, 1815–1920* (Chicago: University of Chicago Press, 2019).

10 Richard L. Bushman, *The Refinement of America: Persons, Houses, Cities*

(New York: Vintage, 1992), especially 402–48; Wendy A. Woloson, "The
Rise of the Consumer in the Age of Jackson," in Sean Patrick Adams,
ed., *A Companion to the Era of Andrew Jackson* (Chichester, UK: Wiley-
Blackwell, 2013), 489–508.

11 Kathryn Kish Sklar, *Catharine Beecher: A Study in American Domesticity*
(New Haven, CT: Yale University Press, 1973), quotes from 155 and
157. On the limitations of the "cult of true womanhood," see Frances
B. Cogan, *All-American Girl: The Ideal of Real Womanhood in Mid-
Nineteenth-Century America* (Athens: University of Georgia Press, 1989).
12 Megan Marshall, *Margaret Fuller: A New American Life* (New York:
Houghton Mifflin Harcourt, 2013), quotes on 233, 235–37; "Our
City Charities," in Jeffrey Steele, ed., *The Essential Margaret Fuller*
(New Brunswick, NJ: Rutgers University Press, 1992), 385–91; Karen
Roggenkamp, *Sympathy, Madness, and Crime: How Four Nineteenth-
Century Journalists Made the Newspaper Women's Business* (Kent, OH:
Kent State University Press, 2016), 34–52.
13 Margaret Fuller, "The Great Lawsuit," *The Dial* 4 (July 1843), 1–48,
quoted in Perry Miller, ed., *The Transcendentalists: An Anthology*
(Cambridge, MA: Harvard University Press, 1950), 458, 460; John
Matteson, *The Lives of Margaret Fuller: A Biography* (New York: W. W.
Norton, 2012), 261–67, quote on 256.
14 Marshall, *Margaret Fuller*, 230–31.
15 Thomas J. Brown, *Dorothea Dix: New England Reformer* (Cambridge,
MA: Harvard University Press, 1998), with quotes from 89, 118, 128,
140, and 158.
16 Brown, *Dorothea Dix*, 146.
17 George Lippard, *The Quaker City; or, The Monks of Monk Hall*, David
S. Reynolds, ed. (Amherst: University of Massachusetts Press, 1995
[1845]), quotes from xii and viii; Philip F. Gura, *Truth's Ragged Edge:
The Rise of the American Novel* (New York: Farrar, Straus & Giroux,
2013), 83–90.
18 Kenneth Silverman, *Edgar Allan Poe: Mournful and Never-Ending
Remembrance* (New York: HarperCollins, 1991), quotes on 234, 240–41,
257, and 249.
19 Laura Dassow Walls, *Henry David Thoreau: A Life* (Chicago: University
of Chicago Press, 2017), 182–201, with quotes from 200, 185, 189, and
191; Robert A. Gross, *The Transcendentalists and Their World* (New York:
Farrar, Straus & Giroux, 2021), 806–22; Elise Virginia Lemire, *Black
Walden: Slavery and Its Aftermath in Concord, Massachusetts* (Philadelphia:
University of Pennsylvania Press, 2009).
20 Lisa Goff, *Shantytown, USA: Forgotten Landscapes of the Working Poor*
(Cambridge, MA: Harvard University Press, 2016).
21 Sarah N. Roth, *Gender and Race in Antebellum Popular Culture*
(Cambridge: Cambridge University Press, 2014), 77–102; Manisha
Sinha, *The Slave's Cause: A History of Abolition* (New Haven, CT: Yale
University Press, 2016), 421–36.

22 *New-York Tribune* review of *Narrative of the Life of Frederick Douglass*, June 10, 1845.

23 Ken Emerson, *Doo-dah! Stephen Foster and the Rise of American Popular Culture* (New York: Simon & Schuster, 1997), 66.

24 Katrina Dyonne Thompson, *Ring Shout, Wheel About: The Racial Politics of Music and Dance in North American Slavery* (Urbana: University of Illinois Press, 2014), 170–72.

25 Laurent Dubois, *The Banjo: America's African Instrument* (Cambridge, MA: Harvard University Press, 2016), 171, 196–97; Richard Crawford, *America's Musical Life: A History* (New York: W. W. Norton, 2001), 213–14; Kristina R. Gaddy, *Well of Souls: Uncovering the Banjo's Hidden History* (New York: W. W. Norton, 2022).

26 Emerson, *Doo-dah!*, 66, 70.

27 Crawford, *America's Musical Life*, 257–58, including the quotes; Brian Roberts, *Blackface Nation: Race, Reform, and Identity in American Popular Music, 1812–1925* (Chicago: University of Chicago Press, 2017); Emerson, *Doo-Dah!*, 75.

28 James D. Bratt, "The Reorientation of American Protestantism, 1835–1845," *Church History* 67 (March 1998): 52–82.

29 Richard Carwardine, *Evangelicals and Politics in Antebellum America* (New Haven, CT: Yale University Press, 1993), 141–73, with quotes from 159–60, 164–66; John R. McKivigan, *The War against Proslavery Religion: Abolitionism and the Northern Churches, 1830–1865* (Ithaca, NY: Cornell University Press, 1984).

30 Beth Barton Schweiger, *The Gospel Working Up: Progress and the Pulpit in Nineteenth-Century Virginia* (New York: Oxford University Press, 2000), 81–86; and Charles F. Irons, *The Origins of Proslavery Christianity: White and Black Evangelicals in Colonial and Antebellum Virginia* (Chapel Hill: University of North Carolina Press, 2008), 196–208, with quotes from 198–99, 199–200, and 202–3.

31 Irons, *Origins*, 187–90; Gregg D. Kimball, *American City, Southern Place: A Cultural History of Antebellum Richmond* (Athens: University of Georgia Press, 2000), 124–25.

32 Beth Barton Schweiger, *A Literate South: Reading before Emancipation* (New Haven, CT: Yale University Press, 2019); Michael O'Brien, *Conjectures of Order: Intellectual Life and the American South, 1810–1860* (Chapel Hill: University of North Carolina Press, 2004); John W. Quist, *Restless Visionaries: The Social Roots of Antebellum Reform in Alabama and Michigan* (Baton Rouge: Louisiana State University Press, 1998); Jonathan Daniel Wells, *The Origins of the Southern Middle Class, 1800–1861* (Chapel Hill: University of North Carolina Press, 2004).

CHAPTER SEVEN: VOYAGES—1845–1850

1 Carl J. Bon Tempo and Hasia R. Diner, *Immigration: An American History* (New Haven, CT: Yale University Press, 2022), 65–82.

2 Kerby A. Miller, *Emigrants and Exiles: Ireland and the Irish Exodus to*

North America (New York: Oxford University Press, 1985), quote from 281; Donald Harman Akenson, *Ireland, Sweden, and the Great European Migration, 1815–1914* (Montreal: McGill-Queen's University Press, 2011), whose revised figures on 156–57 I have cited.

3 Quoted in J. Matthew Gallman, *Receiving Erin's Children: Philadelphia, Liverpool, and the Irish Famine Migration, 1845–1855* (Chapel Hill: University of North Carolina Press, 2000), 2.

4 Gallman, *Receiving Erin's Children*, quote on 220–21. For overviews, see Tyler Anbinder, Cormac Ó Gráda, and Simone A. Wegge, "Networks and Opportunities: A Digital History of Ireland's Great Famine Refugees in New York," *American Historical Review* 124 (December 2019): 1591–629; Hasia R. Diner, *Erin's Daughters in America: Irish Immigrant Women in the Nineteenth Century* (Baltimore: Johns Hopkins University Press, 1983).

5 Hasia Diner, *Jewish Americans: The Immigrant Experience* (New York: Levin, 2002), 65–92.

6 Tyler Anbinder, *Five Points: The 19th-Century New York City Neighborhood That Invented Tap Dance, Stole Elections, and Became the World's Most Notorious Slum* (New York: The Free Press, 2001), 172–75.

7 Malcolm J. Rohrbough, *Days of Gold: The California Gold Rush and the American Nation* (Berkeley: University of California Press, 1997), 1–25; Mae Ngai, *The Chinese Question: The Gold Rushes and Global Politics* (New York: W. W. Norton, 2021); Thomas Richards Jr., *Breakaway Americas: The Unmanifest Future of the Jacksonian United States* (Baltimore: Johns Hopkins University Press, 2020), 235–36; Michael Wallis, *The Best Land under Heaven: The Donner Party in the Age of Manifest Destiny* (New York: Liveright, 2017).

8 Amy K. DeFalco Lippert, *Consuming Identities: Visual Culture in Nineteenth-Century San Francisco* (New York: Oxford University Press, 2018); Richard T. Stillson, *Spreading the Word: A History of Information in the California Gold Rush* (Lincoln: University of Nebraska Press, 2006); Archer Butler Hulbert, *Forty-Niners: The Chronicle of the California Trail* (Boston: Little, Brown, 1931), quote on 167–68; Ken Emerson, *Doo-dah! Stephen Foster and the Rise of American Popular Culture* (New York: Simon & Schuster, 1997), quote on 9.

9 Benjamin Madley, *An American Genocide: The United States and the California Indian Catastrophe, 1846–1873* (New Haven, CT: Yale University Press, 2016), 130–44.

10 Ngai, *Chinese Question*; Susan Lee Johnson, *Roaring Camp: The Social World of the California Gold Rush* (New York: W. W. Norton, 2000); Rohrbough, *Days of Gold*.

11 Ilyon Woo, *Master, Slave, Husband, Wife: An Epic Journey from Slavery to Freedom* (New York: Simon & Schuster, 2023); Richard J. M. Blackett, *Beating against the Barriers: Biographical Essays in Nineteenth-Century Afro-American History* (Baton Rouge: Louisiana State University Press, 1989), 104–7, 119–22.

12 Judith Wellman, *The Road to Seneca Falls: Elizabeth Cady Stanton and*

the First Woman's Rights Convention (Urbana: University of Illinois Press, 2004), with quotes from 60, 63, 199, 200, 210, and 211; Lori D. Ginzberg, *Untidy Origins: A Story of Woman's Rights in Antebellum New York* (Chapel Hill: University of North Carolina Press, 2005); Lisa Tetrault, *The Myth of Seneca Falls: Memory and the Women's Suffrage Movement, 1848–1898* (Chapel Hill: University of North Carolina Press, 2014).

13 Martha S. Jones, *All Bound Up Together: The Woman Question in African American Public Culture, 1830–1900* (Chapel Hill: University of North Carolina Press, 2007), quote on 59–60.

14 Sylvia E. Crane, *White Silence: Greenough, Powers, and Crawford— American Sculptors in Nineteenth-Century Italy* (Coral Gables: University of Miami Press, 1972), 168–269. Quotes on 195, 203–4, 218–19, 220– 21, and 222.

15 Joy S. Kasson, *Marble Queens and Captives: Women in Nineteenth-Century American Sculpture* (New Haven, CT: Yale University Press, 1990), 46– 72; Charmaine Nelson, *The Color of Stone: Sculpting the Black Female Subject in Nineteenth-Century America* (Minneapolis: University of Minnesota Press, 2007), 75–86.

16 Vivien M. Green, "Hiram Powers's 'Greek Slave': Emblem of Freedom," *American Art Journal* 14 (Autumn 1982): 31–39, with quotes from 38.

17 Ann Braude, *Radical Spirits: Spiritualism and Women's Rights in Nineteenth-Century America* (Bloomington: Indiana University Press, 1989, second edition, 2001), 35; Kathryn Troy, *The Specter of the Indian: Race, Gender, and Ghosts in American Seances, 1848–1890* (Albany: State University of New York Press, 2017).

18 Robert S. Cox, *Body and Soul: A Sympathetic History of American Spiritualism* (Charlottesville: University of Virginia Press, 2003); Charles Colbert, *Haunted Visions: Spiritualism and American Art* (Philadelphia: University of Pennsylvania Press, 2011), 10.

19 Quoted in Cox, *Body and Soul*, 7.

20 Cox, *Body and Soul*, 16–20.

21 Quoted in Braude, *Radical Spirits*, 44–45.

22 Fergus M. Bordewich, *America's Great Debate: Henry Clay, Stephen A. Douglas, and the Compromise That Preserved the Union* (New York: Simon & Schuster, 2012), quote on 214; Christoph Irmscher, *Louis Agassiz: Creator of American Science* (New York: Houghton Mifflin, 2013).

23 Irmscher, *Louis Agassiz*, 225–33, with quotes on 237, 231. On Nott and his colleagues, see Michael O'Brien, *Conjectures of Order: Intellectual Life and the American South, 1810–1860* (Chapel Hill: University of North Carolina Press, 2004), 240–52.

24 Ilisa Barbash, Molly Rogers, and Deborah Willis, eds., *To Make Their Own Way in the World: The Enduring Legacy of the Zealy Daguerreotypes* (Boston: Peabody Museum Press/Aperture, 2020).

25 Agassiz quoted in Reginald Horsman, *Race and Manifest Destiny: The Origins of American Racial Anglo-Saxonism* (Cambridge, MA: Harvard

University Press, 1981), 132, and sales figures on 135; Irmscher, *Louis Agassiz*, quotes on 240–41.

26 Laura Dassow Walls, *Henry David Thoreau: A Life* (Chicago: University of Chicago Press, 2017), 254–57, 262–63, 268–72.

27 "Address delivered before the Agricultural society of Rutland County, Sept. 30, 1847, by George P. Marsh," at https://memory.loc.gov/ammem/amrvhtml/cnchron1.html; David Lowenthal, *George Perkins Marsh: Prophet of Conservation* (Seattle: University of Washington Press, 2009). Marsh's influential book, *Man and Nature: Or, Physical Geography as Modified by Human Action*, would appear in 1864, when Marsh served as minister to Italy.

28 Susan Fenimore Cooper, *Rural Hours*, Rochelle Johnson and Daniel Patterson, eds. (Athens: University of Georgia Press, 1998 [1850]), 53, 128, 132; Rochelle Johnson and Daniel Patterson, eds., *Susan Fenimore Cooper: New Essays on* Rural Hours *and Other Works* (Athens: University of Georgia Press, 2001); Tina Gianquitto, *Good Observers of Nature: American Women and the Scientific Study of the Natural World, 1820–1885* (Athens: University of Georgia Press, 2007), 100–131; Vera Norwood, *Made from This Earth: American Women and Nature* (Chapel Hill: University of North Carolina Press, 1993), 25–53.

29 Kenneth Silverman, *Edgar A. Poe: Mournful and Never-Ending Remembrance* (New York: HarperCollins, 1991), and John Tresch, *The Reason for the Darkness of the Night: Edgar Allan Poe and the Forging of American Science* (New York: Farrar, Straus & Giroux, 2021). The quotes that follow are from Tresch, *Reason*, 9–12, 373–74, 377–78, and Silverman, *Edgar A. Poe*, 435–36; Mark Dawidziak, *A Mystery of Mysteries: The Death and Life of Edgar Allan Poe* (New York: St. Martin's Press, 2023).

30 Andrea Wulf, *The Invention of Nature: Alexander von Humboldt's New World* (New York: Alfred A. Knopf, 2015), 249–62; Aaron Sachs, *The Humboldt Current: Nineteenth-Century Exploration and the Roots of American Environmentalism* (New York: Viking, 2006), 73–74.

31 Jeffrey Steele, ed., *The Essential Margaret Fuller* (New Brunswick, NJ: Rutgers University Press, 1992), quotes on xliv–xlv; Megan Marshall, *Margaret Fuller: A New American Life* (Boston: Houghton Mifflin, 2013), quote on 315–16.

32 Steele, *Essential Margaret Fuller*, quote on 434–35; Marshall, *Margaret Fuller*, 366–90; John Matteson, *The Lives of Margaret Fuller* (New York: W. W. Norton, 2012), 420–35; Walls, *Henry David Thoreau*, 290–95.

33 Marshall, *Margaret Fuller*, 387–91.

CHAPTER EIGHT: CONFRONTATIONS—1850–1855

1 James R. Mellow, *Nathaniel Hawthorne in His Times* (Boston: Houghton Mifflin, 1980), quotes on 309–11; Brenda Wineapple, *Hawthorne: A Life* (New York: Alfred A. Knopf, 2003), 107–8, 208–9.

2 Stephen Railton, *Authorship and Audience: Literary Performance in the*

American Renaissance (Princeton, NJ: Princeton University Press, 1991), 107–31; Wineapple, *Hawthorne*, 214–16.

3   Wineapple, *Hawthorne*, 218–25, quotes on 225; Mellow, *Nathaniel Hawthorne in His Times*, 326–84.

4   Andrew Delbanco, *Melville: His World and Work* (New York: Alfred A. Knopf, 2005), 107–13, with quote on 111.

5   Wineapple, *Hawthorne*, quote on 225; Maurice S. Lee, *Overwhelmed: Literature, Aesthetics, and the Nineteenth-Century Information Revolution* (Princeton, NJ: Princeton University Press, 2019); on the influence of the Wilkes expedition, see George Cotkin, *Dive Deeper: Journeys with Moby-Dick* (New York: Oxford University Press, 2012), and David Jaffé, *The Stormy Petrel and the Whale: Some Origins of* Moby-Dick (Washington, DC: University Press of America, 1982 [1976]).

6   Delbanco, *Melville*, 124–75; Aaron Sachs, *Up from the Depths: Herman Melville, Lewis Mumford, and Rediscovery in Dark Times* (Princeton, NJ: Princeton University Press, 2022); Peter West, *The Arbiters of Reality: Hawthorne, Melville, and the Rise of Mass Information Culture* (Columbus: Ohio State University Press, 2008); Robert S. Levine, ed., *The New Cambridge Companion to Herman Melville* (New York: Cambridge University Press, 2014).

7   Delbanco, *Melville*, quote on 124; Railton, *Authorship and Audience*, 163–78. On Melville's possible relationship with the recipient of his warning, see Michael Shelden, *Melville in Love: The Secret Life of Herman Melville and the Muse of* Moby-Dick (New York: HarperCollins, 2016), 102–3.

8   Wineapple, *Hawthorne*, 235–51, quote on 235.

9   Rebecca Rego Barry, "The Wide, Wide World beyond a Tiny, Deserted Island: At Home with Susan and Anna Warner," in Jennifer Harris and Hilary Iris Lowe, eds., *From Page to Place: American Literary Tourism and the Afterlives of Authors* (Amherst: University of Massachusetts Press, 2017), 88–106, quotes from 91–92; Susan Williams, "Widening the World: Susan Warner, Her Readers, and the Assumption of Authorship," *American Quarterly* 42 (December 1990): 565–86.

10 See the pioneering work by Nina Baym, *Women's Fiction: A Guide to Novels by and about Women in America, 1820–1870* (Ithaca, NY: Cornell University Press, 1979).

11 Sharon Estes, "'In Its English Dress': Reading Susan Warner's *The Wild, Wild World* as a Transatlantic Religious Bestseller," in Beth L. Lueck, Brigitte Bailey, and Lucinda L. Damon-Bach, eds., *Transatlantic Women: Nineteenth-Century American Women Writers and Great Britain* (Durham: University of New Hampshire Press, 2012), 208–31, quotes from 209, 223–24.

12 Susan S. Williams, *Reclaiming Authorship: Literary Women in America* (Philadelphia: University of Pennsylvania Press, 2006), 72–96.

13 Yellow Bird [John Rollin Ridge], *The Life and Adventures of Joaquín Murieta: The Celebrated California Bandit*, introduction by Joseph Henry Jackson (Norman: University of Oklahoma Press, 1955); James W.

Parins, *John Rollin Ridge: His Life and Works* (Lincoln: University of Nebraska Press, 1991); Edward Whitley, *American Bards: Walt Whitman and Other Unlikely Candidates for National Poet* (Chapel Hill: University of North Carolina Press, 2010), 116–38.

14 Michael Todd Landis, *Northern Men with Southern Loyalties: The Democratic Party and the Sectional Crisis* (Ithaca, NY: Cornell University Press, 2015), 32–36; Elizabeth R. Varon, *Disunion! The Coming of the American Civil War, 1789–1859* (Chapel Hill: University of North Carolina Press, 2008), 235–36; Joanne B. Freeman, *The Field of Blood: Violence in Congress and the Road to Civil War* (New York: Farrar, Straus & Giroux, 2018); Stephen E. Maizlish, *A Strife of Tongues: The Compromise of 1850 and the Ideological Foundations of the American Civil War* (Charlottesville: University of Virginia Press, 2018); Andrew Delbanco, *The War before the War: Fugitive Slaves and the Struggle for America's Soul from the Revolution to the Civil War* (New York: Penguin, 2018), 258.

15 John L. Brooke, *"There Is a North": Fugitive Slaves, Political Crisis, and Cultural Transformation in the Coming of the Civil War* (Amherst: University of Massachusetts Press, 2019), 81–93; R. J. M. Blackett, *The Captive's Quest for Freedom: Fugitive Slaves, the 1850 Fugitive Slave Law, and the Politics of Slavery* (Cambridge: Cambridge University Press, 2018), 5; Jonathan Daniel Wells, *Blind No More: African American Resistance, Free-Soil Politics, and the Coming of the Civil War* (Athens: University of Georgia Press, 2019), 57–60; Robert H. Churchill, *The Underground Railroad and the Geography of Violence in Antebellum America* (New York: Cambridge University Press, 2020), 15–39, with quote on 15; Steven Kantrowitz, *More than Freedom: Fighting for Black Citizenship in a White Republic, 1829–1889* (New York: Penguin, 2012), 175–85.

16 Nell Irvin Painter, *Sojourner Truth: A Life, a Symbol* (New York: W. W. Norton, 1996), quotes on 125–26.

17 Catherine Clinton, *Harriet Tubman: The Road to Freedom* (Boston: Little, Brown, 2004), quote on 91.

18 Brooke, *"There Is a North,"* 116–27, with quote from 127.

19 Railton, *Authorship and Audience*, 74–87; Brooke, *"There Is a North,"* 128–29; Barbara A. White, *The Beecher Sisters* (New Haven, CT: Yale University Press, 2003), 52–53. For context, see David S. Reynolds, *Mightier than the Sword:* Uncle Tom's Cabin *and the Battle for America* (New York: W. W. Norton, 2011); Sarah Meer, *Uncle Tom Mania: Slavery, Minstrelsy, and Transatlantic Culture in the 1850s* (Athens: University of Georgia Press, 2005); Thomas F. Gossett, Uncle Tom's Cabin *and American Culture* (Dallas: Southern Methodist University Press, 1985).

20 Brooke, *"There Is a North,"* quote from 138; Railton, *Authorship and Audience*, quote on 84.

21 Barbara Hochman, *"Uncle Tom's Cabin" and the Reading Revolution* (Amherst: University of Massachusetts Press, 2011); Brooke, *"There Is a North,"* quote from 141, 148–49; White, *Beecher Sisters*, quote on 54;

Marianne Noble, *Rethinking Sympathy and Human Contact in Nineteenth-Century American Literature: Hawthorne, Douglass, Stowe, Dickinson* (Cambridge: Cambridge University Press, 2019).

22 White, *Beecher Sisters*, 6; Brooke, "*There Is a North*," 183–99.

23 Ezra Greenspan, *William Wells Brown: An African American Life* (New York: W. W. Norton, 2014), 240–55, quote from 241; Manisha Sinha, *The Slave's Cause: A History of Abolition* (New Haven, CT: Yale University Press, 2016), 236–50.

24 Elizabeth Mankin Kornhauser, "George Catlin and the Colt Firearms Series," in Herbert G. Houze, and Elizabeth Mankin Kornhauser, ed., *Samuel Colt: Arms, Art, and Invention* (New Haven, CT: Yale University Press, 2007), 216.

25 Lisa Merrill, "Exhibiting Race 'Under the World's Huge Glass Case': William and Ellen Craft and William Wells Brown at the Great Exhibition in Crystal Palace, London, 1851," *Slavery & Abolition* 33 (June 2012): 321–36; Kenneth Salzer, "Great Exhibitions: Ellen Craft on the British Abolitionist Stage," in Lueck, et al., eds. *Transatlantic Women*, 136–52; Ilyon Woo, *Master, Slave, Husband, Wife: An Epic Journey from Slavery to Freedom* (New York: Simon & Schuster, 2023).

26 Sarah Ruffing Robbins, "Harriet Beecher Stowe, Starring as Benevolent Celebrity Traveler," in Lueck et al., eds., *Transatlantic Women*, 71–88; White, *Beecher Sisters*, 58; Ann duCille, "Where in the World Is William Wells Brown? Thomas Jefferson, Sally Hemings, and the DNA of African-American Literary History," *American Literary History* 12 (Autumn 2000): 443–62.

27 David Blight, *Frederick Douglass: Prophet of Freedom* (New York: Simon & Schuster, 2018), 213–36, quotes on 233, 235–36.

28 Frederick Law Olmsted's letters were later gathered in three volumes and then into a single compilation in 1861. Quotes are here from *A Journey in the Seaboard Slave States, with Remarks on Their Economy* (New York: Dix & Edwards, 1856), 18, 420, 446.

29 Laura Wood Roper, *FLO: A Biography of Frederick Law Olmsted* (Baltimore: Johns Hopkins University Press, 1983), 86–91, quote on 91.

30 Solomon Northup, Henry Louis Gates Jr., and Kevin M. Burke, eds., *Twelve Years a Slave* (New York: W. W. Norton, 2017), quotes from 97–98, 143–46.

31 Zoe Trodd, "A Renaissance-Self: Frederick Douglass and the Art of Remaking," in Christopher Phillips, ed., *The Cambridge Companion to the Literature of the American Renaissance* (New York: Cambridge University Press, 2018), 189–204.

32 Frederick Douglass, *My Bondage and My Freedom* (New York and Auburn: Miller, Orton, and Mulligan, 1855), Appendix: "The Anti-Slavery Movement: Extracts from a Lecture before Various Anti-Slavery Bodies, in the Winter of 1855," 457–64.

33 Brooke, "*There Is a North*," quote on 174; Blight, *Frederick Douglass*, 252–60.

34 Ken Emerson, *Doo-dah! Stephen Foster and the Rise of American Popular*

Culture (New York: Simon & Schuster, 1997), quotes on 55 and 80; Emily Bingham, *My Old Kentucky Home: The Astonishing Life and Reckoning of an Iconic American Song* (New York: Alfred A. Knopf, 2022).

35 Emerson, *Doo-dah!*, 158–74.

36 Emerson, *Doo-dah!*, 179–200; Bingham, *My Old Kentucky Home*.

37 S. Frederick Starr, *Bamboula! The Life and Times of Louis Moreau Gottschalk* (New York: Oxford University Press, 1995); Kristina R. Gaddy, *Well of Souls: Uncovering the Banjo's Hidden History* (New York: W. W. Norton, 2022), 196–202.

38 Robin Bolton-Smith, ed., *Lilly Martin Spencer, 1822–1902: The Joys of Sentiment* (Washington, DC: Smithsonian Institution Press, 1973), 41, 54; Elizabeth Johns, *American Genre Painting: The Politics of Everyday Life* (New Haven, CT: Yale University Press, 1991), 169–75; David M. Lubin, *Picturing a Nation: Art and Social Change in Nineteenth-Century America* (New Haven, CT: Yale University Press, 1994), 159–203.

39 Deborah J. Johnson, "William Sidney Mount: Painter of American Life," in Deborah J. Johnson, ed., *William Sidney Mount: Painter of American Life* (New York: American Federation of Arts, 1998), 61–62; Johns, *American Genre Painting*, 117–18.

40 Johns, *American Genre Painting*, quote on 121; Bruce Robertson, "Stories for the Public, 1830–1860," in H. Barbara Weinberg and Carrie Rebora Barratt, eds., *American Stories: Paintings of Everyday Life, 1765–1915* (New Haven, CT: Yale University Press, 2010), 28–73.

41 Christopher J. Smith, *The Creolization of American Culture: William Sidney Mount and the Roots of Blackface Minstrelsy* (Urbana: University of Illinois Press, 2013), 123–46; Barnard F. Reilly Jr., "Translation and Transformation: The Prints after William Sidney Mount," in Johnson, ed., *William Sidney Mount*, 133–47.

42 Jochen Wierich, *Grand Themes: Emanuel Leutze,* Washington Crossing the Delaware, *and American History Painting* (University Park: Pennsylvania State University Press, 2012); Patricia Hills, "Painting Race: Eastman Johnson's Pictures of Slaves, Ex-Slaves, and Freedmen," in Teresa A. Carbone and Patricia Hills, eds., *Eastman Johnson: Painting America* (Brooklyn, NY: Brooklyn Museum of Art, 1999), 120–65.

43 Wierich, *Grand Themes*, 132–35; Robertson, "Stories for the Public," 28–73.

44 Johns, *American Genre Painting*, quote on 130.

45 Farah Jasmine Griffin, *Read until You Understand: The Profound Wisdom of Black Life and Literature* (New York: W. W. Norton, 2021), 112; Melba Joyce Boyd, *Discarded Legacy: Politics and Poetics in the Life of Frances E. W. Harper, 1825–1911* (Detroit: Wayne State University Press, 1994), 43.

46 Steven Saunders, "The Social Agenda of Stephen Foster's Plantation Melodies," *American Music* 30 (Fall 2012): 275–89, quote on 289.

CHAPTER NINE: CULMINATIONS—1855–1860

1 Robert Wilson, *Barnum: An American Life* (New York: Simon & Schuster, 2019), 1–61; Neil Harris, *Humbug: The Art of P.T. Barnum* (Boston: Little, Brown, 1973), 212–17.

2 Nicholas A. Basbanes, *Cross of Snow: A Life of Henry Wadsworth Longfellow* (New York: Alfred A. Knopf, 2020), 292–98; Christopher Irmscher, *Longfellow Redux* (Urbana: University of Illinois Press, 2006), 106–8; Paul Giles, *The Global Remapping of American Literature* (Princeton, NJ: Princeton University Press, 2011), 77–78.

3 Joyce W. Warren, *Fanny Fern: An Independent Woman* (New Brunswick, NJ: Rutgers University Press, 1992); Nancy A. Walker, *Fanny Fern* (New York: Twayne, 1993); Jennifer L. Brady, "Fern, Warner, and the Work of Sentimentality," in Christopher N. Phillips, ed., *Cambridge Companion to the Literature of the American Renaissance* (Cambridge: Cambridge University Press, 2018), 142–56, quote on 154–55.

4 Karen Roggenkamp, *Sympathy, Madness, and Crime: How Four Nineteenth-Century Journalists Made the Newspaper Women's Business* (Kent, OH: Kent State University Press, 2016), 53–72, quote on 55; Debra J. Rosenthal, *Performatively Speaking: Speech and Action in Antebellum American Literature* (Charlottesville: University of Virginia Press, 2015), 44–62, quote on 45.

5 Elizabeth Johns, *American Genre Painting: The Politics of Everyday Life* (New Haven, CT: Yale University Press, 1991), 169–75; David M. Lubin, *Picturing a Nation: Art and Social Change in Nineteenth-Century America* (New Haven, CT: Yale University Press, 1994), 159–203; Robin Bolton-Smith, ed., *Lilly Martin Spencer, 1822–1902: The Joys of Sentiment* (Washington, DC: Smithsonian Institution Press, 1973), quotes on 54 and 55.

6 Erkki Huhtamo, *Illusions in Motion: Media Archaeology of the Moving Panorama and Related Spectacles* (Cambridge, MA: MIT Press, 2013), 180–85.

7 Naurice Frank Woods Jr., *Race and Racism in Nineteenth-Century Art: The Ascendency of Robert Duncanson, Edward Bannister, and Edmonia Lewis* (Jackson: University of Mississippi Press, 2021), 35–38; Judith Wilson, "The Challenges of the Nineteenth Century: Two Recent Landmark Publications of African American Visual Production," *International Review of African American Art* 1 (January 1995): 45–59; Lubin, *Picturing a Nation*, 106–57.

8 Lubin, *Picturing a Nation*, 107–58; Lucinda Moore, "America's Forgotten Landscape Painter: Robert S. Duncanson," *Smithsonian Magazine*, October 12, 2011. The murals have been restored at the Taft Museum of Art in Cincinnati, located in the former Longworth mansion.

9 Tamera Lenz Muente, "The Power of Art and Freedom: A Look at Duncanson's Cincinnati and His Enduring Freedom," Taft Museum of Art Blog at https://www.taftmuseum.org/blog/posts/2020/august/the-power-of-art-and-freedom.

10 Anne Farrar Hyde, *An American Vision: Far Western Landscape and National Culture, 1820–1920* (New York: New York University Press, 1990), 44–50, quote on 47.

11 Matthew N. Johnston, *Narrating the Landscape: Print Culture and American Expansion in the Nineteenth Century* (Norman: University of

Oklahoma Press, 2016), 9–14; essays by Alan Trachtenberg, Grant B. Romer, and Wendy Wick Reaves and Sally Pierce in Grant B. Romer and Brian Wallis, eds., *Young America: The Daguerreotypes of Southworth & Hawes* (New York: International Center of Photography, 2005).

12 Quoted in Watson G. Branch, *Melville: The Critical Heritage* (London: Routledge and Kegan Paul, 1974), 360.

13 Herman Melville, *The Confidence-Man: His Masquerade* (New York: Dix, Edwards, 1857), 74.

14 Andrew Delbanco, *Melville: His World and Work* (New York: Alfred A. Knopf, 2005), quote on 252–53; Peter West, *The Arbiters of Reality: Hawthorne, Melville, and the Rise of Mass Information Culture* (Columbus: Ohio State University Press, 2008); Robert S. Levine, ed., *The New Cambridge Companion to Herman Melville* (New York: Cambridge University Press, 2014).

15 Ruth Brandon, *A Capitalist Romance: Singer and the Sewing Machine* (Philadelphia: Lippincott, 1977), 124–25; William Cronon, *Nature's Metropolis: Chicago and the Great West* (New York: W. W. Norton, 1991), 313–18; Lynn Downey, *Levi Strauss: The Man Who Gave Blue Jeans to the World* (Amherst: University of Massachusetts Press, 2016). In 1871, another immigrant, Jacob Davis, would suggest a partnership with Strauss, his fabric supplier, for cotton denim work pants reinforced with rivets. They would prove popular.

16 Joseph Messerli, *Horace Mann: A Biography* (New York: Alfred A. Knopf, 1972), 360–61.

17 Bob Johnson, *Carbon Nation: Fossil Fuels in the Making of American Culture* (Lawrence: University Press of Kansas, 2014), 369.

18 Christopher F. Jones, *Routes of Power: Energy and Modern America* (Cambridge, MA: Harvard University Press, 2014), 23–86; Louis C. Hunter, *A History of Industrial Power in the United States, 1780–1930*, Volume 2, *Steam Power* (Charlottesville: University of Virginia Press, 1985), 410–30; Andreas Malm, *Fossil Capital: The Rise of Steam Power and the Roots of Global Warming* (London: Verso, 2015).

19 Jeremy Zallen, *American Lucifers: The Dark History of Artificial Light, 1750–1865* (Chapel Hill: University of North Carolina Press, 2019), with quotes that follow from 58, 61, 62, 65–66, and 68.

20 Jones, *Routes of Power*, 90–98.

21 Robert D. Richardson Jr., *Emerson: The Mind on Fire* (Berkeley: University of California Press, 1996), 527–29.

22 Ralph Waldo Emerson, *Essays and Lectures*, Joel Porte, ed. (New York: Library of America, 1983), 465.

23 Jerome Loving, *Walt Whitman: The Song of Himself* (Berkeley: University of California Press, 1999); David S. Reynolds, *Walt Whitman's America: A Cultural Biography* (New York: Alfred A. Knopf, 1995); Mark Edmundson, *Song of Ourselves: Walt Whitman and the Fight for Democracy* (Cambridge, MA: Harvard University Press, 2021); and Mark Doty, *What Is the Grass: Walt Whitman in My Life* (New York: W. W. Norton,

2020). The Walt Whitman Archive, an invaluable source, is available at https://whitmanarchive.org.

24 *New York Ledger*, May 10, 1856, quoted in Doty, *What Is the Grass*, 191.

25 Quoted in David S. Reynolds, ed., *Leaves of Grass* (New York: Oxford University Press, 2005), 179.

26 Henry David Thoreau, *Walden*, Chapter 9, in *A Week on the Concord and Merrimack Rivers/Walden; Or, Life in the Woods/The Maine Woods/Cape Cod* (New York: Library of America, 1985).

27 Robert A. Gross, *The Transcendentalists and Their World* (New York: Farrar, Straus & Giroux, 2021), especially 817–22.

28 Laura Dassow Walls, *Henry David Thoreau: A Life* (Chicago: University of Chicago Press, 2017), quotes on 359–60.

29 H. Daniel Peck, "Unlikely Kindred Spirits: A New Vision of Landscape in the Works of Henry David Thoreau and Asher B. Durand," *American Literary History* 17 (Winter 2005): 687-713. Durand quoted in *The Crayon*, Letter III, January 31, 1855; Dickinson quoted in Cristanne Miller, ed., *Emily Dickinson's Poems: As She Preserved Them* (Cambridge: Harvard University Press, 2016), 33. For fascinating studies, see Martha Ackman, *These Fevered Days: Ten Pivotal Moments in the Making of Emily Dickinson* (New York: W. W. Norton, 2020), Eliza Richards, ed., *Emily Dickinson in Context* (Cambridge: Cambridge University Press, 2013), and Helen Vendler, *Dickinson: Selected Poems and Commentaries* (Cambridge: Harvard University Press, 2010).

30 Adam W. Sweeting, *Reading Houses and Building Books: Andrew Jackson Downing and the Architecture of Popular Antebellum Literature, 1835–1855* (Hanover: University Press of New Hampshire, 1996).

31 Roy Rosenzweig and Elizabeth Blackmar, *The Park and the People: A History of Central Park* (Ithaca, NY: Cornell University Press, 1992), 18–236; Justin Martin, *Genius of Place: The Life of Frederick Law Olmsted* (New York: Da Capo, 2011), 124–57; Lisa Goff, *Shantytown, USA: Forgotten Landscapes of the Working Poor* (Cambridge, MA: Harvard University Press, 2016), 66–84.

32 Michael E. Woods, *Arguing until Doomsday: Stephen Douglas, Jefferson Davis, and the Struggle for American Democracy* (Chapel Hill: University of North Carolina Press, 2020); Michael A. Morrison, *Slavery and the American West: The Eclipse of Manifest Destiny and the Coming of the Civil War* (Chapel Hill: University of North Carolina Press, 1997); Christopher Childers, *The Failure of Popular Sovereignty: Slavery, Manifest Destiny, and the Radicalization of Southern Politics* (Lawrence: University Press of Kansas, 2012); Michael E. Woods, *Emotional and Sectional Conflict in the Antebellum United States* (Cambridge: Cambridge University Press, 2014).

33 David W. Blight, *Frederick Douglass: Prophet of Freedom* (New York: Simon & Schuster, 2018), quote on 271; James Oakes, *The Radical and the Republican: Frederick Douglass, Abraham Lincoln, and the Triumph of Antislavery Politics* (New York: W. W. Norton, 2007).

34 Blight, *Frederick Douglass*, 275.

35 Len Gougeon and Joel Myerson, eds., *Emerson's Antislavery Writings* (New Haven, CT: Yale University Press, 1995), xliii–xliv, xlv.

36 Walls, *Henry David Thoreau*, 347–48.

37 James Oakes, *Freedom National: The Destruction of Slavery in the United States, 1861–1865* (New York: W. W. Norton, 2013).

38 Speech of the Honorable James H. Hammond, of South Carolina, March 4, 1858, https://babel.hathitrust.org/cgi/pt?id=loc.ark:/13960 /t7jq19w4m;view=1up;seq=3. See Drew Gilpin Faust, *James Henry Hammond and the Old South: A Design for Mastery* (Baton Rouge: Louisiana State University Press, 1982); Claire M. Wolnisty, *A Different Manifest Destiny: U.S. Southern Identity and Citizenship in Nineteenth-Century South America* (Lincoln: University of Nebraska Press, 2020).

39 Eric Foner, *The Fiery Trial: Abraham Lincoln and American Slavery* (New York: W. W. Norton, 2010), quote on 99–100.

40 "The Irrepressible Conflict: A Speech by William H. Seward, Delivered at Rochester, Monday, Oct. 25, 1858," https://babel.hathitrust.org/cgi /pt?id=coo.31924032259578;view=1up;seq=1.

41 Ariel Ron, *Grassroots Leviathan: Agricultural Reform and the Rural North in the Slaveholding Republic* (Baltimore: Johns Hopkins University Press, 2020); James L. Huston, *Securing the Fruits of Labor: The American Concept of Wealth Distribution, 1765–1900* (Baton Rouge: Louisiana State University Press, 1998), 97–98; Adam Dean, *An Agrarian Republic: Farming, Antislavery Politics, and Nature Parks in the Civil War Era* (Chapel Hill: University of North Carolina Press, 2015).

42 Philip Mills Herrington, "Agricultural and Architectural Reform in the Antebellum South: Fruitland at Augusta, Georgia," *Journal of Southern History* 78 (November 2012): 855–86; Steven Stoll, *Larding the Lean Earth: Soil and Society in Nineteenth-Century America* (New York: Hill and Wang, 2002); William M. Mathew, *Edmund Ruffin and the Crisis of Slavery in the Old South: The Failure of Agricultural Reform* (Athens: University of Georgia Press, 1988); Lynn A. Nelson, *Pharsalia: An Environmental Biography of a Southern Plantation, 1780–1880* (Athens: University of Georgia Press, 2007); John Majewski, *Modernizing a Slave Economy: The Economic Vision of the Confederate Nation* (Chapel Hill: University of North Carolina Press, 2009); Sarah T. Phillips, "Antebellum Agricultural Reform, Republican Ideology, and Sectional Tension," *Agricultural History* 74 (Autumn 2000): 799–822; Mark M. Smith, *Mastered by the Clock: Time, Slavery, and Freedom in the American South* (Chapel Hill: University of North Carolina Press, 2007); Marie Jenkins Schwartz, *Birthing a Slave: Motherhood and Medicine in the Antebellum South* (Cambridge, MA: Harvard University Press, 2006).

43 David Brown, *Southern Outcast: Hinton Rowan Helper and* The Impending Crisis of the South (Baton Rouge: Louisiana State University Press, 2006), quotes from 107 and 127.

44 James L. Huston, *The Panic of 1857 and the Coming of the Civil War* (Baton Rouge: Louisiana State University Press, 1987); Jenny Wahl, "*Dred*, Panic,

War: How a Slave Case Triggered Financial Crisis and Civil Disunion," in Paul Finkelman, ed., *Congress and the Crisis of the 1850s* (Miami, OH: Ohio University Press, 2012), 159–202; Craig Miner, *A Most Magnificent Machine: America Adopts the Railroad, 1825–1862* (Lawrence: University Press of Kansas, 2010); William G. Thomas, *The Iron Way: Railroads, the Civil War, and the Making of Modern America* (New Haven, CT: Yale University Press, 2011); Leonard L. Richards, *The California Gold Rush and the Coming of the Civil War* (New York: Alfred A. Knopf, 2007); Kevin Waite, *West of Slavery: The Southern Dream of a Transcontinental Empire* (Chapel Hill: University of North Carolina Press, 2021).

45 Huston, *Securing the Fruits of Labor*, 84–85; Jonathan A. Glickstein, *American Exceptionalism, American Anxiety: Wages, Competition, and Degraded Labor in the Antebellum United States* (Charlottesville: University of Virginia Press, 2002), 8.

46 Ken Emerson, *Doo-dah! Stephen Foster and the Rise of American Popular Culture* (New York: Simon & Schuster, 1997), 223–26, quotes on 223; Aaron Skirboll, "The Gritty Realism of Genre Artist David Blythe," *Belt Magazine*, January 13, 2015.

47 Kathryn Teresa Long, *The Revival of 1857–58: Interpreting an American Religious Awakening* (New York: Oxford University Press, 1998); John Corrigan, *Business of the Heart: Religion and Emotion in the Nineteenth Century* (Berkeley: University of California Press, 2002); Richard Carwardine, *Evangelicals and Politics in Antebellum America* (New Haven, CT: Yale University Press, 1993), 294–96.

48 Mitchell Snay, *Gospel of Disunion: Religion and Separatism in the Antebellum South* (New York: Cambridge University Press, 1997); Ben Wright, *Bonds of Salvation: How Christianity Inspired and Limited American Abolitionism* (Baton Rouge: Louisiana State University Press, 2020); John R. McGivigan and Mitchell Snay, *Religion and the Antebellum Debate over Slavery* (Athens: University of Georgia Press, 1998).

49 Lindsay Schakenbach Regele, "Industrial Manifest Destiny: American Firearms Manufacturing and Antebellum Expansion," *Business History Review* 92 (Spring 2018): 57–83; Herbert C. Houze, "Samuel Colt and the World," and Elizabeth Mankin Kornhauser, "George Catlin and the Colt Firearms Series," both in Houze, Cooper, and Kornhauser, eds., *Samuel Colt: Arms, Art, and Invention*; Randolph Roth, *American Homicide* (Cambridge, MA: Harvard University Press, 2009), 299–301; Pekka Hämäläinen, *Indigenous Continent: The Epic Contest for North America* (New York: Liveright, 2022), 432–36; Leonard Arrington and Davis Bitton, *The Mormon Experience: A History of the Latter-day Saints* (New York: Alfred A. Knopf, 1979), 164–68.

50 For fresh and often conflicting perspectives on the politics of the 1850s, see Woods, *Arguing until Doomsday*; John L. Brooke, *"There Is a North": Fugitive Slaves, Political Crisis, and Cultural Transformation in the Coming of the Civil War* (Amherst: University of Massachusetts Press, 2019); Michael Todd Landis, *Northern Men with Southern Loyalties: The Democratic Party*

and the Sectional Crisis (Ithaca, NY: Cornell University Press, 2015); Rachel A. Shelden, *Washington Brotherhood: Politics, Social Life, and the Coming of the Civil War* (Chapel Hill: University of North Carolina Press, 2013); Childers, *The Failure of Popular Sovereignty*; Peter Wirzbicki, *Fighting for the Higher Law: Black and White Transcendentalists against Slavery* (Philadelphia: University of Pennsylvania Press, 2021); Corey M. Brooks, *Liberty Power: Antislavery Third Parties and the Transformation of American Politics* (Chicago: University of Chicago Press, 2016); Michael J. Gerhardt, *The Forgotten Presidents: Their Untold Constitutional Legacy* (New York: Oxford University Press, 2013); Jason Phillips, *Looming Civil War: How Nineteenth-Century Americans Imagined the Future* (New York: Oxford University Press, 2019). I offer my own perspective in *In the Presence of Mine Enemies: Civil War in the Heart of America, 1859–1863* (New York: W. W. Norton, 2003), and the essays in *What Caused the Civil War? Reflections on the South and Southern History* (New York: W. W. Norton, 2007).

EPILOGUE: THE SWORD AND THE NOOSE—1859–1861

1 Len Gougeon and Joel Myerson, eds., *Emerson's Antislavery Writings* (New Haven, CT: Yale University Press, 1995), xlvii; Farah Jasmine Griffin, *Read until You Understand: The Profound Wisdom of Black Life and Literature* (New York: W. W. Norton, 2021), quotes on 114 and 115. Watkins married in 1860 and took the name of Harper, by which she would become well-known in future years.

2 Henry David Thoreau, "A Plea for Captain John Brown," in *Echoes of Harper's Ferry*, James Redpath, ed. (Boston: Thayer and Eldridge, 1860), 17–42.

3 Laura Dassow Walls, *Henry David Thoreau: A Life* (Chicago: University of Chicago Press, 2017), 450–56; Philip F. Gura, *Man's Better Angels: Romantic Reformers and the Coming of the Civil War* (Cambridge, MA: Harvard University Press, 2017) and Peter Wirzbicki, *Fighting for the Higher Law: Black and White Transcendentalists against Slavery* (Philadelphia: University of Pennsylvania Press, 2021) offer conflicting perspectives on the involvement of Emerson, Thoreau, and others with abolitionists.

4 Lydia Moland, *Lydia Maria Child: A Radical American Life* (Chicago: University of Chicago Press, 2022), quoted on 314–24.

5 Harriet Jacobs, *Incidents in the Life of a Slave Girl: Written by Herself*, edited and with an introduction by Jean Fagan Yellin (Cambridge, MA: Harvard University Press, 2000); Moland, *Lydia Maria Child*, 343–57; Jean Fagan Yellin, *Harriet Jacobs: A Life* (New York: Basic, 2004); William L. Andrews, *Slavery and Class in the American South: A Generation of Slave Narrative Testimony, 1840–1865* (New York: Oxford University Press, 2019).

6 David W. Blight, *Frederick Douglass: Prophet of Freedom* (New York: Simon & Schuster, 2018), quotes on 320–21, 336–37; Van Gosse, *The First Reconstruction: Black Politics in America from the Revolution to the Civil War* (Chapel Hill: University of North Carolina Press, 2021), 544.

7 Gougeon and Myerson, eds., *Emerson's Antislavery Writings*, xlviii–xlix.

Illustration Credits

George Catlin, *Múk-a-tah-mish-o-káh-kaik, Black Hawk, Prominent Sac Chief*
Smithsonian American Art Museum
Gift of Mrs. Joseph Harrison, Jr., 1985.66.2
Creative Commons

INSERT PAGE 5

Ralph Waldo Emerson
Library of Congress, Prints and Photographs Division

Margaret Fuller
Library of Congress, Prints and Photographs Division

INSERT PAGE 6

William Lloyd Garrison
National Portrait Gallery, Smithsonian Institution
Bequest of Garrison Norton
Public Domain

Frederick Douglass
My Bondage and My Freedom (New York: Miller, Orton and Mulligan, 1855).
Internet Archive

INSERT PAGE 7

Thomas Cole, *The Oxbow*
Metropolitan Museum of Art
Gift of Mrs. Russell Sage
Open Access Program

INSERT PAGE 8

Edgar Allan Poe
Library of Congress, Prints and Photographs Division

George Lippard
Library of Congress, Prints and Photographs Division

INSERT PAGE 9

William Henry Lane
Charles Dickens, *American Notes for General Circulation* (London: Chapman and Hall, 1842).
When suddenly the lively hero Dashes in to the Rescue by A. B. Frost (engraved by Edward G. Dalziel), in Charles Dickens's *Pictures from Italy* and *American Notes* (1880), Chapter VI, "New York," facing 277.
Internet Archive; Public Domain; scan from Alamy

Stephen C. Foster
The Melodies of Stephen C. Foster (Pittsburgh: T. M. Walker, 1909).
International Music Score Library Project / Petrucci Music Library
Creative Commons

INSERT PAGE 10

Dorothea Dix
Library of Congress, Prints and Photographs Division

Elizabeth Cady Stanton
Library of Congress, Prints and Photographs Division

INSERT PAGE 11

Herman Melville
Library of Congress, Rare Book Division

Nathaniel Hawthorne
Library of Congress, Rare Book Division

INSERT PAGE 12

Fanny Fern
Library of Congress, Prints and Photographs Division

Walt Whitman
Leaves of Grass (Brooklyn, NY: W. Whitman, 1855).
The Walt Whitman Archive; Creator of master digital image: Beeghly
    Library, Ohio Wesleyan University

INSERT PAGE 13

Sojourner Truth
Library of Congress, Rare Book and Special Collections Division
Library of Congress, The Alfred Whital Stern Collection of Lincolniana

Harriet Tubman
Library of Congress, Prints and Photographs Division
Emily Howland Photograph Album

INSERT PAGE 14

William Sidney Mount, *The Banjo Player*
Long Island Museum, Stony Brook, New York
Reproduced with permission

William Sidney Mount, *The Power of Music*
Cleveland Museum of Art
Leonard C. Hanna, Jr. Fund 1991.110
Open Access

INSERT PAGE 15

Susan Augusta Fenimore Cooper
Fenimore Art Museum, Cooperstown, New York
Reproduced with permission

Henry David Thoreau
National Portrait Gallery, Smithsonian Institution; gift of anonymous donor
Object Number NPG.72.119

INSERT PAGE 16

John Brown
Library of Congress, Prints and Photographs Division
Copyright by Small, Maynard & Co., defunct since 1927

Lydia Maria Child
Library of Congress, Prints and Photographs Division
Emily Howland Photograph Album

Frances Ellen Watkins (Harper)
Library of Congress, Prints and Photographs Division

Index

Blackstone, Lord, 68
Blithedale Romance, The (Hawthorne), 220
Blue Ridge Mountains, 62
Blythe, David Gilmour, 276
Boston
    African Masonic Hall, 69
    Faneuil Hall, 121, 184
    Harvard, 89, 92–95, 98, 205–8
Boston Athenaeum, 83
Boston Society of Natural History, 207
Boudinot, Elias, 48, 222
Brent, Linda. *See* Jacobs, Harriet
Britain. *See* England
Brontë, Charlotte, 210
Brontë, Emily, 210
Brook Farm, 220
Brower, Frank, 182–83
Brown, Charles Brockden, 34–35, 38, 174–75
Brown, Henry "Box," 179, 249
Brown, John, 267–69, 280–82
Brown, William Wells, 179, 228–30
buffalo, 77, 126
Burns, Anthony, 268, 269
"Bury Me in a Free Land" (Watkins), 243

California
    in the American imagination, 250
    exploration of, 138, 143–44
    gold rush, 192–94
    manifest destiny and, 153
    Native Americans in, 192–93
    Pantoscope of California, 250
    San Francisco, 193, 252
    settlement and acquisition of, 153, 159, 162, 192–94, 223
    Sierra Nevada mountains, 143, 192, 193, 250
Calvinists, 25, 39
Cambridge Scientific Club, 206
camphene, 254–55
"Camptown Races" (Foster), 239
Canada, 11, 74

Black migration to, 61, 122, 224–25
French Canadians, 141
immigrants from, 100
Maine's border with, 133–34
Carlyle, Thomas, 90
Carroll, Charles, 56–57
Cary, Lott, 16
Catholics
    abortion and, 166
    conflicts with Protestant Christians, 27–28, 151
    Democrats and, 127
    Irish immigrants, 102, 166, 190
    of Mexico, 80, 155
    nativism vs., 191
    Protestants missionizing to, 186, 190
    public education and, 102–3
    Sabbatarians and, 27–28
    Whig view of, 72
Catlin, George, 76, 155–56, 229
Celtic race, 155
Chapman, John (Johnny Appleseed), 31–32
Cherokee Phoenix and Indians' Advocate, The (newspaper), 47–48
Cherokees, 2, 4–6, 13, 47–49, 72, 74–76, 78, 126–27, 141, 222
Chesapeake Bay, 11
Cheyennes, 76, 126, 278
Chickasaws, 2, 5, 22, 47, 78, 126–27
Child, David, 81–82, 282
Child, Maria (Lydia Maria Francis), 81–83, 113, 158, 282–85
China
    the gold rush and, 193–94
    Opium Wars, 125, 137
    trade with, 135, 137, 159
Choctaws, 2, 5, 47, 78, 126
Chopin, Frédéric, 240
Christianity. *See* Catholics; Protestants; *other specific denominations*
Christian Observer, 152
Christopolis (Monrovia), 15–16
Christy's Minstrels, 183, 238
Church of Jesus Christ of Latter-day Saints. *See* Mormons